THE POWER OF JAPANESE
CANDLESTICK CHARTS

THE POWER OF JAPANESE CANDLESTICK CHARTS

Advanced Filtering Techniques for Trading Stocks, Futures, and Forex

REVISED EDITION

Fred K. H. Tam

WILEY

Cover image: © iStockphoto.com/P2007
Cover design: Wiley

Copyright © 2015 by John Wiley & Sons Singapore Pte. Ltd.

Published by John Wiley & Sons Singapore Pte. Ltd.
1 Fusionopolis Walk, #07-01, Solaris South Tower, Singapore 138628

Other Wiley Editorial Offices
John Wiley & Sons, 111 River Street, Hoboken, NJ 07030, USA
John Wiley & Sons, The Atrium, Southern Gate, Chichester, West Sussex, P019 8SQ, United Kingdom
John Wiley& Sons (Canada) Ltd., 5353 Dundas Street West, Suite 400, Toronto, Ontario, M9B 6HB, Canada
John Wiley& Sons Australia Ltd., 42 McDougall Street, Milton, Queensland 4064, Australia
Wiley-VCH, Boschstrasse 12, D-69469 Weinheim, Germany

ISBN 978-1-118-73292-2 (Hardcover)
ISBN 978-1-118-73294-6 (ePDF)
ISBN 978-1-118-73295-3 (ePub)
ISBN 978-1-118-77714-5 (o-Book)

Typeset in 12/14 pt, Perpetua Std Regular by Aptara

Printed and bound by CPI Group (UK) Ltd, Croydon, CR0 4YY

C9781118732922_261023

CONTENTS

This book is about applying the popular time-tested Japanese candlestick technique to spot market turning points. After all, making money from the markets is all about predicting correctly when the market is about to turn, and the Japanese candlestick technique does this job superbly.

I find the candlestick technique very applicable for trading actively traded financial instruments such as stock indices, foreign exchange (forex), commodities futures, and stocks. This is because most, if not all, financial instruments tend to exhibit short-term rallies only to be followed by short-term corrections regardless of their time frames. Their trading cycle ranges from 5 to 15 candles (see Figure P.1 and Figure P.2).

It is fun to be on the right side of the market, buying at or near market bottoms and selling at or near market tops. But the question is, "How do I know if today's market action constitutes a market bottom?" Conversely, after a sharp rally of a few sessions, what signals are there to tell you that your stocks have topped out and are due for a correction?

Questions like "Is this the right time to buy?" or "Is this the right time to sell?" have always been a talking point amongst traders and investors. The objective of this book is to provide an answer to these questions.

There are many techniques out there, mainly from the West, like the moving average, relative strength index, moving average convergence divergence (MACD), stochastic, momentum, Bollinger bands, Elliott waves, and so on, that can help you time your entry and exit. I strongly believe that these Western techniques should be part of a trader's arsenal.

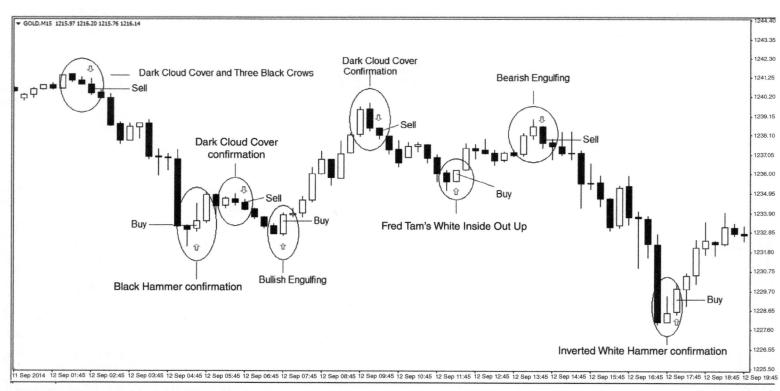

FIGURE P.1   Gold 15-Minute (2014)—Trading cycles range from 5 to 15 candles

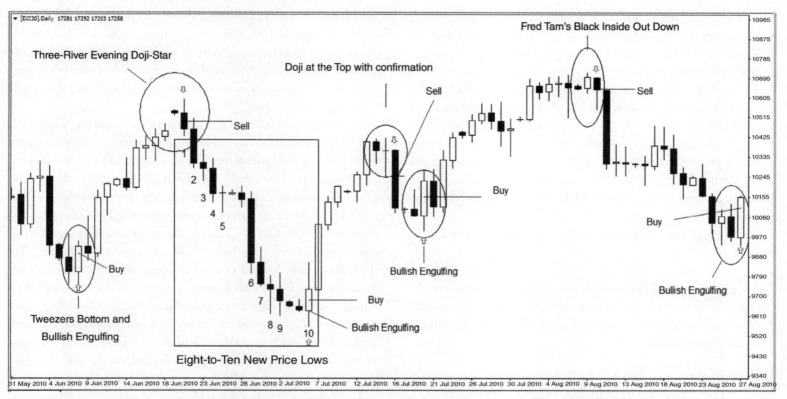

FIGURE P.2 Dow Jones Industrial Average Daily (2010)—Trading cycles range from 5 to 15 candles regardless of the periodicity of the chart

But complementing Western techniques with that of Japanese candlesticks will give you that extra edge in getting a much better price—a lower price if you are buying and a higher price if you are selling. You will be convinced from the hundreds of charts illustrated in this book that Japanese candlestick signals lead the Western technical indicators in timing market entry and exit.

The candlestick technique is the most leading of all technical indicators that I have come across. The reason why the Japanese candlestick technique triggers buy or sell signals at least 2 periods and sometimes up to 10 periods earlier than Western indicators is that candlestick signals are based on an analysis of price itself.

When you are analysing the candle chart, you are in effect analysing the psychology of the market participants that is reflected in its price. No indicators can beat a technique that analyses price in itself.

This passage taken from the Sakata Goho sums up the candlesticks' raison d'être:

> The psychology of the market participant, the supply and demand equation and the relative strength of the buyers and sellers are all reflected in the one candlestick or in a combination of candlesticks.

Western indicators, on the other hand, use formulas that take into account prices of several periods. The MACD, for example, uses a 12-day, 26-day, and 9-day exponential moving average as its parameter. Once parameters are used more than two periods, the resultant signal, when it is triggered, tends to lag behind price (see Figure P.3). This is the reason Western indicators tend to call a buy or sell between 3 and 10 periods (and sometimes more) from the market's bottom or top. The longer the parameters used, the more distant is the signal.

This book is written for the beginner as well as for the advanced trader. Part I takes you through, from the technique's historical background, to the construction of the candle chart to defining and interpreting single to multiple candles. It not only explains the psychology behind each pattern, but also offers suggestions on the proper action to take as well as a stop-loss point to exit if the signal fails.

As the candlestick technique prides itself on spotting market U-turns, I have devoted many pages in this book to describe popular reversal patterns and how to apply them to enter and exit the markets. Continuation patterns are also covered to alert the trader when a trend is only pausing momentarily but will continue with its run after a rest.

Part II of this book covers the more advanced aspects of trading with candlesticks. It emphasizes the importance of using candlesticks together with Western technical indicators to improve the accuracy of candle signals. Several popular Western technical indicators are covered in this book with examples drawn from widely traded financial instruments like forex; U.S., European, Japanese, Singapore, and Malaysian stocks; and stock indices, as well as from the futures markets to illustrate that this technique works for all markets. This technique, however, will not work if the instrument traded is controlled by a small group of players in a thinly traded environment.

The Japanese candlestick technique is a very powerful short-term trading technique if it is used on 1-minute, 5-minute, 15-minute, or 1-hour charts, as markets exhibit rallies and declines between 5 and 15 cycles on every time frame. It is therefore very suitable for use by remisiers, stockists, scalpers, day traders, and short-term position traders.

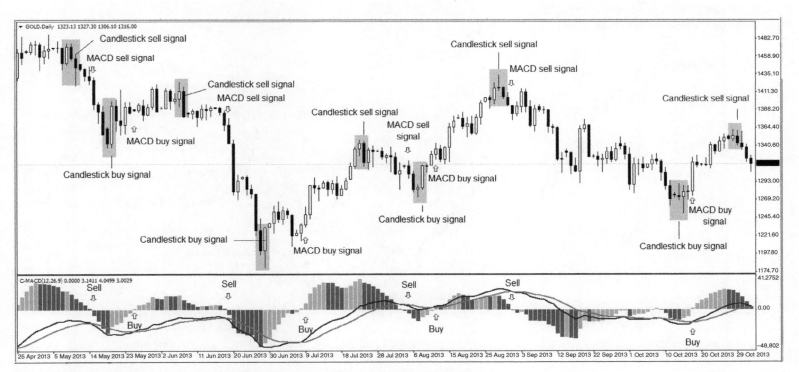

FIGURE P.3   Gold Daily (2013)—Western indicators (e.g., MACD) tend to lag behind candlesticks

FIGURE P.4   Kuala Lumpur Composite Index Weekly (1999)—Weekly candle charts are best for long-term investors

This technique is equally useful for medium-term and long-term forecasting through the use of 4-hour, daily, weekly, and monthly candlestick charts in combination with longer-term Western technical indicators (see Figure P.4).

Herein lies the adaptability of technical analysis in that it works irrespective of the time frame used. You can apply this technique for intra-day trading through the use of a 1-minute chart, a 5-minute chart, a 15-minute chart, a 30-minute chart, or an hourly chart.

For longer-term investors like fund managers who tend to hold stocks for a period of more than a month, I have found that the weekly candle charts provide the most consistent buy and sell signals.

Winning from the market requires two ingredients. The first is that you must have a proven trading technique. The second is that you must practice sound money management. This book will provide you with the first ingredient.

Knowing when to exit the market when you are wrong is part of money management. To that extent, this book will also cover the second ingredient.

Good luck and happy trading.

A book on Japanese candlesticks is not easy to write, mainly because of the lack of literature on the subject until 1991 when an American analyst by the name of Steve Nison revealed this ancient technique to the Western world through his classic book, *Japanese Candlestick Charting Techniques: A Contemporary Guide to the Ancient Investment Techniques of the Far East.*

This book was my first contact with candlesticks. Nison's second, *Beyond Candles*, is another masterpiece. After putting his research into practice, I am convinced of the candlesticks' usefulness in forecasting market U-turns as well as trend continuations and am now a faithful disciple of this age-old technique. Nison has my utmost respect for introducing candlesticks to the Western world and to me. He is, to me, the "granddaddy" of candlesticks.

I would also like to thank Gary S. Wagner and Brad L. Matheny for furthering my knowledge on candles. We met when I attended a U.S. International Trading and Markets Conference called "Futures West '94" in Los Angeles. Wagner and Matheny's book, *Trading Applications of Japanese Candlestick Charting,* taught me, besides additional candlestick techniques, the importance of computerization of candle patterns.

Though I have never had a chance to meet Greg Morris, I give him credit for his well-formatted book, *Candlepower*. He had obviously done extensive research to produce this book, including painstakingly giving each pattern a Japanese name. His interview with renowned Japanese technician Takehiro Hikita is recommended reading.

Last but not least, I want to acknowledge the guidance, support, and patience of the editors and management team at John Wiley & Sons Singapore Pte. Ltd., namely, Nick Wallwork, Chris Gage, Emilie Herman, Jeremy Chia, and Gladys Ganaden, who patiently helped me bring this book to fruition.

Basic Candlestick Techniques

CHAPTER 1

Introduction

The Japanese candlestick charting technique dates back to the 1700s when bar charting and point-and-figure charting were not even discovered. Japanese traders, on the other hand, were already using this technique to trade their rice markets. Yet this technique of charting was confined strictly to Japan until the Americans discovered this technique from Japanese traders who traded the U.S. financial markets in the 1980s.

What fascinated the U.S. traders in the late 1980s was its uncanny trading accuracy in the purchase and sale of stocks, stock index and commodity futures, currency and treasury bonds on the New York and Chicago exchanges. Yet, the Americans were unaware of the techniques used by the Japanese. Strong interest emerged amongst the U.S. traders as to how the Japanese arrived at their buy and sell decisions.

They reasoned that if they were going to beat the Japanese at their game, the American traders would have to fully understand how the Japanese traders' minds worked. That entails knowing their charting technique. Understanding how

Japanese traders use their charts would help the American traders answer the question "What are the Japanese going to do next?" This accounts for the resurgence of interest in the West into this previously obscure technique of technical analysis.

More information is now available on candlestick charting after extensive research by an American analyst, Steve Nison. His two books, *Japanese Candlestick Charting Techniques* and *Beyond Candles*, offered the outside world a first glimpse into this ancient methodology of the Japanese traders.

As Nison's research into this mystically obscure charting technique became available through his two books, traders in the United States and the rest of the world began to realise its forecasting value. When combined with Western technical concepts, forecasting and trading the markets can be—in the words of Steve Nison—exciting, powerful, fun, and much more rewarding.

Even as recently as the late 1980s, real-time quote and chart services offered to investors in the United States, Europe, and the rest of the world did not feature candlestick charts—only bar charts. Yet within two years after Nison's first book, published in 1991, almost every real-time technical service and end-of-day technical analysis software package offered candlestick charts to their clients. In Malaysia, every major real-time technical chart service provider such as Thomson-Reuters, Bloomberg, Updata, Meta-Trader, and Bursa Station supports real-time candlestick charts. The inclusion candlestick charts into these companies' services underscores their popularity and usefulness.

■ Historical Background

After the unification of Japan under the Tokugawa Shogunate (Eighth Shogunate) from 1615 to 1867, its agrarian economy grew. By the seventeenth century, Osaka was regarded as Japan's capital and commercial centre. Osaka's easy access to the sea made it a national port for the shipping of supplies, including rice. Strategically located, Osaka soon became the centre for the rice trade, and rice brokerage became the foundation of Osaka's prosperity. The Dojima Rice Exchange became the centre of rice trade for physical delivery.

Into this background, Munehisa Homma (1716–1803) was born in the city of Sakata, Yamagata Prefecture, Japan. His real name was Kosaku Kato, but he took up the name Munehisa Homma later in his life after his adoption by the wealthy Homma family. At that time, the port of Sakata was a distribution centre for *shonai* (rice). Homma concentrated his attention on the rice market and later on the popular fixed rice market. By 1750 he was trading at his local rice exchange in Sakata. After the death of his father, he was placed in charge of managing his family's assets. With this money he went to the Dojima Rice Exchange in Osaka and began to trade rice futures.

His detailed attention to the markets and his understanding of candlesticks propelled him to become a very wealthy man. He was considered an elusive and feared trader because of his effective understanding of candlesticks and the psychology of the rice markets. He would keep records of yearly weather conditions. To analyse the psychology of investors, Homma analysed rice prices going back to the time when the rice exchange started. Using his own network of communication links he made a killing in the Osaka Rice Exchange and later in the Edo (now Tokyo) exchange.

It was believed that Homma even achieved the feat of 100 consecutive winning trades. Munehisa Homma was perhaps the first person in recorded Japanese history to have used past prices to predict futures price movements—and he did it successfully.

His charismatic personality and highly effective trading methods gained him the nickname "Dewa's long-nosed goblin" and an honour as the "god of the markets." He was such a legend that a folk song from Edo was composed to honour his feats. "When it is sunny in Sakata [Homma's hometown], it is cloudy in Dojima [the Dojima Rice Exchange in Osaka] and rainy in Kuramae [the Kuramae Exchange in Edo]." Interpreted, it means: When there is a good rice harvest in Sakata, rice prices fall on the Dojima Rice Exchange and collapse in Edo. This song underscores Homma's control over the rice markets during his time.

In later years, Homma became the financial consultant to the Japanese government and was given the title of "Samurai." He died in 1803, but his books about the markets (*Sakata Senho* and *Soba Sani No Den*), which revealed his trading principles, evolved into the candlestick charting technique that we know today.

■ Reasons Candlestick Charts Are So Popular Today

Here are six reasons that candlestick charts are so popular amongst professional traders today:

1. **Leading indicator:** Candlestick charts have the ability to show reversal signals earlier than Western charting techniques. As such, candlestick charts are a true leading indicator of market action. They regularly identify potential moves before they become apparent with Western technical tools. Many Japanese candlestick patterns are not found in Western chart techniques. Figure 1.1 shows an example of how candlesticks lead moving average convergence divergence (MACD) in timing entry and exit.

2. **Pictorial:** Candlestick charts are very pictorial and describe the state of players' psychology at a particular moment, which can be utilised to make meaningful trading decisions. Terminology like the "hangman," "shooting star," "dark cloud cover," "hammer," and "abandoned baby" paints indelible word pictures that can assist the trader to remember the pattern through recalling its name. The candlestick technique consists of hundreds of different pattern groups that accurately identify specific traits and tendencies.

3. **Versatile:** Candlestick charts are versatile in that they can be used alone or in combination with Western technical tools. They are unlike point-and-figure charts, which cannot be used alongside other Western technical indicators. Candlesticks use the same price data as bar charts, yet the candlestick technique better promotes the ability to recognise complex pattern groups and predict the next possible outcome based on them.

4. **Can be applied to any time dimension:** Candlestick charting techniques can be adapted for either short- or long-term trading. Candlestick charts are excellent for short-term

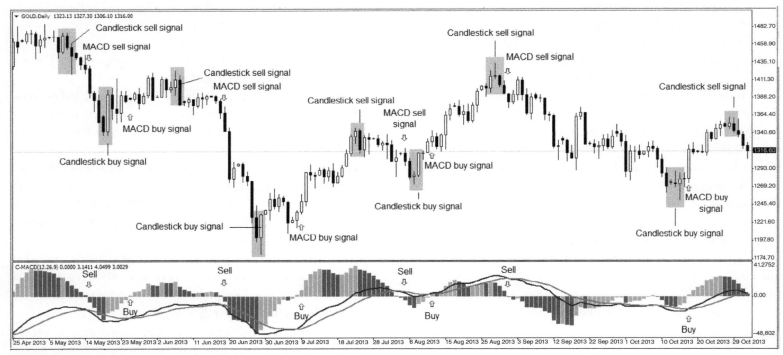

FIGURE 1.1   Gold Daily (2013)—An example of how candlesticks lead MACD in timing entry and exit

trading through the use of intra-day charts like the 1-minute, 5-minute, 15-minute, 30-minute, and 1-hour charts. They can also be applied for longer-term forecasting through the use of daily, weekly, and monthly charts.

5. **Flexibility and adaptability:** Candlestick charts can be applied to follow as many markets as desired—be they stocks, futures, currency, or commodities. In other words, a trader can apply candlestick principles to analyse or trade Malaysian stocks, index futures, or crude palm oil futures. If traders wish to diversify their portfolio, they can trade, for example, U.S. stocks, U.S. futures, foreign currency, Japanese or U.S. Treasury bonds, and for that matter any commodity in any market around the world.

6. **Time-tested, dependable, and useful:** The candlestick charting technique is time-tested and had been refined by generations of use in Japan. The fact that it is still very much in use today after more than 300 years since its discovery is testimony to its usefulness.

■ Construction of the Candlestick Chart

The word *candlestick* is a Western term coined by Steve Nison. In Japan it is called *Ashi*, which means "leg" or "foot." A daily chart is called *Hi Ashi*, a weekly chart *shu ashi*, and a monthly chart *tsuki ashi*. The word for *foot* is used by the Japanese to describe a chart probably because, while the foot reveals a person's past records, a chart reveals the activities of market players. *Ashi* can also mean "footprint," and the Japanese could have used it to describe the

candle chart, because footprints left behind in the sand will offer clues as to where a person is heading.

Drawing a candlestick chart requires four elements of price data:

1. The open   3. The low
2. The high   4. The close

Here are the four simple steps to draw a candlestick chart.

Step 1: Mark the open and the close.

Step 2: Box up the open and the close. This boxed up rectangle is called the "real body." The real body represents the range between the open and close of the session. If the close is higher than the open, the real body is coloured red (or white in some software). If the close is lower than the open, the real body is coloured black.

Step 3: Mark the high and join this to the top of the box (real body). This thin line above the box is called the "upper shadow." Shadows represent the session's price extreme. The peak of the shadow is thus the high of the session.

Step 4: Mark the low and join this to the bottom of the box (real body). This thin line below the box is called the lower shadow. The trough of the shadow is thus the low of the session.

If a candlestick line has no upper shadow, it is said to have a shaven head. A candlestick with no lower shadow has a shaven bottom. A candlestick line where the open and close are at the same or nearly the same price level is called a doji (pronounced *do-gee*). A doji implies indecision and reflects a market where the bulls and bears are in equilibrium. A doji has no box (real body).

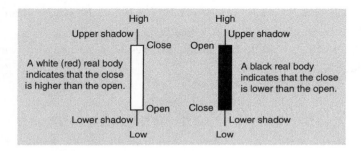

The Real Body

The box that is joined by the open and the close is called the real body of the candlestick. If the close is higher than the open, the real body is coloured white (or red in some software). Conversely, if the close is lower than the open, the real body is coloured black. A white real body depicts an up-day or a strong day, that is, a day where the bulls are victorious over the bears, while a black real body depicts a down-day or weak day, a day where the bears are victorious. The length of the real body measures the strength of the move.

The Shadow

The lines above and below the real body are called shadows. The line above the real body is called the upper shadow, and the line below the real body is called the lower shadow. The upper and lower shadows reflect price fluctuations during the session. The high of the upper shadow represents the high price reached during the session while the low of the lower shadow represents the low price reached during the session.

■ Construction of a Bar Chart

Drawing a Western bar chart requires only three elements of price data.

1. The high
2. The low
3. The close

Sometimes the open is also drawn into the chart, in which case the open will be represented by a slash to the left of the high-low range.

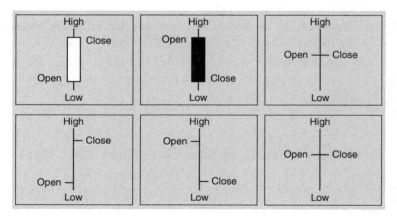

Comparison between a Candlestick and a Bar Chart

Figure 1.2 and Figure 1.3 show examples of a candle chart and a bar chart for S&P 500 Hourly (2013).

FIGURE 1.2 S&P 500 Hourly (2013)—A candle chart describes the state of players' psychology much better than a bar chart

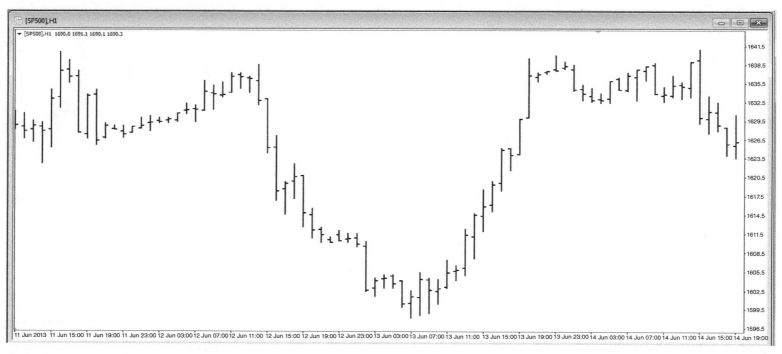

FIGURE 1.3   S&P 500 Hourly (2013)—A bar chart is flat and makes it difficult to spot changes in players' psychology

CHAPTER 2

Single Candle Types

■ Single Candles

Reading the single candle marks the beginning of Japanese candlestick analysis. A single candle can represent any trading period, but in my examples that follow, each candle represents a trading day.

The three purposes of identifying the single candle are:

1. To understand the players' psychology behind the formation of the candle.

2. To investigate the relationship between one candle and the candles that preceded it and from this investigation, interpret any changes to the players' psychology that arise from the patterns that emerge.

3. To act by making a decision on whether to buy, hold, or sell through the patterns that emerge.

Basic Candlestick Formation

There are three basic candle types:

1. A white, or empty, candle indicates that the closing price is higher than the opening price for the trading session.
2. A black, or full, candle indicates that the closing price is lower than the opening price for the trading session.
3. A doji occurs when the opening and the closing price are equal, or very close to each other.

The following diagram shows these three basic candle types.

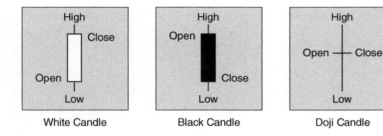

White Candle   Black Candle   Doji Candle

Size, Location, and Colour

To interpret the psychology behind the single candle, there are three elements to look for:

1. Size
2. Location
3. Colour

A large *size* candle, for example, suggests tremendous strength and power behind the move. A large candle is also indicative of more volatile market conditions.

Though its large size makes it a very powerful candle, the *location* of the long candle is important in analysing whether it will be a continuation or reversal pattern. Its interpretation depends on whether it is found at a low price or high price area.

The *colour* of the candle is also important in determining whether the bulls or bears are in control on a particular trading day. A white candle denotes that the bulls are in control (also called an up-day) and a black candle denotes that the bears are in control (also called a down-day). The only category of candles where colour is unimportant is the Umbrella Candles. As I go into the various candle types, you will understand how their location, size, and colour play important roles in interpreting the psychology behind a candle or a collection of candles.

The Long Candle

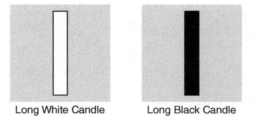

Long White Candle   Long Black Candle

A long candle is defined as one where the open and close (real body) are far apart. It has a greater than average price range. Long candles can be white (bullish) or black (bearish) as shown in the previous diagrams.

A long candle reflects a day with a larger price movement. A long white candle is generally interpreted as a very bullish day and a long black candle is interpreted as a very bearish day.

Though its large size makes it a significant candle, it is important to note the location of this large candle and the candle that follows, as their combinations may signal a reversal pattern (see Figure 2.1).

The Short Candle

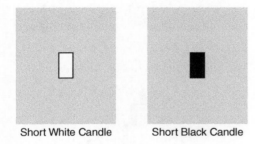

Short White Candle   Short Black Candle

A short candle is defined as one where the difference between the open and close (real body) is small. It may or may not have shadows. When there are shadows, their short upper and/or lower shadows have a less than average price range. A short candle reflects a day of narrow price movement. It is generally viewed as an insignificant candle and is indicative of a consolidation or indecisive market. Relatively small volumes accompany their occurrence. Short candles can be either white or black as shown in the preceding diagrams.

Though its small size makes it an insignificant candle, it is important to note the location of this small candle along with the candles preceding it, as their combination may signal a reversal pattern.

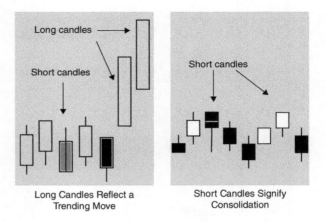

Long Candles Reflect a
Trending Move

Short Candles Signify
Consolidation

Exception to the rule: A short candle is normally viewed as an insignificant candle because of its small real body, short shadows, small volume, and a less than average price range. But the exception to this rule is when short candles are a part of an umbrella group (i.e., the Hammer, Hangman, Inverted Hammer, and Shooting Star) or when they have very long upper and lower shadows (called high wave Spinning Tops or doji). If these candles of the umbrella group or high wave Spinning Tops or doji are spotted at the top or bottom of a market trend, they are signals of a market top or bottom. In such a situation the *location* of these candles will be a more significant factor than their small size.

Ten White Candle Types and Their Interpretations

Following are the definitions and interpretations of the 10 white candle types.

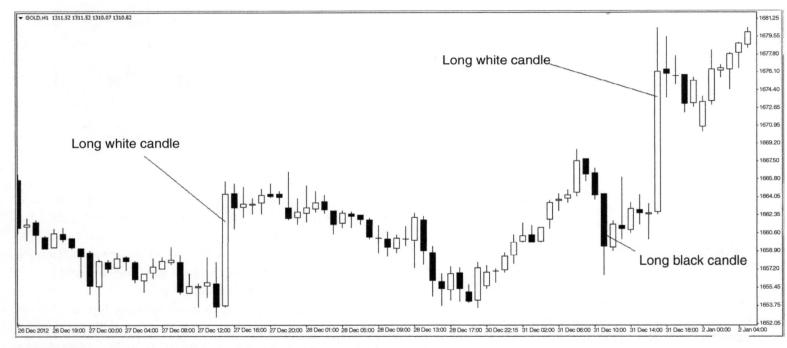

FIGURE 2.1 Gold Hourly (2012)—Locations of long candles may signal a reversal

1. Long Marubozu White Candle

- **Definition:** This candle's close is greater than the open during a greater than average daily range. The close must be equal to the high, and the open must be equal to the low. It has no upper or lower shadows.
- **Interpretation:** *Marubozu* has several meanings in Japanese, one of which is "bald" or "shaven." In describing a candle it means there is no upper or lower shadow. A Long Marubozu White Candle is considered extremely bullish because it has no shadows. It is the most bullish of all long white candles as it opens at the low and closes at the high. The bulls are in total control of the market on this day.

2. Long White Candle

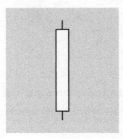

- **Definition:** This candle's close is greater than the open during a greater than average daily range. The close must be near but not at the high, and the open must be near but not at the low. It has a short upper and lower shadow.
- **Interpretation:** The long white candle is a bullish candle. It is a strong candle, but not as strong as the Long Marubozu White Candle because there is some selling close to the open and to the close, giving rise to a small lower and upper shadow. Still, the bulls are in control on this day.

3. Long Closing Bozu White Candle

- **Definition:** This candle's close is greater than the open during a greater than average daily range. The close must be at the high, and the open must be near but not at the low. It has a short lower shadow.
- **Interpretation:** The Long Closing Bozu White Candle is a bullish candle. It is as strong as the Marubozu White Candle because it closed at the high. It is viewed as a strong day, and the interpretation of this Long Closing Bozu Candle is similar to that in analysing the Long Marubozu White Candle.

4. Long Opening Bozu White Candle

- **Definition:** This candle's close is greater than the open during a greater than average daily range. The close must be near but not at the high, and the open must be at the low. It has a short upper shadow.

- **Interpretation:** The Long Opening Bozu White Candle is a bullish candle. Though it did not close at the high, it is a strong candle but not as strong as the Long Marubozu White Candle or the Long Closing Bozu White Candle because there is some selling near the close giving rise to a short upper shadow. Still, the bulls are in control on this day.

5. Inverted White Umbrella Candle

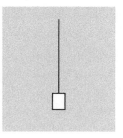

- **Definition:** This candle's close is greater than the open during an average or large range day. The upper shadow must be at least twice the length of the real body. It has a small real body and a long upper shadow. This formation is called a shooting star if it is found at the top of the market or an Inverted Hammer if it is found at the bottom. It can be recognised by its tight opening and closing real body.

- **Interpretation:** The Inverted Umbrella Candle has strong reversal implications. In interpreting an Inverted Umbrella Candle, the colour of the real body is not important. Rather it is its *location* that is of the essence. This inverted Umbrella Candle becomes a shooting star and has bearish implications if found after a market advance. It becomes an Inverted Hammer and has bullish implications if found after a market decline.

5A. Shooting Star (Inverted Umbrella Candle at the Top)

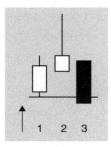

- **Definition:** This Inverted Umbrella Candle becomes a Shooting Star and has bearish implications if found after a market advance.

- **Interpretation:** The sighting of a Shooting Star signals a possible market top, but a bearish confirmation is required before selling. Candle 3 must close lower than the low of candles 2 and 1 to generate a sell signal (see Figure 2.2).

5B. Inverted Hammer (Inverted Umbrella Candle at the Bottom)

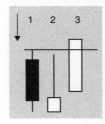

- **Definition:** This Inverted Umbrella Candle becomes an Inverted Hammer and has bullish implications if found after a market decline.

- **Interpretation:** The Inverted Hammer is an indication of a possible end of a decline, but a bullish confirmation is required before buying. Candle 3 must close higher than the high of candles 2 and 1 to generate a buy signal.

6. White Umbrella Candle

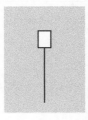

- **Definition:** This candle's close is greater than the open during an average or large range day. The lower shadow must be at least twice the length of the real body. This formation is called a Hammer if it is found at the bottom of the market or a Hanging Man if it is found at the top. It can be recognised by its tight opening and closing real body.

- **Interpretation:** The Umbrella Candle has strong reversal implications. In interpreting an Umbrella Candle, the colour of the real body is not important. Rather it is its *location* that is of the essence. This Umbrella Candle becomes a Hanging Man and has bearish implications if found after a market advance. It becomes a Hammer and has bullish implications if found after a market decline.

6A. Hanging Man (Umbrella Candle at the Top)

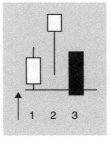

- **Definition:** This Umbrella Candle becomes a Hanging Man and has bearish implications if found after a market advance.

- **Interpretation:** The sighting of a Hanging Man signals a possible market top, but bearish confirmation is required before selling. Candle 3 must close lower than candles 2 and 1 to generate a sell signal.

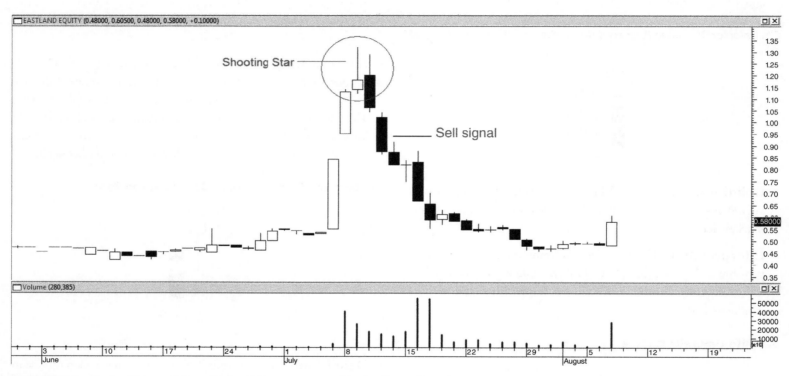

FIGURE 2.2 Eastland Equity Malaysia Daily (2013)—An Inverted Umbrella Candle at the top becomes a Shooting Star

6B. Hammer (Umbrella Candle at the Bottom)

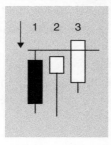

- **Definition:** This Umbrella Candle becomes a Hammer and has bullish implications if found after a market decline.

- **Interpretation:** The Hammer is an indication of a possible end of a decline, but a bullish confirmation is required before buying. Candle 3 must close higher than the high of candles 2 and 1 to generate a buy signal.

7. Short White Candle

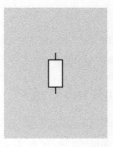

- **Definition:** This candle's close is greater than the open with a less than average daily range. The close should be near but not at the high, and the open should be near but not at the low. It has an upper and a lower shadow. The total length of the real body must be larger than the sum of its upper and lower shadow. If there are no upper or lower shadows, it will be called a Short White Marubozu Candle.

- **Interpretation:** It is a bullish candle as its close is above its open, but due to its smaller than average range, it is not as significant as a long white candle. The short white candle is generally viewed as a trend continuation pattern.

8. White Spinning Top

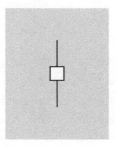

- **Definition:** This candle's close is greater than the open with a less than average daily range. The total length of the real body must be smaller than the sum of its upper and lower shadow.

- **Interpretation:** A Spinning Top (white or black does not matter as colour is unimportant in this type of candle) is a sign of market indecision and is considered neutral in a sideways trend. In a trending market, it can be part of a continuation pattern. Found after a strong rally, it could signal a possible reversal to the downside, but found after a decline, it could signal a reversal to the upside. In analysing a Spinning Top its colour is unimportant but its *location* is.

Analysed in conjunction with another candle before it, they help to form Stars or harami patterns and transform into a reversal pattern.

When a Spinning Top Becomes a Top Reversal Pattern

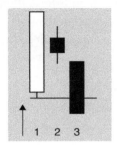

Seen after a rally, a Spinning Top (black) and another long white candle before it take the form of a Bearish Harami, a top reversal pattern. Bearish confirmation is required before selling.

Candle 3 must close below candle 2 (Spinning Top) and candle 1 to generate a sell signal. If the colour of the Spinning Top is white (very rare), this two-candle pattern is called a bearish Homing Pigeon.

When a Spinning Top Becomes a Bottom Reversal Pattern

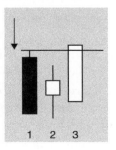

Seen after a decline, a Spinning Top (white) with another long black candle before it takes the form of a Bullish Harami pattern, a bottom reversal pattern. Bullish confirmation is required before buying.

Candle 3 must close above candle 2 (Spinning Top) and candle 1 to generate a buy signal. If the colour of the Spinning Top is black, this two-candle pattern is called a Homing Pigeon.

9. White Lower Shadow

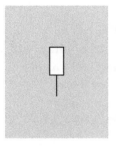

- **Definition:** This candle's close is greater than the open during an average or small daily range. The close must be equal to the high. The length of its real body must be larger than the length of its lower shadow.

- **Interpretation:** It is a bullish candle as the close is greater than the open, and the close is at the high. It is likely to be a continuation pattern as the bulls are still in control. This candle's bullishness will only be threatened if there is a close below its low on the next day (see Figure 2.3).

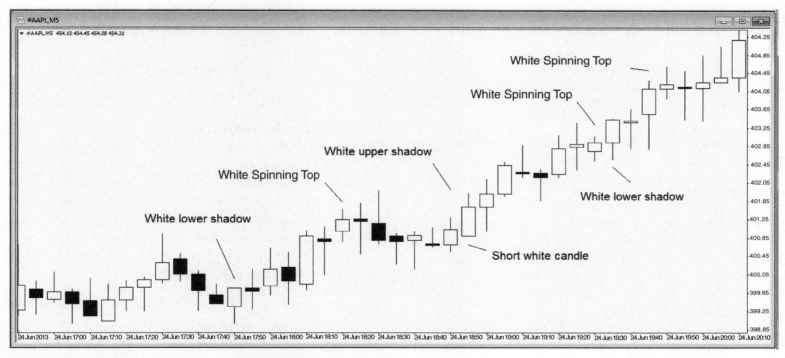

FIGURE 2.3 Apple 5-Minute (2013)—Short candles as continuation patterns

10. White Upper Shadow

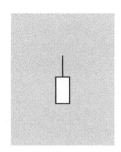

- **Definition:** This candle's close is greater than the open during an average or small daily range. The open must be equal to the low. The length of its real body must be larger than the length of its upper shadow.

- **Interpretation:** It is a bullish candle as the close is greater than the open although the close is off the high. Though the bulls are still in control, there is some profit taking at the close. As such, this candle is less bullish than the White Lower Shadow Candle. Despite its close off the high, it is still considered a bullish day and is a likely continuation pattern unless confirmed by a close below its low (which is also the open).

When a Long White Candle Breaks Resistance A long white candle reflects extreme power and strength behind the move. Found after a series of small candles at a low price area, it is a strong signal of a breakout on the upside. Relatively higher volume accompanying this long white candle will confirm that the breakout is genuine and implies that bigger players are ready to buy this stock further up (see Figure 2.4).

Proper action: It is appropriate to take up a long position.

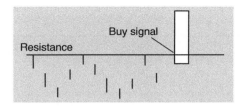

Long White Candle Breaks Resistance

Long White Candle Seen at a Low Price Area Long white candles seen at a low price area represent bulls attempting to take control. But it may take some time for bulls to garner enough strength to absorb stale bull liquidations before lifting themselves out of the sideways trend. Ideally, oscillators like the relative strength index (RSI) should be at oversold levels, and volume registered on white candles should exceed volume on black candles (see Figure 2.5).

Proper action: Look for a breakout on the upside for a buy signal. Stronger volume registered on the breakout day is proof of bull intentions to drive prices higher.

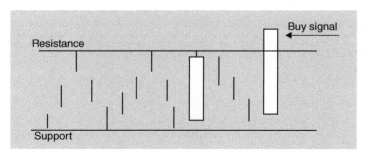

Long White Candle at a Low Price Area

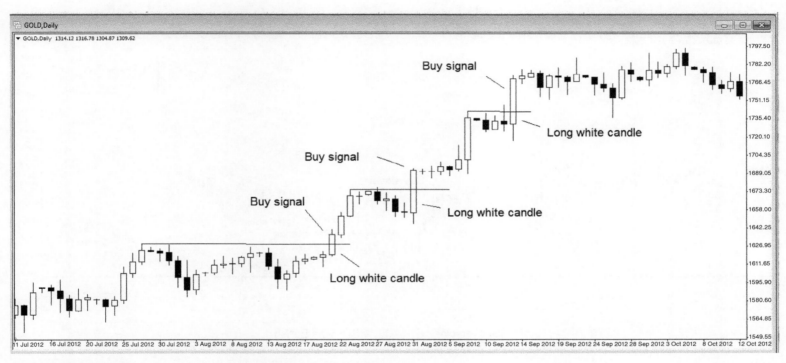

FIGURE 2.4 Gold Daily (2012)—Long white candle breaks resistance; buy signal

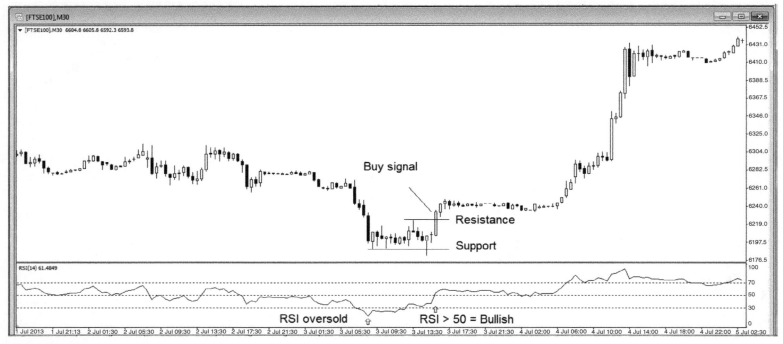

FIGURE 2.5   FTSE 30-Minute (2013)—White candles at a low price area; buy on breakout of resistance

Long White Candle Seen at a High Price Area A long white candle seen at a high price area, especially when oscillators like the RSI display overbought signals, should be approached with caution. It could well signify a market top or buying climax. It may or may not result in a trend reversal, but it is not wise to buy into it as it signifies resistance (see Figure 2.6).

Proper action: If its high is not exceeded and a black candle follows this, it is an indication of a market top. It would be wise to take some profits on long positions if a bearish candle results the next day. Bearish confirmation is required before selling.

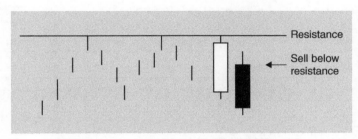

Long White Candle Seen at a High Price Area Acts as Resistance

Long White Candle in an Inverted V Shape or Spike Formation

1. Occasionally prices rally 5 to 10 days in a row making new highs every day in a dynamic move. In this scenario, there are no previous highs to gauge resistance. Here, an exceptionally long white candle's high or close provides the resistance. Check the volume for a hint of a buying climax; also check oscillators like the RSI for overbought levels. An RSI above 70 warns of an overbought market.

2. A sell signal comes only if there is one or a series of bearish candles appearing over the next few days closing lower than the long white candle's low.

3. In the event of an uptrend resumption, the highs of either of the two candles will be your buy-stop (see Figure 2.7).

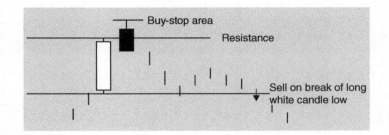

Ten Black Candle Types and Their Interpretations

Following are the definitions and interpretations of the 10 black candle types.

1. Long Marubozu Black Candle

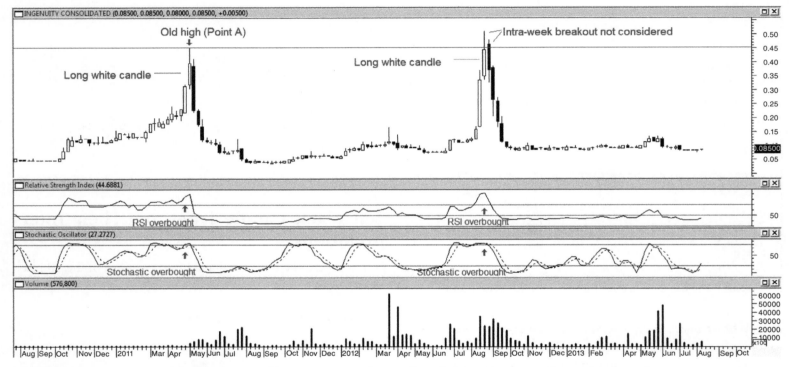

FIGURE 2.6 Ingenuity Consolidated Malaysia Weekly (2011)—Long white candles at high price area warn of an overbought market

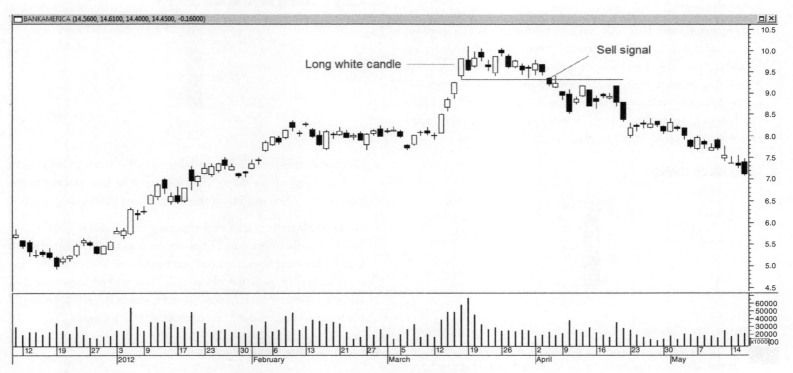

FIGURE 2.7 Bank of America Daily (2012)—Long white candle's low acts as support; sell below support

- **Definition:** This candle's close is less than the open during a greater than average daily range. The close must be equal to the low, and the open must be equal to the high. It has no upper or lower shadows.

- **Interpretation:** *Marubozu* has several meanings in Japanese, one of which is "bald" or "shaven." When applied to describe a candle, it means there is no upper or lower shadow. A Long Marubozu Black Candle is considered extremely bearish because it has no shadows. It is the most bearish of all long black candles as it opens at the high and closes at the low. The bears are in total control of the market on this day.

2. Long Black Candle

- **Definition:** This candle's close is less than the open during a greater than average daily range. The close must be near but not at the low, and the open must be near but not at the high. It has a short upper and lower shadow.

- **Interpretation:** The long black candle is a bearish candle. It is a weak candle but not as weak as the Marubozu Black Candle because there is some buying near the open and the close, creating an upper and lower shadow. Still, it is viewed as a weak day, and the interpretation of this long black candle is

similar to that of the Long Marubozu Black Candle. The bears are in total control.

3. Long Opening Bozu Black Candle

- **Definition:** This candle's close is less than the open during a greater than average daily range. The close must be near but not at the low, and the open must be at the high. It has a short lower shadow.

- **Interpretation:** The Long Opening Bozu Black Candle is a bearish candle. It is weak, but not as weak as the Marubozu Black Candle because it closes near but not at the low. Some buying support is seen near the close. Still, it is viewed as a weak day, and the interpretation of this Long Opening Bozu Black Candle is similar to that of the Long Marubozu Black Candle.

4. Long Closing Bozu Black Candle

- **Definition:** This candle's close is less than the open during a greater than average daily range. The close must be at the low, and the open must be near but not at the high, indicating some buying near the open. It has a short upper shadow.

- **Interpretation:** The Long Closing Bozu Black Candle is a bearish candle. Though it opened and made a slightly higher high, it closed at the low. It is as weak as the Long Marubozu Black Candle and is a day where bears are in total control.

5. Inverted Black Umbrella Candle

- **Definition:** This candle's close is less than the open during an average or large range day. The upper shadow must be at least twice the length of the real body. It has a small real body and a long upper shadow. This formation is called a Shooting Star if it is found at the top of the market or an Inverted Hammer if it is found at the bottom. It can be recognised by its tight opening and closing real body.

- **Interpretation:** This Black Inverted Umbrella Candle (white or black does not matter as colour is unimportant in this candle type) has strong reversal implications. In interpreting an Inverted Umbrella Candle, the colour of the real body is not important. Rather, it is its *location* that is of the essence.

6. Black Umbrella Candle

- **Definition:** This candle's close is less than the open during an average or large range day. The lower shadow must be at least twice the length of the real body. This formation is called a Hammer if it is found at the bottom of the market, or a Hanging Man if it is found at the top. It can be recognised by its tight opening and closing real body.

- **Interpretation:** This Black Umbrella Candle (white or black does not matter as colour is unimportant in this candle type) has strong reversal implications. In interpreting an Umbrella Candle, the colour of the real body is not important. Rather, it is its *location* that is of the essence.

7. Short Black Candle

- **Definition:** This candle's close is less than the open with a less than average daily range. The close should be near but not at the low, and the open should be near but not at the high. It has an upper and a lower shadow. The total length of the real body must be larger than the sum of its upper and lower shadow. If there is no upper or lower shadow, it is called a Short Marubozu Black Candle.

- **Interpretation:** The short black candle is considered a weak candle as the close is below the open. But due to its smaller than average real body, it is not as weak as a long black candle. Still, the short black candle is interpreted as weak. It can appear in a consolidation pattern or as part of a trend continuation pattern.

8. Black Spinning Top

- **Definition:** This candle's close is less than the open with a less than average daily range. The total length of the real body must be smaller than the sum of its upper and lower shadows.

- **Interpretation:** The Spinning Top (white or black does not matter as colour is unimportant in this candle type) is considered a neutral candle as the open and the close are

near one another while its upper and lower shadows are longer than the length of its real body. This candle reflects a tug-of-war between the bulls and the bears with no party emerging victorious at the end of battle. The market is said to be indecisive or uncertain. In a trending market, it is part of a continuation pattern. Found after a strong rally, it may indicate a possible reversal to the downside. Found after a decline, it may point to a possible reversal to the upside. In analysing a Spinning Top, its colour is unimportant but its *location* is.

Analysed in relation with another candle before it, they help to form Stars or harami patterns and transform into a reversal pattern.

9. Black Lower Shadow

- **Definition:** This candle's close is less than the open during an average or small range, but the length of its real body must be larger than the length of its lower shadow.

- **Interpretation:** The Black Lower Shadow Candle is considered a weak candle, as the close is less than the open. The lower shadow implies some buying support towards the close. But the lower close meant the bears were still in control. It can appear in a consolidation pattern or as part of a trend continuation pattern.

10. Black Upper Shadow

- **Definition:** This candle's close is less than the open during an average or small range, but the length of its real body must be larger than the length of its upper shadow.

- **Interpretation:** The Black Upper Shadow Candle is considered a weak candle, as the close is less than the open. Though there is an attempt by the bulls to control price at some point during the day, the weak close at the end of the day implies weakness. This candle is more bearish than the Black Lower Shadow Candle because it closed at the low. It can appear in a consolidation pattern or as part of a trend continuation pattern.

Short Black Candles as Continuation Patterns Figure 2.8 shows an example of short black candles as continuation patterns.

Short Black Candles as Consolidation Patterns Figure 2.9 shows an example of short black candles as consolidation patterns.

Note: When a market is in a consolidation mode, one can gauge its tone by observing the frequency of occurrence of white candles over black candles. In the previous example on Apple, Quadrant A consists of seven white candles compared to only three black candles and two doji. With more white candles than black, the predominance of white candles tells us that the bulls are in control. Note that Apple's price continues to rise.

Similarly, in Quadrant B, the number of white candles over black comes to five against three. On March 13, 2012, Apple's price broke out of this quadrant to rise further.

When a Long Black Candle Breaks Support A long black candle reflects extreme power and strength behind the move. Found breaking a support after a series of small candles (consolidation), it is a strong signal of a breakout on the downside. Relatively higher volume accompanying this long black candle will confirm this breakout and is a signal that bigger players are ready to depress this stock further (see Figure 2.10).

Proper action: It is appropriate to take up a short position.

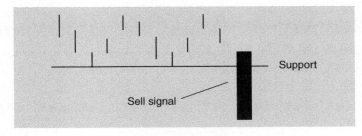

Long Black Candle Breaks Support

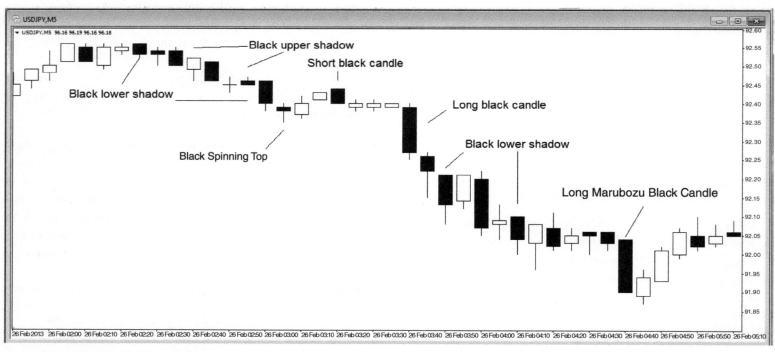

FIGURE 2.8 UsdJpy 5-Minute (2013)—Short black candles as continuation patterns

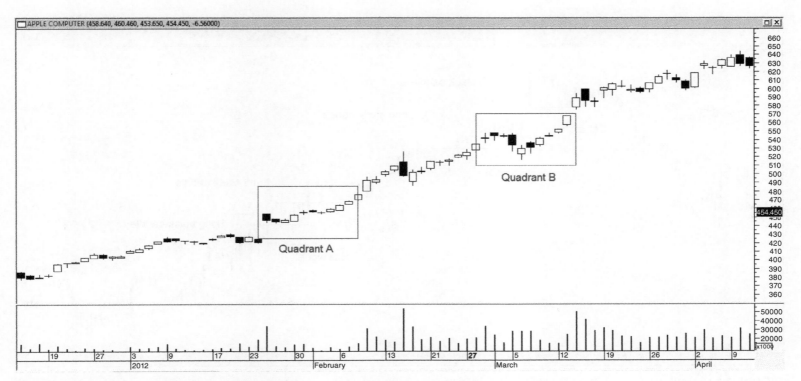

FIGURE 2.9   Apple Daily (2012)—Predominance of white candles over black candles has bullish implications

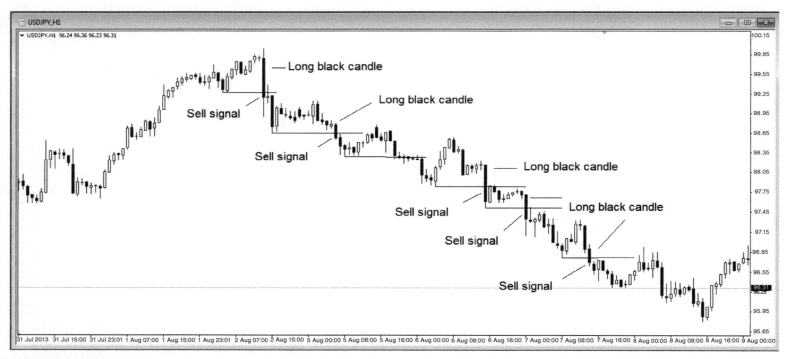

FIGURE 2.10 UsdJpy Hourly (2013)—Long black candle breaks support: sell signal

Long Black Candle Seen at a Low Price Area A long black candle seen at a low price area should be approached with caution. It could well signify a market bottom or selling climax. It may not be wise to sell into this candle as it may signify support (see Figure 2.11).

Proper action: If its low is not exceeded and is followed by a white candle, it is an indication of a market bottom. Take profits on short positions. In the event of a resumption of the downtrend, place a sell-stop below the low of the support. A long black candle seen after a protracted decline is indicative of a selling climax.

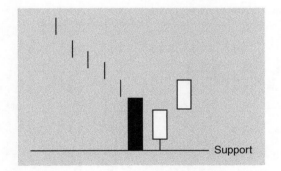

Long Black Candle at a Low Price Area Acts as Support

Long Black Candle Seen at a High Price Area A long black candle seen at a high price area should be approached with caution. It could warn of a market top or buying climax if it could not exceed previous highs. It may be a good selling area (see Figure 2.12).

Proper action: If its high is not exceeded and is preceded by a white candle forming a bearish reversal pattern group (like a

bearish engulfing pattern in this example), it is wise to take profits or take up a short position. In the event of an uptrend resumption, place a buy-stop above the resistance.

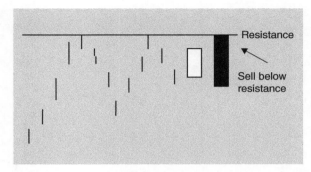

Long Black Candle at High Price Area Acts as Resistance

■ The Doji

The doji is one of the more important single candles. It is created when its opening price and its closing price are the same. A doji does not have a real body. The upper and lower shadows can be long or short. More weight is given in analysing a doji with longer shadows. Doji with longer shadows reflect a volatile day while doji with shorter shadows reflect a dull and quiet day.

Interpretation: A doji is classified as a neutral candle if it is found within a sideways market. It takes on significance when it is spotted at a high price area, for example after an uptrend, or at a low price area after a downtrend. In such a situation, the doji is likely to warn of a market reversal. A doji seen after a long white

FIGURE 2.11   Gold Daily (2013)—Long black candle at low price area acts as support

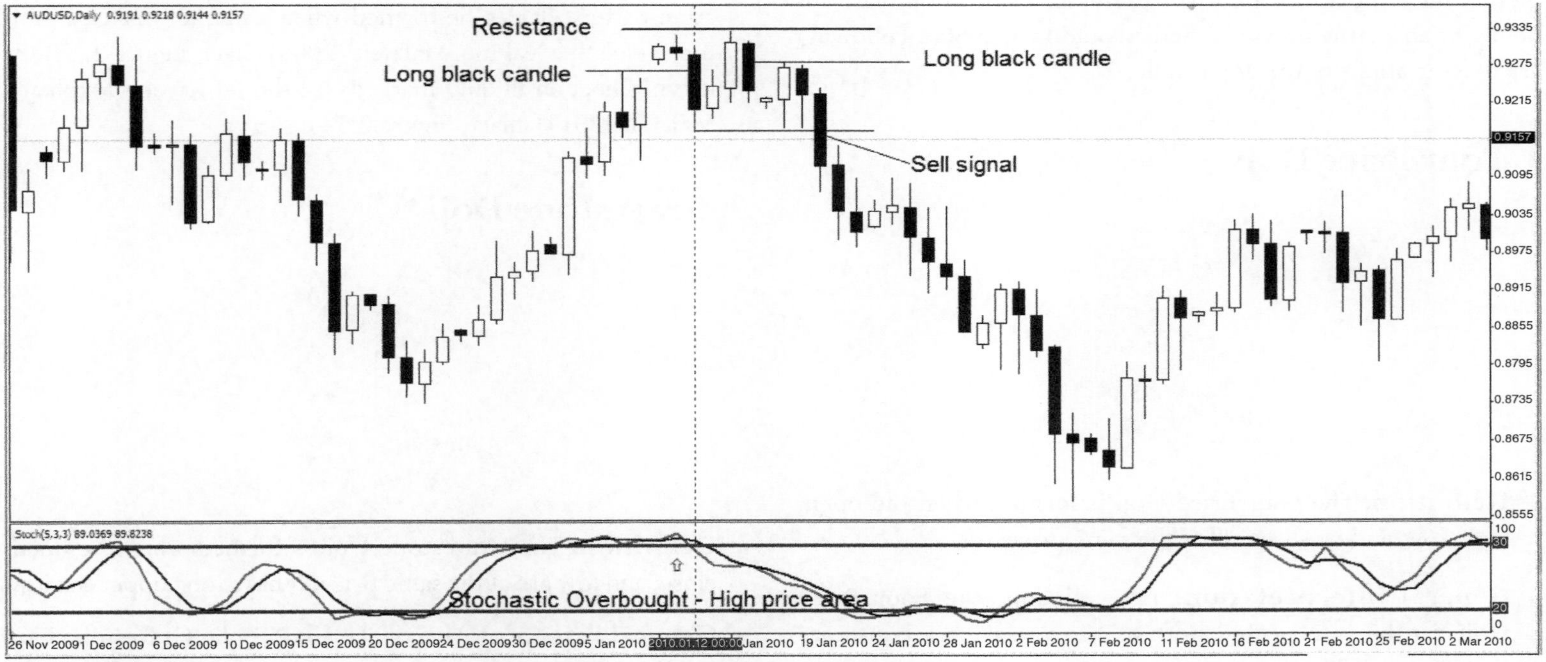

FIGURE 2.12 AudUsd Daily (2010)—Long black candle at high price area acts as resistance

or black candle will also hint of a possible reversal. The location of the doji is of significance.

A doji should be read in conjunction with other patterns before it. The advance pattern group that is created gives a clearer picture on its next direction. For example, a small doji that gaps below or above the previous candle could form a Star. Following are five variations of the doji candle.

1. Four Price Doji

- **Definition:** The Four Price Doji is formed when the open, high, low, and close are all at the same price.

- **General interpretation:** Like all doji, the Four Price Doji can be interpreted both as a reversal or a continuation pattern. The important criterion is to identify where the doji is found. If the doji is found after a rally or at a high price area, it is generally viewed as a potential bearish reversal pattern. If it is found after a downtrend or at a low price area, it has potential bullish reversal implications. But if found in a sideways market, it is viewed as a neutral candle.

- **Proper action:** Possible reversal candle but wait for a confirmation candle before buying or selling.

- **Specific interpretation:** The Four Price Doji is a rare occurrence. It can be interpreted both as a reversal or a continuation pattern. It can be formed when a market makes a limit move (see the Seal Inc. Malaysia [2005] chart, Figure 2.13), or it can reflect an illiquid market (see the Tai Kwong Yokohama Malaysia [2014] chart, Figure 2.14).

2. Gravestone Doji

- **Definition:** The Gravestone Doji is formed when the open, close, and low are at the same price. It has a long upper shadow.

- **General interpretation:** Like all doji, the Gravestone Doji can be interpreted both as a reversal or a continuation pattern. The important criterion is to identify where the doji is found. If the doji is found after a rally or in a high price area, it is generally viewed as a potential bearish reversal pattern. If it is found after a downtrend or at a low price area, it has potential bullish reversal implications. But if found in a sideways market, it is viewed as neutral.

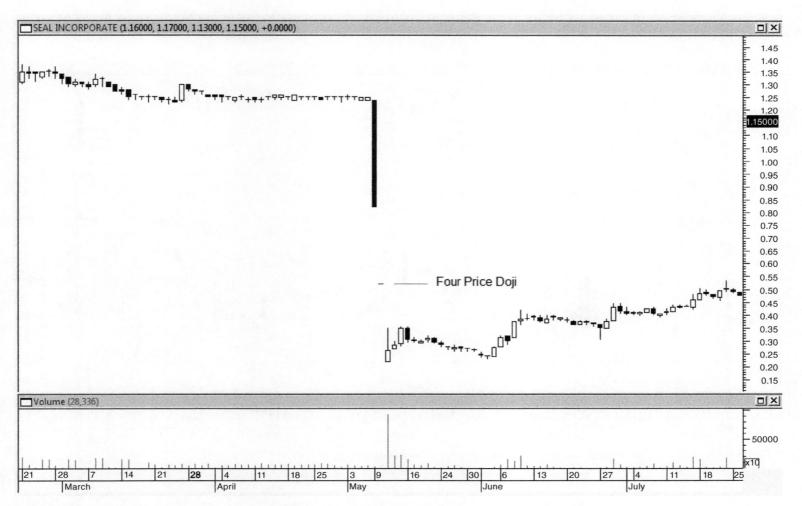

FIGURE 2.13 Seal Inc. Malaysia Daily (2005)—Four Price Doji making a limit move in an extremely bearish market

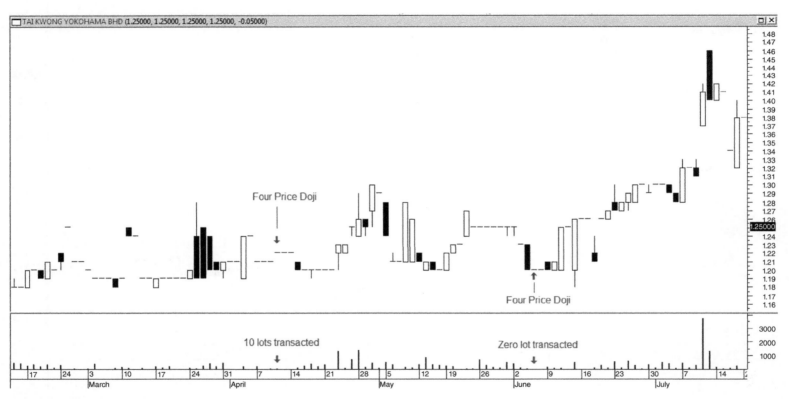

FIGURE 2.14   Tai Kwong Yokohama Malaysia (2014)—Four Price Doji in an illiquid market

Gravestone Doji at the Top

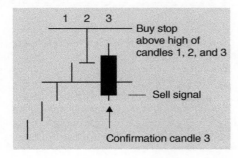

1 2 3
— Buy stop above high of candles 1, 2, and 3

— Sell signal

↑ Confirmation candle 3

Rules
1. Sell if confirmation candle 3 closes below lowest of candles 1 and 2.
2. In case of a resumption of uptrend, place buy-stop above the highest of candles 1, 2, and 3.

Specific interpretation: The Gravestone Doji is bearish if seen after a strong uptrend or at a high price area. It is a bearish candle because of its long upper shadow and a close at its low. A low close implies that the bears dominate prices even though they were traded higher all day. If the open and close are near each other but not at the same price, it is called a Shooting Star, also a bearish candle.

Proper action: Possible major reversal candle but wait for a confirmation candle before selling. A close below the lowest low of the Gravestone Doji (candle 2) and the candle before it (candle 1) is your sell confirmation. The Gravestone Doji candle is, however, a rare pattern in Malaysian stocks and futures as well as in most financial instruments. I managed to find one perfect example in the forex pair UsdJpy 15-Minute chart (Figure 2.15). Its variation, the Shooting Star, is a much more common occurrence as a bearish reversal signal, as shown in the Gold Hourly chart (Figure 2.16).

Example of Gravestone Doji and Shooting Star Figure 2.15 and Figure 2.16 show an example of a Gravestone Doji and its variation, the Shooting Star.

Gravestone Doji at the Bottom

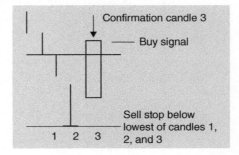

↓ Confirmation candle 3

— Buy signal

Sell stop below lowest of candles 1, 2, and 3

1 2 3

Rules
1. Buy if confirmation candle 3 closes above high of candles 1 and 2.
2. In case of a resumption of downtrend, place sell-stop below the lowest of candles 1, 2, and 3.
   - **Specific interpretation:** The Gravestone Doji formed in a low price area or after a downtrend is seen as a bullish candle. If the open and close are near each other but not at the same price, it is called an Inverted Hammer, a bullish candle (see Figure 2.17).

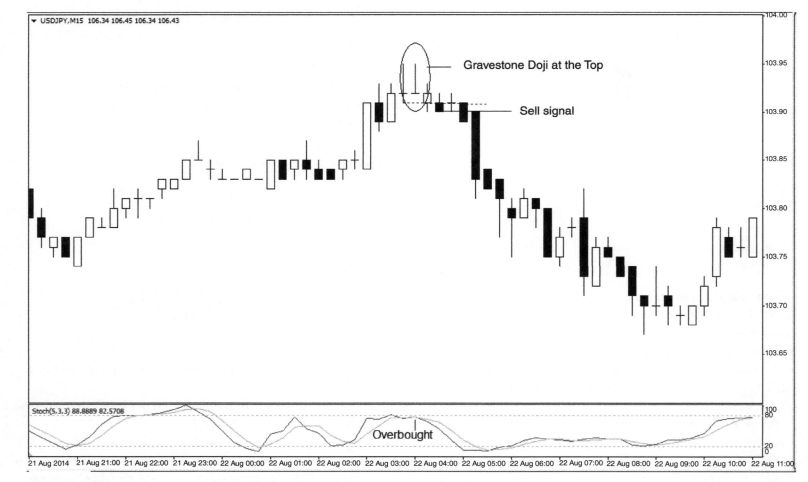

FIGURE 2.15   UsdJpy 15-Minute (2014)—Example of a Gravestone Doji

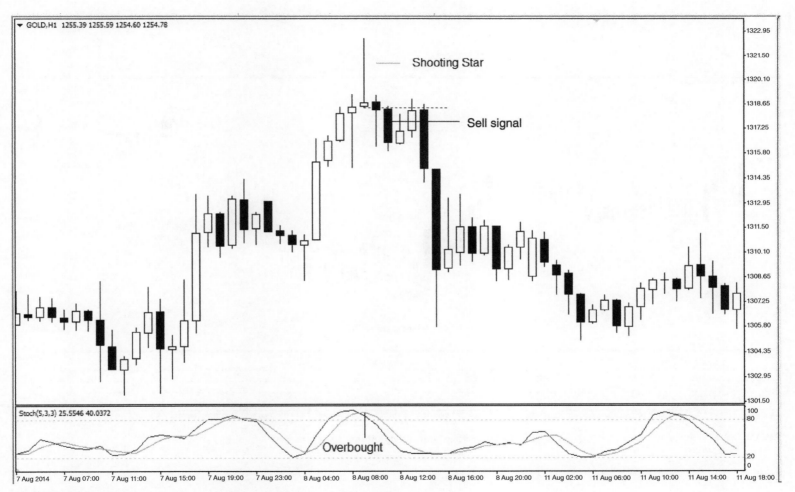

FIGURE 2.16 Gold Hourly (2014)—Shooting Star: A variation of the Gravestone Doji

FIGURE 2.17 Silver 15-Minute (2013)—Example of a Gravestone Doji at the Bottom

- **Proper action:** Possible major reversal candle but wait for a confirmation candle before buying. A close above the highest high of the Gravestone Doji (candle 2) and the candle before it (candle 1) is your buy confirmation. The Gravestone Doji candle is, however, a rare pattern in Malaysian stocks and futures as well as in most financial instruments. In more active issues, its variation, the Inverted Hammer, is a much more common occurrence as a bullish reversal signal.

3. Long-Legged Doji (Also Called High-Wave Doji)

- **Definition:** The Long-Legged or High-Wave Doji is formed when the open and close are at the same price during a larger than average daily range. The open and the close must be at the midpoint of its range. It has a long upper and lower shadow. It is the long upper and lower shadow that gives it the alternative name of a High-Wave Doji. When it emerges after an uptrend or downtrend, the Japanese say that the market has lost its sense of direction. This lack of orientation puts the prior trend into doubt (see Figure 2.18).

- **General interpretation:** Like all doji, the Long-Legged Doji can be interpreted both as a reversal or a continuation pattern. The important criterion is to identify where the doji is found. If the doji is found after a rally or at a high price area, it is generally viewed as a potential bearish reversal pattern. If it is found after a downtrend or at a low price area, it has potential bullish reversal implications. But if found in a lateral market, it is viewed as neutral.

Long-Legged Doji at the Top

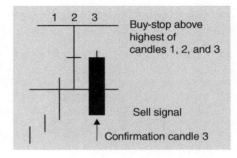

Rules
1. Sell if confirmation candle 3 closes below the low of candle 2.
2. In case of a resumption of uptrend, place buy-stop above the highest of candles 1, 2, and 3.
3. For conservative traders, sell only below candles 1 and 2.
   - **Specific interpretation:** The Long-Legged Doji is bearish if seen after a strong uptrend or at a high price area. It is a bearish candle because of its long upper and lower shadow, which reflects extreme market volatility. The inability of either the buyers or sellers to control price, resulting in a doji, implies indecision. Found after a rally, it marks the

FIGURE 2.18 Gold 15-Minute (2014)—A Long-Legged Doji found after a rally is viewed as bearish

exhaustion of the uptrend. If the open and close are near each other but not at the same price, it can still be called a Long-Legged Doji or High-Wave Doji (see Figure 2.19).

- **Proper action:** Possible major reversal candle but wait for a confirmation candle before selling. For conservative traders, wait for break below candles 1 and 2 before selling.

Long-Legged Doji at the Bottom

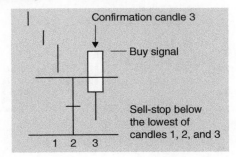

Rules

1. Buy if confirmation candle 3 closes above high of candle 2.
2. In case of a resumption of downtrend, place sell-stop below the lowest of candles 1, 2, and 3.
3. For conservative traders, buy only above candles 1 and 2.

   - **Specific interpretation:** If the Long-Legged Doji is located at a low price area or after a downtrend, it is seen as a bullish reversal candle. If the open and close are near each other but not at the same price, it is still labelled a Long-Legged Doji or a High-Wave Doji (see Figure 2.20).

   - **Proper action:** Possible major reversal candle but wait for a confirmation candle before buying. A close above the high of the Long-Legged Doji (candle 2) is your buy

confirmation. For conservative traders, wait for break above candles 1 and 2 before buying.

4. Dragonfly Doji

Definition: The Dragonfly Doji is formed when the open, close, and high are at the same price during an average or larger daily range. It has a long lower shadow.

General interpretation: Like all doji, the Dragonfly Doji can be interpreted both as a reversal or a continuation pattern. The important criterion is to identify where the doji is found. If the doji is found after a rally or at a high price area, it is generally viewed as a potential bearish reversal pattern. If it is found after a downtrend or at a low price area, it has potential bullish reversal implications. But if found in a sideways market, it is viewed as neutral.

The Dragonfly Doji at the Top

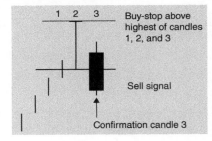

FIGURE 2.19 Soyoil Daily (2014)—A Long-Legged Doji at a high price area warns of a market top

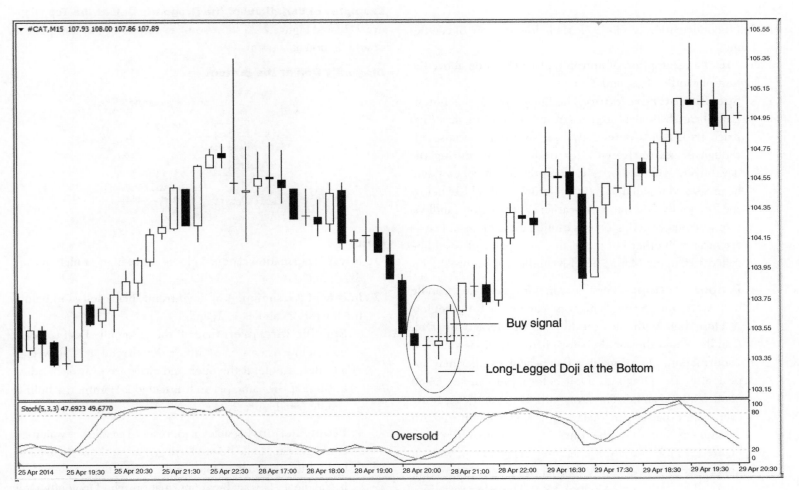

FIGURE 2.20   Caterpillar 15-Minute (2014)—A Long-Legged Doji found after a decline is a bullish reversal pattern

Rules

1. Sell if confirmation candle 3 closes below the low of candles 1 and 2.
2. In case of a resumption of uptrend, place buy-stop above the highest of candles 1, 2, and 3.

- **Specific interpretation:** The Dragonfly Doji is potentially bearish if seen after a strong uptrend or at a high price area. It is a potentially bearish candle because, although prices recovered after trading lower during the day, buyers who had bought along the lower shadow will be pressured to sell if the confirmation candle closes below the Dragonfly Doji's low. A bearish confirmation candle is required before acting on this candle. If the open and close are near each other but not at the same price, it would be called a Hanging Man, a bearish candle (see Figure 2.21).

- **Proper action:** Possible major reversal candle but wait for a confirmation candle before selling. A close below the lowest low of the Dragonfly Doji (candle 2) and the candle before it (candle 1) is your sell confirmation. Occasionally, a few bearish candles may appear after the Dragonfly Doji before you can see a sell confirmation candle. The Dragonfly Doji candle is, however, a rare pattern in Malaysian stocks and futures. An example is found in the EurAud 5-Minute chart (see Figure 2.21). Its variation, the Long-Legged Doji, with an upper shadow, occurs more frequently as signs of a market top (Gold 5-Minute; see Figure 2.22). The other variation, appearing with a small real body, called the Hanging Man, is a much more common occurrence (Silver 15-Minute; see Figure 2.23).

Examples of Variations of the Dragonfly Doji at the Top Figure 2.22 and Figure 2.23 show some examples of variations of the dragonfly doji at the top.

Dragonfly Doji at the Bottom

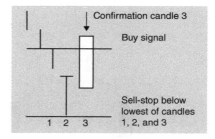

Rules

1. Buy if confirmation candle 3 closes above highest high of candles 1 and 2.
2. In case of a resumption of downtrend, place sell-stop below the lowest of candles 1, 2, and 3.

- **Specific interpretation:** If the Dragonfly Doji is located at a low price area or after a downtrend, it is viewed as a bullish candle. If the open and close are near each other but not at the same price, it is called a Hammer, a bullish candle (see Figure 2.24).

- **Proper action:** Possible major reversal candle but wait for a confirmation candle before buying. A close above the highest high of the Dragonfly Doji (candle 2) and the candle before it (candle 1) is your buy confirmation. The Dragonfly Doji candle is, however, a rare pattern in Malaysian stocks and futures. Its variations, the Hammer and Long-Legged Doji, are much more common occurrences as bullish reversal signals.

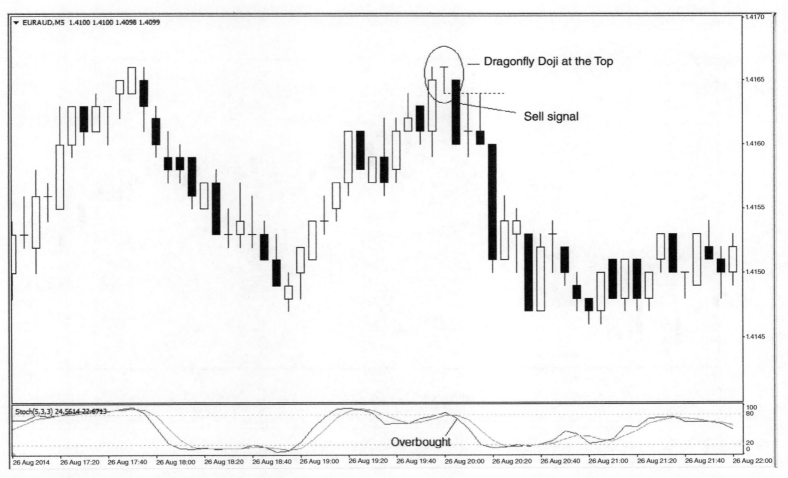

FIGURE 2.21 EurAud 5-Minute (2014)—Dragonfly Doji at the Top

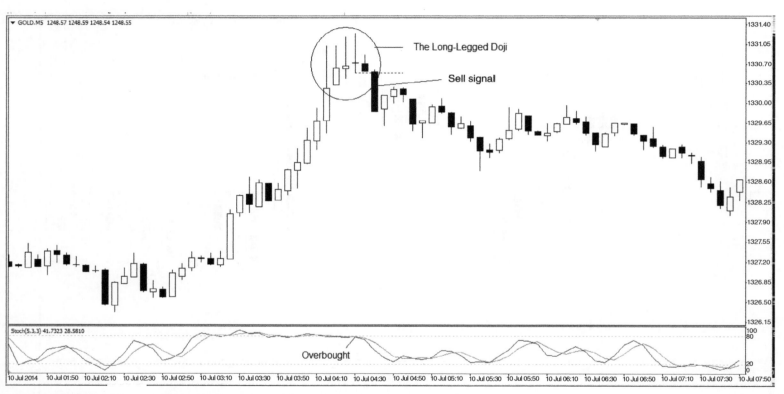

FIGURE 2.22 Gold 5-Minute (2014)—The Long-Legged Doji: A variation of the Dragonfly Doji

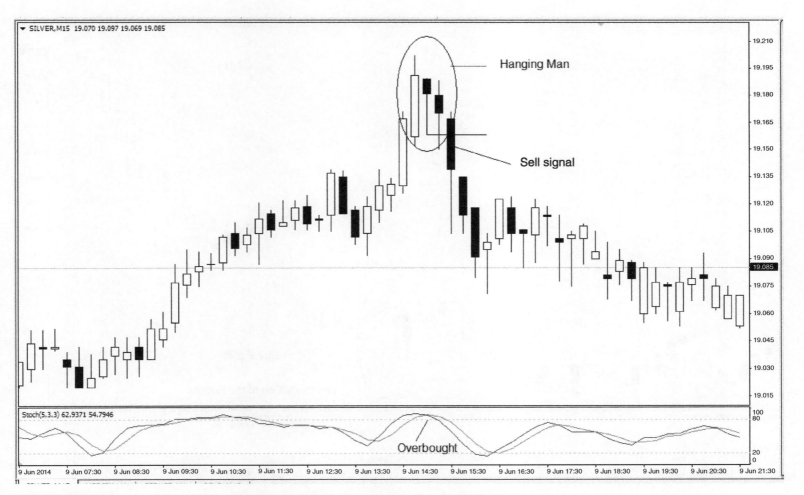

FIGURE 2.23 Silver 15-Minute (2014)—The Hanging Man: Another variation of the Dragonfly Doji

FIGURE 2.24 UsdJpy Daily (2014)—Dragonfly Doji at the Bottom

5. Small Doji

- **Definition:** This candle is formed when the open and close are equal during a smaller than average daily range. The bodyline (open and close) should be at the mid-range of the high and low (see Figure 2.25).

- **Interpretation:** This type of doji is interpreted as a consolidation pattern with a decrease in market activity because of its small range. But seen after a rally or decline, it could signal a major market top or bottom.

- **Proper action:** This doji signals a possible major market reversal if found after an advance or decline. But wait for confirmation. It is an excellent candle if it has gapped above or below to form a Star. The Doji Star indicates possible termination of a trend.

6. Small White Doji

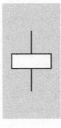

- **Definition:** The Small White Doji is formed when the open and close are almost equal during a smaller than average daily range. The close must be greater than the open. The real body should be at the mid-range of the high and low.

- **Interpretation and proper action:** The interpretation and proper action for this Small White Doji is similar to that of the Small Doji. Colour is not important.

7. Small Black Doji

- **Definition:** The Small Black Doji is formed when the open and close are almost equal during a smaller than average daily range. The close must be less than the open. The real body should be at the mid-range of the high and low (see Figure 2.26).

- **Interpretation and proper action:** The interpretation and proper action for this Small Black Doji is similar to that of the Small Doji. Colour is not important.

FIGURE 2.25 AudUsd Daily (2010)—A doji seen after a rally warns of a market top

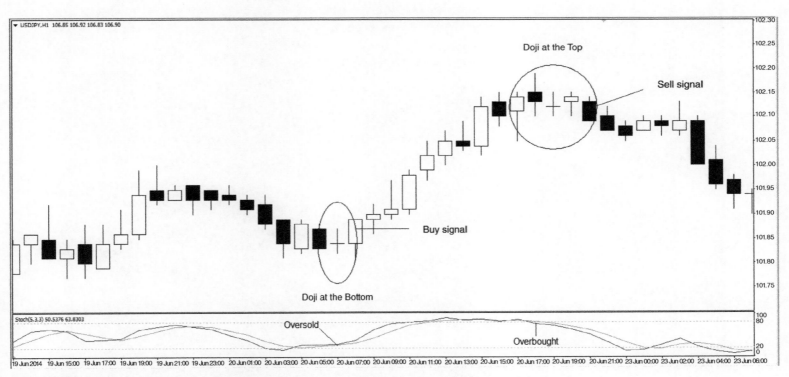

FIGURE 2.26 UsdJpy Hourly (2014)—A doji seen after a sharp decline or rally warns of market reversal

CHAPTER 3

The Umbrella Group

This group of candles is known in Japanese as *karakasa*, or paper umbrellas, because of their similarity in shape to the umbrella. In naming and interpreting umbrella group candles *location* and *shape* are the important determinants. Colour is unimportant in interpreting the umbrella group pattern because the opening and closing range (real body) is small. Being of small range, it is not a significant day as neither the bulls nor the bears are in absolute control. But its significance stems from the appearance of the long upper or lower shadow. The long shadow makes it a larger than average candle. Read in conjunction with its small real body, it has reversal implications.

■ White Hammer or Hanging Man (Also Called White Umbrella Candle)

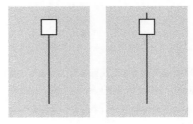

- **Definition:** The open and close are near each other (small real body). The lower shadow must be at least twice the length of the real body (three times or more is better). The close must be equal to the high or should have only a short upper shadow (see the right column in the previous diagram in this section). Although the close is greater than the open (and therefore coloured white), colour is insignificant as its real body is small.

- **Location:** If located after a downtrend or at a low price area, it is called a White Hammer. If it is found after an uptrend or at a high price area, it is called a White Hanging Man.

- **Interpretation:** A Hammer (regardless of colour) is a potentially bullish signal. A Hanging Man is a potentially bearish signal.

- **Proper action:** For conservative traders, confirmation is required before acting on this candle.

■ Black Hammer or Hanging Man (Also Called Black Umbrella Candle)

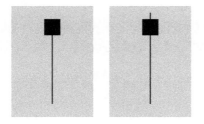

- **Definition:** The open and close are near each other (small real body). The lower shadow must be at least twice the length of the real body. (Three times or more is better.) The open may have

a slight upper shadow, but it should be very short (see the right column in the previous diagram in this section). Although the close is less than the open (and therefore coloured black), colour is insignificant. Its significance stems from its long shadow.

- **Location:** If located after a downtrend or at a low price area, it is called a Black Hammer. If it is found after a rally or at a high price area, it is called a Black Hanging Man.

- **Interpretation:** A Hammer (regardless of colour) is a potentially bullish signal. A Hanging Man (regardless of colour) is a potentially bearish signal. For conservative traders, confirmation is required before acting on this candle.

■ White Inverted Hammer or Shooting Star (Also Called Inverted White Umbrella Candle)

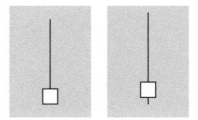

- **Definition:** The open and close are near each other (small real body). There is a long upper shadow that must be at least twice the length of the real body. (Three times or more is better). The open must be at the low or should have only a short lower shadow (see the right column in the previous diagram in this section). Although the close is greater than the open (and therefore coloured white), colour is insignificant. Its significance stems from its long shadow.

- **Location:** If located after a downtrend or at a low price area, it is called an Inverted White Hammer. If it is found after a rally or at a high price area, it is called a White Shooting Star.

- **Interpretation:** An Inverted Hammer (regardless of colour) is a potentially bullish signal. A Shooting Star (regardless of colour) is a potentially bearish signal. For conservative traders, confirmation is required before acting on this candle.

■ Black Inverted Hammer or Shooting Star (Also Called Inverted Black Umbrella Candle)

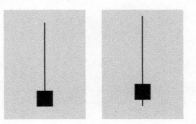

- **Definition:** The open and close are near each other (small real body). There is a long upper shadow that must be at least twice the length of the real body. (Three times or more is better.) The open must be at the low or should have only a short lower shadow (see the right column in the previous diagram in this section). Although the close is less than the open (and therefore coloured black), colour is insignificant. Its significance stems from its long shadow.

- **Location:** If located after a downtrend or at a low price area, it is called an Inverted Black Hammer. If it is found after a rally or at a high price area, it is called a Black Shooting Star.

- **Interpretation:** An Inverted Hammer (regardless of colour) is a potentially bullish signal. A Shooting Star (regardless of colour) is a potentially bearish signal. For conservative traders, confirmation is required before acting on this candle.

Figure 3.1 to Figure 3.4 show some examples of the umbrella candle group.

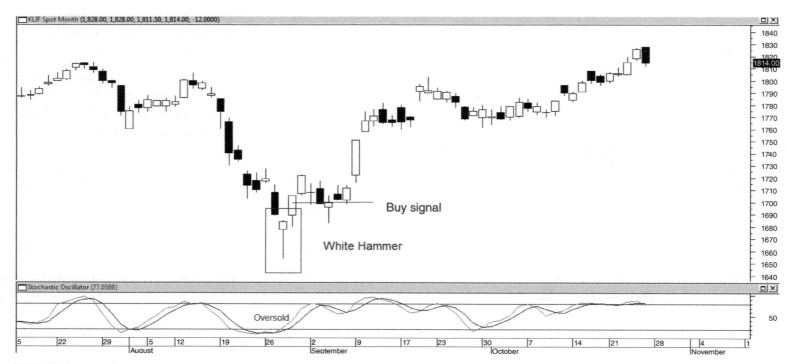

FIGURE 3.1 Kuala Lumpur Composite Index Futures Malaysia Daily (2013)—Seen after a decline this umbrella candle is called a Hammer

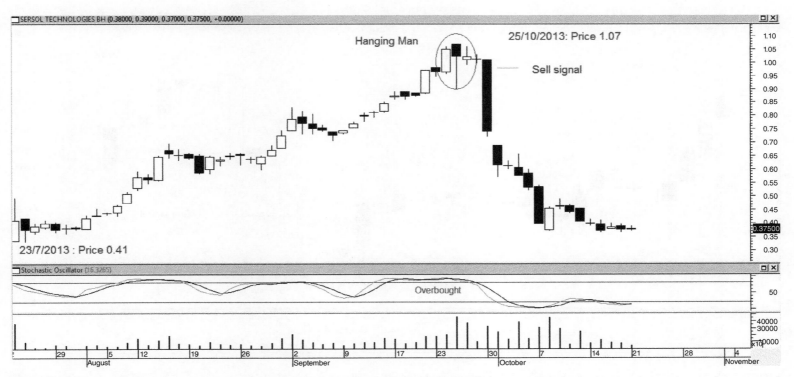

SERSOL TECHNOLOGIES BH (0.38000, 0.39000, 0.37000, 0.37500, +0.00000)

Hanging Man

25/10/2013: Price 1.07

Sell signal

23/7/2013 : Price 0.41

Stochastic Oscillator (16.3265)

Overbought

| 29 | August | 5 | 12 | 19 | 26 | 2 September | 9 | 17 | 23 | 30 October | 7 | 14 | 21 | 28 | 4 November |

FIGURE 3.2 Sersol Industries Daily (2013)—Seen after an advance this umbrella candle is called a Hanging Man

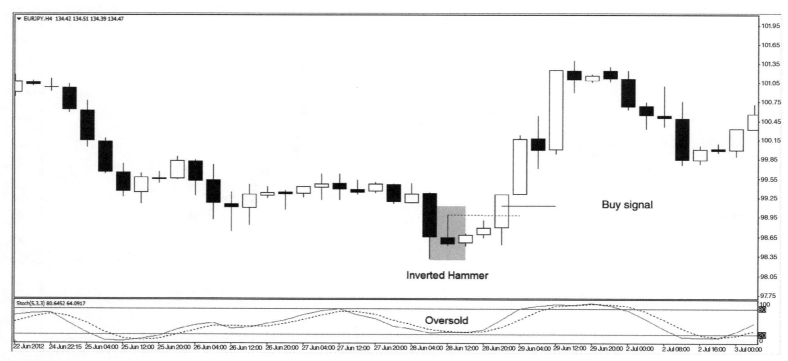

FIGURE 3.3 EurJpy Hourly (2013)—Seen after a decline this inverted umbrella candle is called an Inverted Hammer

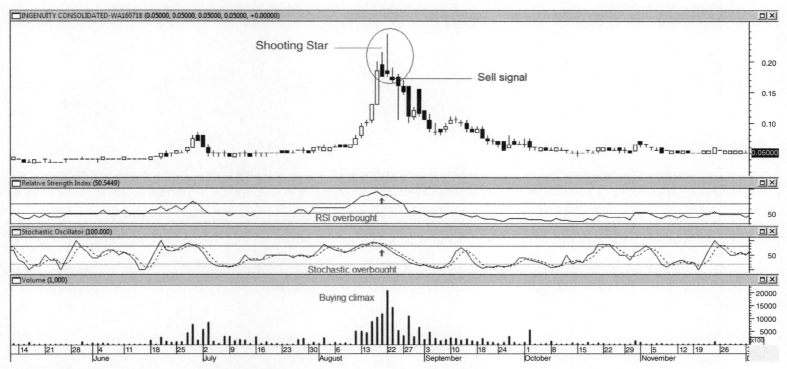

FIGURE 3.4 Ingenuity Malaysia Daily (2013)—Seen after an advance this inverted umbrella candle is called a Shooting Star

CHAPTER 4

Reversal Patterns

■ Introduction

In charting, pattern groups are divided into two major categories: reversal and continuation patterns.

Reversal patterns tell us that a trend reversal is taking place, be it short or long term. Continuation patterns, on the other hand, tell us that the market is only resting momentarily due to an overbought or oversold situation, after which the prior trend will resume.

The job of an analyst or trader is therefore to distinguish between the two types of patterns as early as possible during their formation and to trade in the direction of the breakout. In Western charting theory, the Head-and-Shoulders Top and Bottom, Double Tops and Bottoms, Triple Tops and Bottoms, Saucers, Spike or V Tops and Bottoms, Wedges, Broadening, and Diamond Formations are examples of the eight most common types of reversal patterns.

Japanese charting theory also recognizes the existence of reversal and continuation patterns, although they are called by different names. In Chapter 9 on Sakata's Five Methods, you will see that the Japanese have also identified some of these Western reversal patterns.

But where the Japanese and Western theories differ is in the number of patterns and names given to them. Further, Japanese theory has more short-term patterns in identifying market reversals when compared to Western theory.

For example, Western charting theory has basically three short-term reversal patterns—the key reversal day, two-day key reversal, and inside day. But Japanese charting theory has more than 50 reversal pattern types, with at least 8 of them found frequently in all financial markets.

Western Reversal Patterns Candlestick (Only Three Common Patterns)	Equivalent in Japanese (Eight Common Reversal Patterns)
1. Key reversal day	Bullish or Bearish Engulfing
2. Inside day	Bullish or Bearish Harami
3. Two-day key reversal	None
4. None	Piercing Line and Dark Cloud Cover
5. None	Hammer, Hangman, Inverted Hammer, Shooting Star
6. None	Fred Tam's White Inside Out Up/Black Inside Out Down
7. None	Doji
8. None	Tweezers Bottom and Top

Best Time to Rely on Reversal Patterns

Reversal patterns show extreme accuracy when they are spotted after a sharp rally or decline (of between 5 and 15 cycles). In other words, candlestick reversal patterns are best applied for spotting V or Spike Tops or Bottoms (see following diagram).

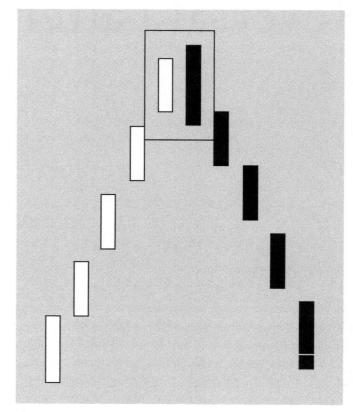

Example of a V or Spike Top

This pattern usually occurs after a runaway bull trend. The turnaround is usually accompanied a reversal pattern—in this example, a Bearish Engulfing pattern. Volume is heavy on the reversal day or the day prior to the reversal day.

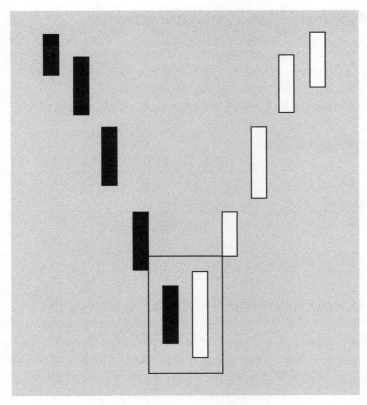

Example of a V or Spike Bottom

The downtrend quickly reverses into an uptrend without warning. But the Bullish Engulfing pattern signals the market's bottom. Volume is heavy on the reversal day or the day prior to the reversal day.

Reversal Patterns Are Reliable If Seen at a Low Price or High Price Area

A low price area can be defined as an area where the Western oscillators like Relative Strength Index, stochastic, momentum, or Williams' Percent R (these will be explained in later chapters) are oversold or where a previous support existed. A high price area can be defined as an area where the Western oscillators are overbought or where a previous resistance existed. Reversal patterns found at low or high price areas are reliable indications of trend reversal.

■ Index of Reversal Patterns

Candlestick reversal patterns can be a single candle or a group of candles. When one, two, three, or more candles combine in various formations, patterns evolve that will reveal to the trader the change in players' psychology. These candlestick reversal patterns will be the trader's guide as to whether one should enter or exit the market.

For every bullish reversal pattern, there is almost always a bearish equivalent. In this chapter I have grouped these reversal patterns into single, double, triple, and multiple candlestick patterns (see Table 4.1 to Table 4.4):

TABLE 4.1	Single Candlestick Patterns	
Bullish Reversal Patterns	**Bearish Reversal Patterns**	**Pages**
Spinning Top	Spinning Top	70–72
Hammer	Hanging Man	72–73
Inverted Hammer	Shooting Star	75–78
Doji at the Bottom	Doji at the Top	78–81
Bullish Meeting Line	Bearish Meeting Line	81–84
Bullish Belt-Hold Line	Bearish Belt-Hold Line	84–87

TABLE 4.2	Double Candlestick Patterns	
Bullish Reversal Patterns	**Bearish Reversal Patterns**	**Pages**
Bullish Engulfing	Bearish Engulfing	90–91
Fred Tam's White Inside Out Up	Fred Tam's Black Inside Out Down	95–96
Piercing Line	Dark Cloud Cover	99–100
Thrusting Line	Incomplete Dark Cloud Cover	100–104
Bullish Harami Line	Bearish Harami Line	104–107
Bullish Harami Cross	Bearish Harami Cross	110–111
Homing Pigeon	Bearish Homing Pigeon	114–115
Tweezers Bottom	Tweezers Top	115–119

TABLE 4.3	Triple Candlestick Patterns	
Bullish Reversal Patterns	**Bearish Reversal Patterns**	**Pages**
Doji-Star at the Bottom	Doji-Star at the Top	119–123
Three-River Morning Doji-Star	Three-River Evening Doji-Star	123–126
Abandoned Baby Bottom	Abandoned Baby Top	126–131
Three-River Morning Star	Three-River Evening Star	131–134
Tri-Star Bottom	Tri-Star Top	134–137
Breakaway Three-New-Price Bottom	Breakaway Three-New-Price Top	137–140
Bullish Black Three Gaps	Bearish White Three Gaps	143–144
Three White Soldiers	Three Black Crows	147–148
—	Advance Block	151–153
—	Deliberation	153–154
—	Upside Gap Two Crows	154–156

TABLE 4.4	Multiple Candlestick Patterns	
Bullish Reversal Patterns	**Bearish Reversal Patterns**	**Pages**
Concealing Baby Swallow	—	156–158
Ladder Bottom	—	158–160
Tower Bottom	Tower Top	160–163
Eight-to-Ten New Record Lows	Eight-to-Ten New Record Highs	163–167

■ Single Candlestick Patterns

Single candlestick patterns such as the Spinning Top, Hammer, Hanging Man, Inverted Hammer, Shooting Star, Doji at the Bottom, Doji at the Top, Bullish Meeting and Bearish Meeting Lines, and Bullish Belt-Hold and Bearish Belt-Hold Lines are discussed next.

Spinning Top

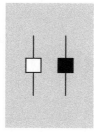

In Chapter 2, I described the Spinning Top as a short candlestick with a small real body (black or white) but with an upper and lower shadow that is longer than the length of its real body. The location of this Spinning Top is important. It is neutral if found within a consolidation market. But seen after a rally, the Spinning Top has the potential of signalling a market top; seen after a decline, it could signal a market bottom.

When a Spinning Top Becomes a Top Reversal Pattern

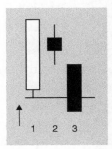

After a rally, a Black Spinning Top analysed in conjunction with the long white candle before it takes the form of a Bearish Harami, a possible top reversal pattern. Confirmation is required via a black candle closing below the lowest low of the two candles before it. Candle 3 must close below candle 2 (Spinning Top) and candle 1 to generate a sell signal. If the colour of the Spinning Top is white in colour, this two-candle pattern is called a Bearish Homing Pigeon.

When a Spinning Top Becomes an Evening Star

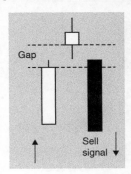

The Spinning Top will take the form of a Star if it gaps above the previous white candle. Followed by a black candle closing below the low of the white candle, this Spinning Top transforms itself into an Evening Star. An Evening Star is a top reversal pattern.

To generate a sell signal, the long black candle must close below the low of the long white candle.

When a Spinning Top Becomes a Bottom Reversal Pattern

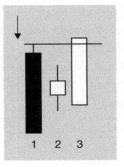

After a decline, a White Spinning Top analysed in conjunction with a long black candle (candle 1) takes the form of a Bullish Harami pattern, a possible bottom reversal pattern. Confirmation is required via a white candle closing above the highest high of the two candles before it. Candle 3 must close above candle 2 (Spinning Top) and candle 1 to generate a buy signal. If the Spinning Top is black in colour, this two-candle pattern is called a Homing Pigeon.

When a Spinning Top Becomes a Morning Star

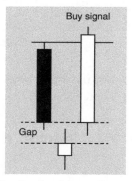

The Spinning Top will take the form of a Star if it gaps below the previous black candle. If the next white candle closes above the high of the black candle, this Spinning Top will transform itself into a Morning Star, a bottom reversal pattern.

To generate a buy signal, the long white candle must close above the high of the long black candle.

Hammer

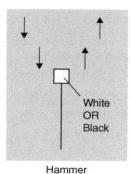

Hammer

Pattern description: The Hammer is a single candle with a long lower shadow and a small real body. The longer the shadow,

the more significant is the pattern. A Hammer is an Umbrella Candle found after a decline or at a low price area.

Rules of Recognition

1. A downtrend must be in progress.
2. The open and close have a very tight range (small real body).
3. The lower shadow must be at least twice the length of the real body (three times or more is better).
4. It should have no, or a very short, upper shadow.
5. Colour of the real body is unimportant.
6. The sharper the prior decline, the higher will be the probability of a market bottom.

Interpretation: Bullish signal.

Proper action: Buy signal if followed by a bullish confirmation candle.

Buying on the Hammer Pattern

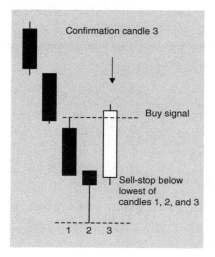

Rules
1. Buy if confirmation candle 3 closes above the highest high of candles 1 and 2.
2. In case of a resumption of a downtrend, place sell-stop below the lowest low of candles 1, 2, and 3.

Figure 4.1 shows an example of a Hammer bottoming out pattern after a sharp fall.

Hanging Man

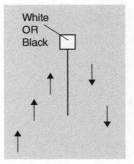

Pattern description: The Hanging Man is a single candle with a long lower shadow and a small real body. The longer the shadow the more significant is the pattern. A Hanging Man is an Umbrella Candle found after an advance or at a high price area.

Rules of Recognition
1. An uptrend must be in progress.
2. The open and close have a very tight range (small real body).

3. The lower shadow must be at least twice the length of the real body (three times or more is better).
4. It should have no, or a very short, upper shadow.
5. Colour of the real body is unimportant.
6. The sharper the prior rally, the higher will be the probability of a market top.

Interpretation: Bearish signal.
Proper action: Sell signal if followed by a bearish confirmation candle.

Selling on the Hanging Man Pattern

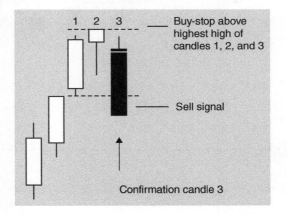

Rules
1. Sell if confirmation candle 3 closes below the lowest low of candles 1 and 2.
2. In case of a resumption of an uptrend, place buy-stop above the highest high of candles 1, 2, and 3.

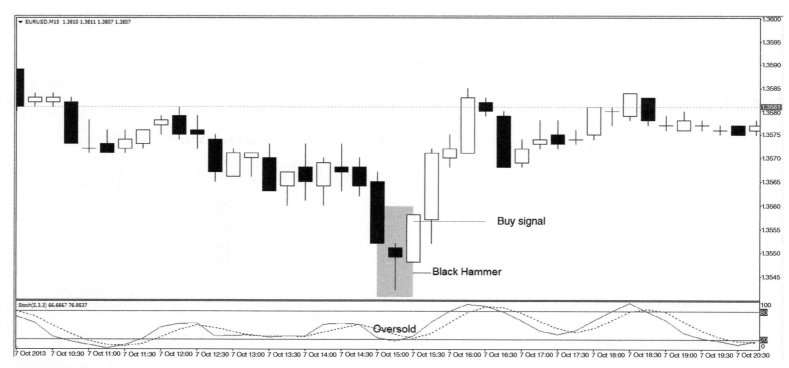

FIGURE 4.1 EurUsd 15-Minute (2013)—A Hammer is a great bottoming out pattern after a sharp fall

Inverted Hammer

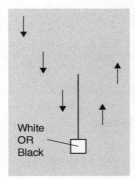

Pattern description: The Inverted Hammer is a single candle with a long upper shadow and a small real body. The longer the shadow, the more significant is the pattern. An Inverted Hammer is an Inverted Umbrella Candle found after a decline or at a low price area.

Rules of Recognition
1. A downtrend must be in progress.
2. The open and close have a very tight range (small real body).
3. The upper shadow must be at least twice the length of the real body (three times or more is better).
4. It should have no, or a very short, lower shadow.
5. Colour is unimportant.
6. The sharper the prior decline, the more significant is the subsequent rebound.

Interpretation: Bullish signal.

Proper action: Buy signal if followed by a bullish confirmation candle.

Buying on the Inverted Hammer Pattern

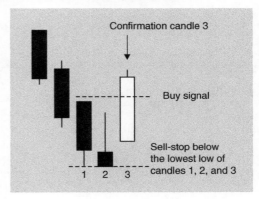

Rules
1. Buy if confirmation candle 3 closes above the highest high of candles 1 and 2.
2. In case of a resumption of a downtrend, place sell-stop below the lowest low of candles 1, 2, and 3.

Figure 4.2 and Figure 4.3 show some examples of Hanging Man and Inverted Hammer patterns.

Shooting Star

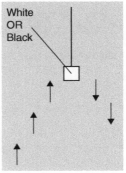

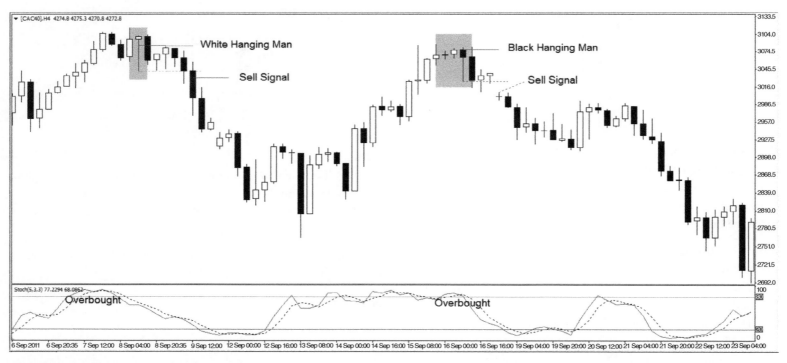

FIGURE 4.2   CAC 40 4-Hour (2013)—Hanging Man seen after a rally is bearish

FIGURE 4.3 UsdJpy Hourly (2013)—Inverted Hammer seen after a decline is bullish

Pattern description: The Shooting Star is a single candle with a long upper shadow and a small real body. The longer the shadow the more significant is the pattern. A Shooting Star is an Inverted Umbrella Candle found after an advance or at a high price area.

Rules of Recognition

1. An uptrend must be in progress.
2. The open and close have a very tight range (small real body).
3. The upper shadow must be at least twice the length of the real body (three times or more is better).
4. It should have no, or a very short, lower shadow.
5. Colour is unimportant.
6. The sharper the prior rally, the higher is the probability of a market top.

Interpretation: Bearish signal.

Proper action: Sell signal if followed by a bearish confirmation candle.

Selling on the Shooting Star Pattern

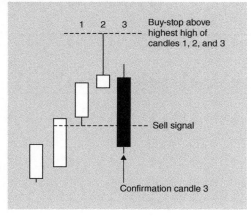

Buy-stop above highest high of candles 1, 2, and 3

Sell signal

Confirmation candle 3

Rules

1. Sell if confirmation candle 3 closes below the lowest low of candles 1 and 2.
2. In case of a resumption of an uptrend, place buy-stop above the highest high of candles 1, 2, and 3.

Figure 4.4 shows an example of selling on the Shooting Star pattern.

Doji at the Bottom

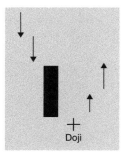

Doji

Pattern description: A doji is a single candle where the open and close are at the same price. It has no real body. The upper and lower shadows can be long or short.

Rules of Recognition

1. A downtrend must be in progress.
2. The first day is a long black day followed by a doji.
3. A doji found within the real body of the prior candle is called a Harami Cross pattern.
4. A doji that gaps below the real body of the prior candle forms a Doji-Star.

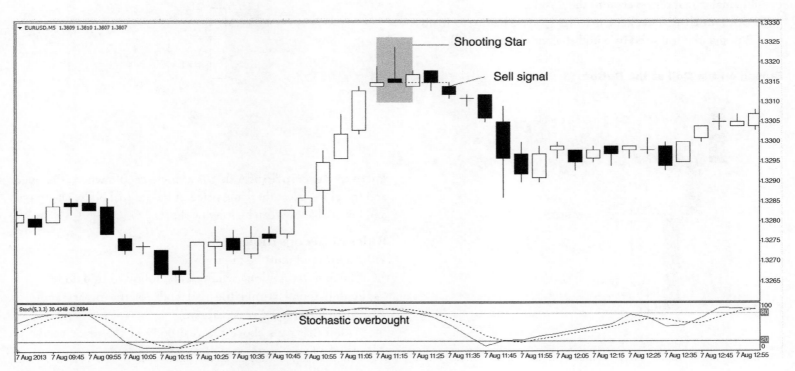

FIGURE 4.4 EurUsd 5-Minute (2013)—Shooting Star seen after an advance is bearish

Interpretation: Normally a doji is a sign of market indecision, hence a neutral candle. But seen after a decline or at the bottom of a trend, a doji has bullish potential. It could signal a possible major market reversal to the upside.

Proper action: Excellent if it has gapped below to form a Star. Buy signal if followed by a bullish confirmation candle.

Buying on the Doji at the Bottom

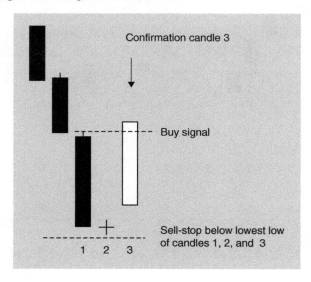

Rules

1. Buy if confirmation candle 3 closes above the highest high of candles 1 and 2.
2. In case of a resumption of a downtrend, place sell-stop below the lowest low of candles 1, 2, and 3.

Doji at the Top

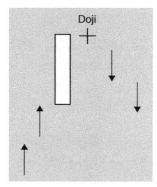

Pattern description: A doji is a single candle where the open and the close are at the same price. It has no real body. The upper and lower shadows can be long or short.

Rules of Recognition

1. An uptrend must be in progress.
2. The first day is a long white candle followed by a doji.
3. A doji found within the real body of the prior candle is called a Harami Cross pattern.
4. A doji that gaps above the real body of the prior candle is called a Doji-Star.

Interpretation: Normally, a doji is a neutral candle, but seen after a rally or at the top of a trend, a doji has bearish potential. It could signal a possible major market reversal.

Proper action: Excellent if it has gapped above to form a Star. Sell signal if followed by a bearish confirmation candle.

Selling on the Doji at the Top

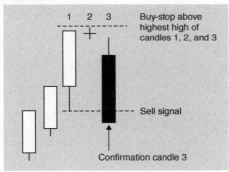

Rules

1. Sell if confirmation candle 3 closes below the lowest low of candles 1 and 2.
2. In case of a resumption of an uptrend, place buy-stop above the highest high of candles 1, 2, and 3.

Figure 4.5 and Figure 4.6 show some examples of doji at the bottom and top patterns.

Bullish Meeting and Bearish Meeting Lines

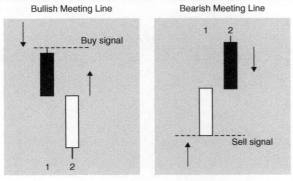

The Bullish Meeting and Bearish Meeting Lines pattern descriptions, rules of recognition, interpretations, and proper actions are explained here together with some examples.

Bullish Meeting Line (Bullish)

Pattern description: The Bullish Meeting Line is formed when a black candle is followed by a white candle, which gaps down on the open but rallies to close at the same price as the black candle.

Rules of Recognition

1. A downtrend must be in progress.
2. The Bullish Meeting Line starts with a long black candle on the first day.
3. The second day gaps lower on the opening, but buying pushes the market to close at the first day's close.
4. Both days have long real bodies of the opposite colour.

Interpretation: Meeting lines are sometimes called counterattack lines. The Bullish Meeting Line is almost like a Piercing Line except that in the Bullish Meeting Line, the close of the current candle is at the same price as the close of the first candle. Unlike the Piercing Line, it does not penetrate into the black real body of the first candle. The Bullish Meeting Line is therefore less bullish than the Piercing Line.

Proper action: Possible bullish reversal. Buy only if there is a bullish confirmation candle that closes above the high of candle 1. Otherwise, the downtrend can continue.

Bearish Meeting Line (Bearish)

Pattern description: The Bearish Meeting Line is formed when a white candle is followed by a gapping black candle on the open but declines to close at the same price as the white candle.

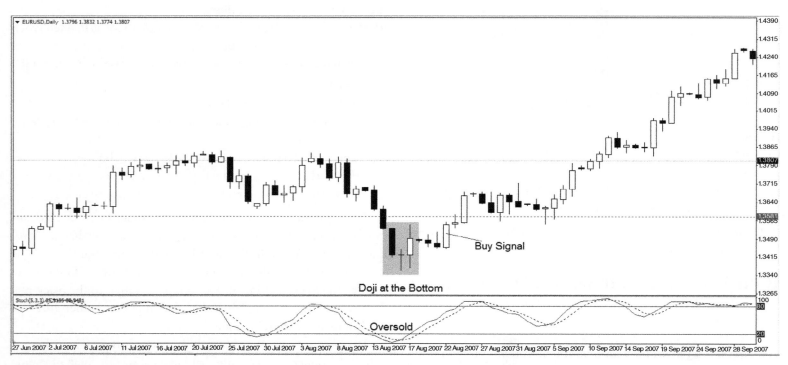

FIGURE 4.5 EurUsd Daily (2013)—A doji seen after a decline is bullish

FIGURE 4.6 UsdChf 15-Minute (2013)—A doji seen after an advance is bearish

Rules of Recognition

1. An uptrend must be in progress.
2. The first day is a long white candle.
3. The second day gaps higher on the opening, but selling push-es the market to close at the first day's close.
4. Both days have long real bodies of the opposite colour.

Interpretation: Meeting lines are sometimes called coun-terattack lines. The Bearish Meeting Line is almost like a Dark Cloud Cover except that in the Bearish Meeting Line, the cur-rent close is at the same price as the close of the previous white candle. Unlike the Dark Cloud Cover, it does not penetrate into the white real body of the first candle. The Bearish Meeting Line is therefore less bearish than the Dark Cloud Cover.

Proper action: Possible bearish reversal. Sell only if there is a bearish confirmation candle that closes below the low of candle 1. Otherwise, the uptrend can continue.

Trading the Bullish Meeting and Bearish Meeting Lines Figure 4.7 and Figure 4.8 show some examples of the Bullish and Bearish Meeting Line patterns.

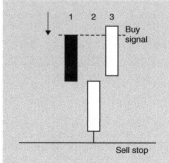

The close on candle 3 must exceed the high of candle 1 to trigger a buy signal. Place sell-stop below the lowest low of candles 1 and 2.

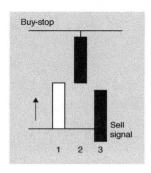

The close on candle 3 must exceed the low of candle 1 to trigger a sell signal. Place buy-stop above the highest high of candles 1 and 2.

Bullish Belt-Hold and Bearish Belt-Hold Lines

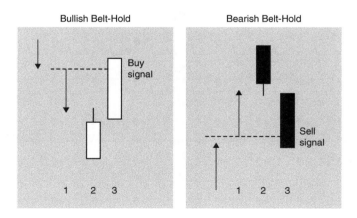

Bullish Belt-Hold and Bearish Belt-Hold pattern descriptions, rules of recognition, interpretations, and proper actions are ex-plained here together with some examples.

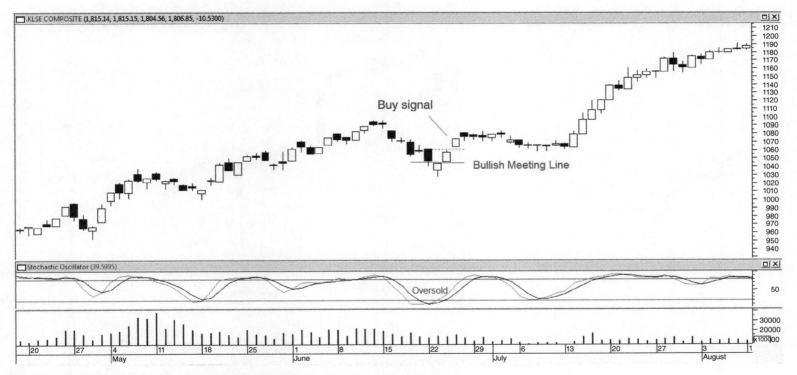

Chart labels (inside chart):
- .KLSE COMPOSITE (1,815.14, 1,815.15, 1,804.56, 1,806.85, -10.5300)
- Buy signal
- Bullish Meeting Line
- Stochastic Oscillator (39.5995)
- Oversold

FIGURE 4.7   Kuala Lumpur Composite Index Malaysia Daily (2010)—Bullish Meeting Line

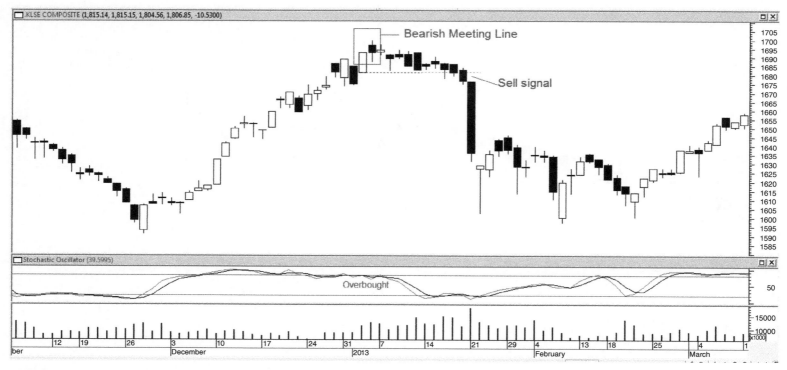

FIGURE 4.8 Kuala Lumpur Composite Index Malaysia Daily (2013)—Bearish Meeting Line

Bullish Belt-Hold Line (Bullish)

Pattern description: The Bullish Belt-Hold Line is a White Opening Bozu candle seen in a downtrend. It opens at the low but closes back up near the high, rallying against the downtrend.

Rules of Recognition

1. A downtrend must be in progress.
2. In a bullish scenario, the market opens with a down gap in the direction of the downtrend but thereafter rallies all the way up to close near the day's high.
3. The Bullish Belt-Hold Line is also called a White Opening Bozu Line where it does not have a lower shadow because it opens at the low but closes near its high, leaving an upper shadow.
4. The Japanese name for Belt-Hold is the sumo wrestling term *yorikiri*, which means "pushing your opponent out of the ring while holding on to his belt."

Interpretation: The Bullish Belt-Hold Line is classified as a bullish reversal pattern because of its appearance after a defined downtrend. It is similar to the counterattack line or Bullish Meeting Line except that it is a White Opening Bozu Line.

Proper action: Possible bullish reversal. Buy only if there is a bullish confirmation candle that closes above the highest high of candles 1 and 2. Otherwise, the downtrend can continue.

Bearish Belt-Hold Line (Bearish)

Pattern description: A Bearish Belt-Hold Line is a Black Opening Bozu candle seen in an uptrend. It opens at the high but closes back down near the low, correcting the uptrend.

Rules of Recognition

1. An uptrend must be in progress.

2. In a bearish scenario, the market opens with an up gap in the direction of the uptrend but thereafter declines all the way down to close near the day's low.
3. The Bearish Belt-Hold Line is also called an Black Opening Bozu Line where it does not have an upper shadow because it opens at the high but closes near its low, leaving a lower shadow.
4. The Japanese name for Belt-Hold is the sumo wrestling term *yorikiri*, which means "pushing your opponent out of the ring while holding on to his belt."

Interpretation: The Bearish Belt-Hold Line is a bearish reversal pattern because of its appearance after a defined uptrend. It is similar to the counterattack line or Bearish Meeting Line except that it is a Black Opening Bozu Line.

Proper action: Possible bearish reversal. Sell only if there is a bearish confirmation candle that closes below the lowest low of candles 1 and 2. Otherwise, the uptrend can continue.

Trading the Bullish Belt-Hold and Bearish Belt-Hold Lines

Figure 4.9 and Figure 4.10 show some examples of Bullish and Bearish Belt-Hold Line patterns.

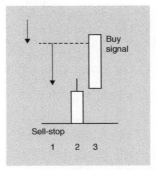

The close on candle 3 must exceed the high of candles 1 or 2 to trigger a buy signal. Place sell-stop below the lowest low of candles 1 and 2.

FIGURE 4.9   S&P 500 Daily (2014)—Bullish Belt-Hold

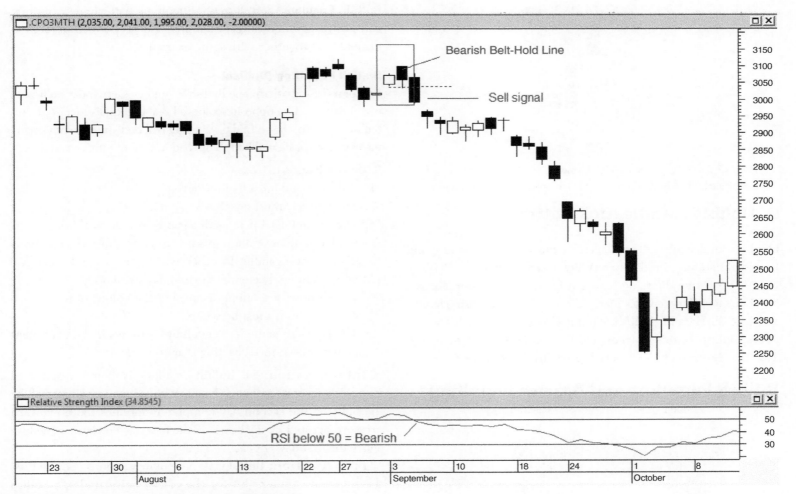

.CPO3MTH (2,035.00, 2,041.00, 1,995.00, 2,028.00, -2.00000)

Bearish Belt-Hold Line

Sell signal

Relative Strength Index (34.8545)

RSI below 50 = Bearish

| 23 | 30 | 6 | 13 | 22 | 27 | 3 | 10 | 18 | 24 | 1 | 8 |

August

September

October

FIGURE 4.10   Crude Palm Oil Daily—Bearish Belt-Hold

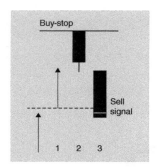

The close on candle 3 must exceed the low of candles 1 and 2 to trigger a sell signal. Place buy-stop above the highest high of candles 1 and 2.

■ Double Candlestick Patterns

Double candlestick patterns such as the Bullish Engulfing and Bearish Engulfing, Fred Tam's White Inside Out Up and Black Inside Out Down, Piercing Line and Dark Cloud Cover, Thrusting Line and Incomplete Dark Cloud Cover, Bullish Harami and Bearish Harami, Bullish Harami Cross and Bearish Harami Cross, Bullish Homing Pigeon and Bearish Homing Pigeon, and Tweezers Bottom and Tweezers Top are discussed next.

Bullish Engulfing and Bearish Engulfing

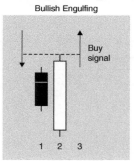
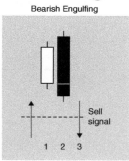

Bullish Engulfing and Bearish Engulfing pattern descriptions, rules of recognition, interpretations, and proper actions are explained here together with some examples.

Bullish Engulfing (Bullish)

Pattern description: The Bullish Engulfing is a two-day bullish reversal pattern. Two opposite-coloured real bodies distinguish it. In a bullish scenario, the second day's white real body must totally engulf the first day's black real body. The shadows are not important here.

Rules of Recognition

1. A downtrend must be in progress.
2. The first day must be a black candle.
3. The second day opens with a gap below the real body of the black candle but rallies upwards to close above the real body of the black candle. In other words, the second day's real body completely engulfs the first day's real body.
4. The shadows are unimportant, but the colour of the second day's real body must be white.
5. The Japanese name for "engulfing" is *tsutsumi*. The equivalent pattern in Western charting is an "outside day."

Interpretation: The Bullish Engulfing is the most bullish of all bullish reversal patterns. This is because the counterattack by the bulls on the second day completely nullifies the downward pressure exerted by the bears on the first day by virtue of a close above the first day's open.

Proper action: Buy signal. No confirmation is required for the aggressive trader. But for the conservative trader, a bullish confirmation is suggested. To confirm a buy, the third candle must close above the highest high of candles 1 and 2. Place sell-stop below the lowest low of candles 1 and 2. Best if found at a low price area or when the market is oversold.

Bearish Engulfing (Bearish)

Pattern description: The Bearish Engulfing is a two-day bearish reversal pattern. Two opposite-coloured real bodies distinguish it. In a bearish scenario, the second day's black real body must totally engulf the first day's white real body. The shadows are not important here.

Rules of Recognition

1. An uptrend must be in progress.
2. The first day must be a white candle.
3. The second day opens with a gap above the real body of the white candle but declines sharply to close below the real body of the first candle. In other words, the second day's real body completely engulfs the first day's real body.
4. The shadows of either day are unimportant. But the colour of the second day's real body must be black. A greater than average black real body on the second day increases the likelihood of a successful bearish reversal.
5. The Japanese name for "engulfing" is *tsutsumi*. The equivalent pattern in Western charting is an "outside day."

Interpretation: The Bearish Engulfing is the most bearish of all bearish reversal patterns because the counterattack by the bears on the second day completely nullifies the control exerted by the bulls on the first day. The second day's close below the first day's open implies a complete change in the psychology of the big players who have now turned bearish.

Proper action: Sell signal. No confirmation is required for the aggressive trader. But for the conservative trader, a bearish confirmation is suggested. To confirm a sell, the third candle must close below the lowest low of candles 1 and 2. Place buy-stop above the highest high of candles 1 and 2. Best if found at a high price area or when market is overbought.

Trading the Bullish Engulfing and Bearish Engulfing Figure 4.11 to Figure 4.13 show some examples of Bullish Engulfing and Bearish Engulfing patterns.

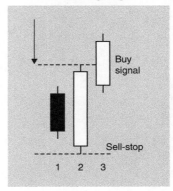

Bullish Engulfing

The close on candle 3 must exceed the high of candles 1 and 2 to trigger a buy signal. Place sell-stop below the lowest low of candles 1 and 2.

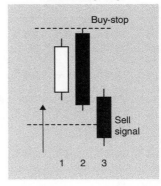

Bearish Engulfing

The close on candle 3 must exceed the low of candles 1 and 2 to trigger a sell signal. Place buy-stop above the highest high of candles 1 and 2.

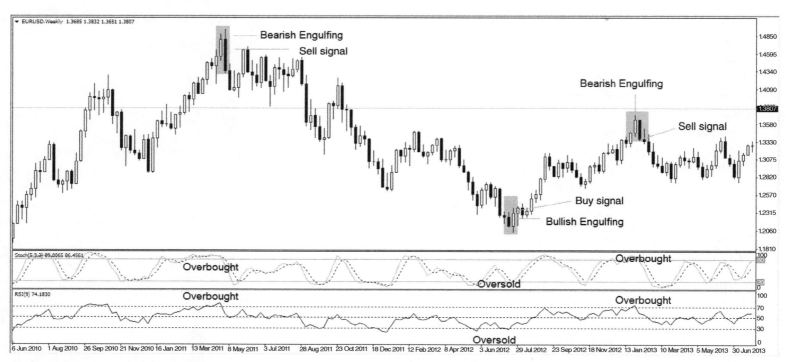

FIGURE 4.11 EurUsd Weekly (2010–2013)—Bullish Engulfing and Bearish Engulfing patterns mark turning points

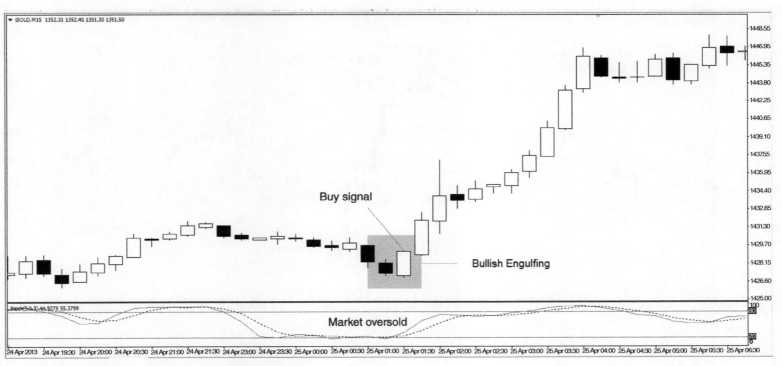

FIGURE 4.12   Gold 15-Minute (2013)—Bullish Engulfing

FIGURE 4.13   EurUsd 15-Minute (2013)—Bearish Engulfing

Fred Tam's White Inside Out Up and Black Inside Out Down

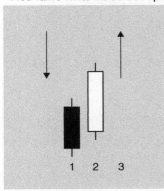

Fred Tam's White Inside Out Up

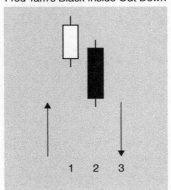

Fred Tam's Black Inside Out Down

Fred Tam's White Inside Out Up and Black Inside Out Down pattern descriptions, rules of recognition, interpretations, and proper actions are explained here together with some examples.

Fred Tam's White Inside Out Up (Bullish)

Pattern description: Fred Tam's White Inside Out Up is a two-day bullish reversal pattern identified by the author. Two opposite-coloured real bodies distinguish it. In a bullish scenario, the second day's white real body opens within the first day's black real body but closes above the first day's open. The shadows are not important here.

Rules of Recognition

1. A downtrend must be in progress.
2. The first day must be a black candle.

3. The second day opens within the first day's black real body, rallies, and closes above the black candle's real body. In other words, the second day's real body partially engulfs the first day's real body. The colour of the second day is white. The shadows are unimportant.
4. This pattern is a variation of the Bullish Engulfing. The difference between these two patterns is that in the Bullish Engulfing, the second day opens below the first day's black real body whereas in this pattern the second day opens within the first day's black real body.

Interpretation: Fred Tam's White Inside Out Up is as bullish as the Bullish Engulfing and is a frequently recurring pattern in all markets. This pattern depicts a scenario where the sharp fall, as represented by the black candle, is overdone. An oversold situation arises, which is taken advantage of by market participants. The higher open on the second day reflects this oversold first day. The second day's rally to close higher than the first day's black candle real body represents a successful counterattack by the bulls.

Proper action: Buy signal. No confirmation is required for the aggressive trader. But for the conservative trader, a bullish confirmation is suggested. To confirm a buy, the third candle must close above the highest high of candles 1 and 2. Place sell-stop below the lowest low of candles 1 and 2 in the event of a failure. Best if found at a low price area or when the market is oversold.

Fred Tam's Black Inside Out Down (Bearish)

Pattern description: Fred Tam's Black Inside Out Down is a two-day bearish reversal pattern identified by the author. Two opposite-coloured real bodies distinguish it. In a bearish scenario, the second day's black real body opens within the first day's white real body but closes below the first day's open. The shadows are not important here.

Rules of Recognition

1. An uptrend must be in progress.
2. The first day must be a white candle.
3. The second day opens within the first day's white real body, declines, and closes below the white candle's real body. In other words, the second day's real body partially engulfs the first day's real body. The colour of the second day is black.
4. This pattern is a variation of the Bearish Engulfing. The difference between these two patterns is that in the Bearish Engulfing, the second day opens above the first day's white real body whereas in this pattern, it opens within the first day's white real body.

Interpretation: Fred Tam's Black Inside Out Down is as bearish as the Bearish Engulfing and is a frequently recurring pattern in all markets. This pattern depicts a scenario where the sharp rally, as represented by the white candle, is overdone. An overbought situation arises, which is taken advantage of by market participants. The lower open on the second day reflects this overbought first day. The second day's decline to close lower than the first day's white candle's real body represents a successful counterattack by the bears.

Proper action: Sell signal. No confirmation is required for the aggressive trader. But for the conservative trader, a bearish confirmation is suggested. To confirm a sell, the third candle must close below the lowest low of candles 1 and 2. Place buy-stop above the highest high of candles 1 and 2 in the event of a failure. Best if found at a high price area or when market is overbought.

Trading Fred Tam's White Inside Out Up and Black Inside Out Down Figure 4.14 and Figure 4.15 show some examples of Fred Tam's White Inside Out Up and Black Inside Out Down patterns.

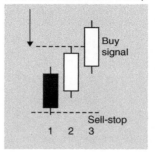

The close on candle 3 must exceed the highest high of candles 1 and 2 to confirm a buy. Place sell-stop below the lowest low of candles 1 and 2.

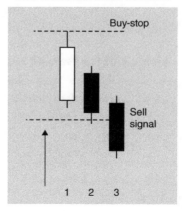

The close on candle 3 must exceed the lowest low of candles 1 and 2 to confirm a sell signal. Place buy-stop above the highest high of candles 1 and 2.

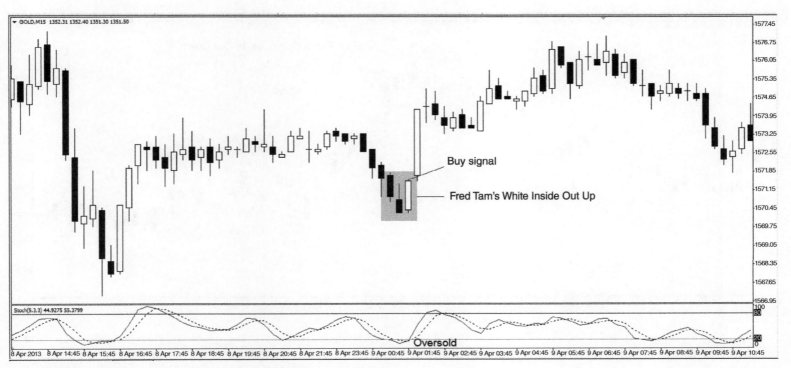

Buy signal

Fred Tam's White Inside Out Up

FIGURE 4.14   Gold 15-Minute (2013)—Fred Tam's White Inside Out Up

FIGURE 4.15 AudUsd 5-Minute (2013)—Fred Tam's Black Inside Out Down

Piercing Line and Dark Cloud Cover

Piercing Line

Dark Cloud Cover

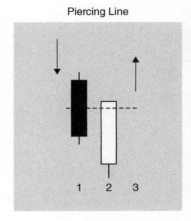
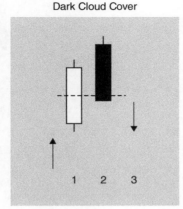

Piercing Line and Dark Cloud Cover pattern descriptions, rules of recognition, interpretations, and proper actions are explained here together with some examples.

Piercing Line (Bullish)

Pattern description: The Piercing Line is a two-day bullish reversal pattern. This pattern is distinguished by the second day's white real body piercing back into or above the midpoint of the first day's black real body.

Rules of Recognition

1. A downtrend must be in progress.
2. The first candle is black, reflecting the continuing bearish mood.
3. The second day's candle gaps lower on the opening, giving the impression of a very weak market ahead, but buyers stage a counterattack resulting in a close that penetrates back into the real body of the first day's white candle.

4. To qualify as a Piercing Line, the white candle on the second day must close at or above the midpoint of the first day's black candle's real body.
5. The Japanese name for Piercing Line is *kirikomi*, which means "a cutback or a switchback."

Interpretation: The Piercing Line can be interpreted as a counterattack by the bulls. Although the second day opens lower, the bulls are strong enough to absorb the selling pressure and stage a rally. Found after a period of decline or at a low price area, the Piercing Line hints at a potential bottom. The Piercing Line is more bullish than the Bullish Meeting Line but less bullish than the Bullish Engulfing.

Proper action: Possible bullish reversal. Buy if there is a bullish confirmation candle that closes above the high of candles 1 and 2. Otherwise, the downtrend can continue.

Dark Cloud Cover (Bearish)

Pattern description: The Dark Cloud Cover is a two-day bearish reversal pattern. This pattern is distinguished by the second day's black real body penetrating into or below the midpoint of the first day's white real body.

Rules of Recognition

1. An uptrend must be in progress.
2. The first candle is white, reflecting the continuing bullish mood.
3. The second day's candle gaps higher on the opening, giving an impression of a strong market ahead, but sellers surface and pressure prices lower throughout the day, resulting in a close that penetrates back into the real body of the first day's black candle.
4. To qualify as a Dark Cloud Cover, the black candle on the second day must close at or below the midpoint of the first day's white candle's real body.

5. The Japanese name for Dark Cloud Cover is *kabuse*, which means "to get covered or to hang over."

Interpretation: The Dark Cloud Cover is a bearish reversal pattern. It can be interpreted as a counterattack by the bears. Although the second day opens higher, the bulls are not strong enough to withstand selling pressure. As a result of heavy selling, the bulls retreat, and hints of a potential top appear. The Dark Cloud Cover is more bearish than the Bearish Meeting Line but less bearish than the Bearish Engulfing.

Proper action: Possible bearish reversal. Sell if there is a bearish confirmation candle that closes below the low of candles 1 and 2. Otherwise, the uptrend can continue.

Trading the Piercing Line and Dark Cloud Cover

Figure 4.16 and Figure 4.17 show some examples of Piercing Line and Dark Cloud Cover patterns.

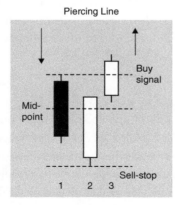

Piercing Line

The close on candle 3 must exceed the high of candles 1 and 2 to trigger a buy signal. Place sell-stop below the lowest low of candles 1 and 2.

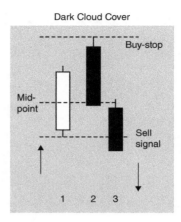

Dark Cloud Cover

The close on candle 3 must exceed the low of candles 1 and 2 to trigger a sell signal. Place buy-stop above the highest high of candles 1 and 2.

Thrusting Line and Incomplete Dark Cloud Cover

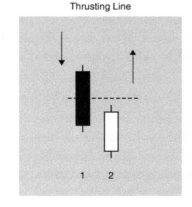

Thrusting Line

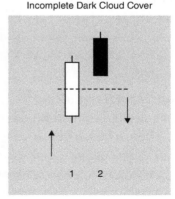

Incomplete Dark Cloud Cover

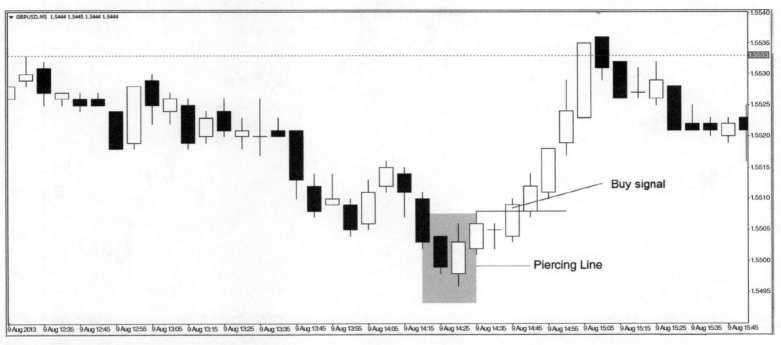

FIGURE 4.16   GbpUsd 5-Minute (2013)—Piercing Line

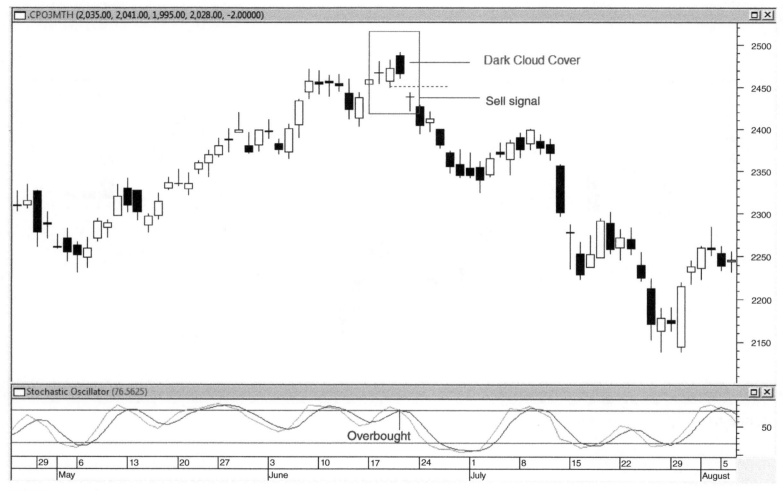

FIGURE 4.17 Crude Palm Oil Daily (2013)—Dark Cloud Cover

Thrusting Line and Incomplete Cloud Cover pattern descriptions, rules of recognition, interpretations, and proper actions are discussed here together with some examples.

Thrusting Line (Bullish)

Pattern description: The Thrusting Line can be both a continuation and a reversal pattern. It is distinguished by the second day's real body piercing back into but close just below the midpoint of the first day's black real body.

Rules of Recognition

1. A downtrend must be in progress.
2. The first candle is black, reflecting the continuing bearish mood.
3. The second day's candle gaps lower on the opening, but buyers stage a counterattack, resulting in a close that penetrates back into the real body of the first day's black candle but below its midpoint.
4. To qualify as a Thrusting Line, the white candle on the second day must close below the midpoint of the first day's black candle's real body.

Interpretation: The Thrusting Line can be interpreted as a counterattack by the bulls. Although the second day opens lower, the bulls are strong enough to absorb the selling pressure and stage a rally, resulting in a higher close back into the bears' territory (which is the first day's black candle). But unlike the Piercing Line, the white candle in the Thrusting Line did not close at or above the midpoint of the black candle. Its inability to close at or above the midpoint implies that this pattern is not as strong as the Piercing Line.

Proper action: Possible bullish reversal. Buy if there is a bullish confirmation candle that closes above the high of candle 1 and 2. Otherwise, the downtrend can continue.

Incomplete Dark Cloud Cover (Bearish)

Pattern description: The Incomplete Dark Cloud Cover is a two-day bearish reversal pattern. This pattern is distinguished by the second day's real body penetrating back into but closing just above the midpoint of the first day's white real body.

Rules of Recognition

1. An uptrend must be in progress.
2. The first candle is white, reflecting the continuing bullish mood.
3. The second day's candle gaps higher on the opening, but sellers stage a sell-off resulting in a close that penetrates back into the real body of the first day's white candle but above its midpoint.
4. To qualify as an Incomplete Dark Cloud Cover, the black candle on the second day must close above the midpoint of the first day's white candle's real body.

Interpretation: The Incomplete Dark Cloud Cover is a bearish reversal pattern. But unlike the Dark Cloud Cover, the black candle in the Incomplete Dark Cloud Cover did not close at or below the midpoint of the first day's white candle. Its inability to close at or below the midpoint implies that this pattern is not as weak as the Dark Cloud cover.

Proper action: Possible bearish reversal. Sell if there is a bearish confirmation candle that closes below the low of candles 1 and 2. Otherwise, the uptrend can continue.

Trading the Thrusting Line and Incomplete Dark Cloud Cover Figure 4.18 and Figure 4.19 show some examples of Thrusting Line and Incomplete Dark Cloud Cover patterns.

Thrusting Line

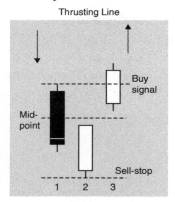

The close on candle 3 must exceed the low of candles 1 and 2 to trigger a sell signal. Place buy-stop above the highest high of candles 1 and 2.

Incomplete Dark Cloud Cover

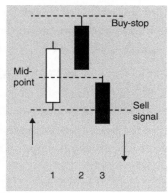

The close on candle 3 must exceed the high of candles 1 and 2 to trigger a buy signal. Place sell-stop below the lowest low of candles 1 and 2.

Bullish Harami and Bearish Harami

Bullish Harami

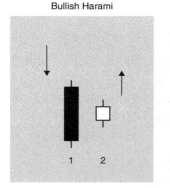

Bearish Harami

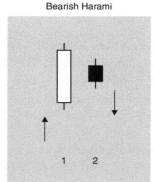

Bullish Harami and Bearish Harami pattern descriptions, rules of recognition, interpretations, and proper actions are explained here together with some examples.

Bullish Harami (Bullish)

Pattern description: The Bullish Harami is a two-day bullish reversal pattern. A long black candle followed by a small white candle distinguishes this pattern. The second day's white real body must reside within the first day's black real body.

Rules of Recognition

1. A downtrend must be in progress.
2. The first candle is black, reflecting the continuing bearish mood.
3. The second day's candle gaps above the previous close on the opening, trades, and closes within the first day's black real body.

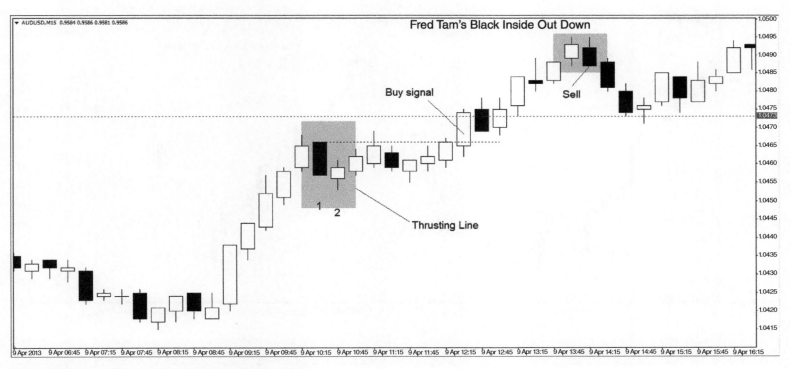

FIGURE 4.18 AudUsd 15-Minute (2013)—Thrusting Line

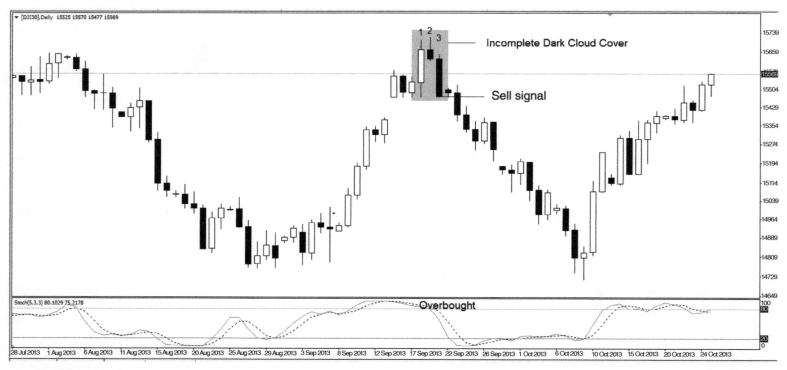

FIGURE 4.19   Dow Jones Industrial Average Daily (2013)—Incomplete Dark Cloud Cover

4. The second day is a short day and must be white in colour.
5. The English translation of *harami* is "pregnant." The first black candle depicts the mother candle while the second short white candle depicts the fetus.

Interpretation: A harami is normally viewed as an "indecision" day. The Western pattern equivalent is an "inside day." After a strong downtrend (black candle) the bears are not selling down any further on the second day, hence the higher opening and close on the second day. Its short white candle reflects this indecision on the second day. Seen after a strong downtrend or at a low price area, this pattern hint of a market reversal to the upside.

Proper action: Possible bullish reversal. Confirmation is required. Buy if there is a bullish confirmation candle that closes above the high of candles 1 and 2. Otherwise, the downtrend can continue.

Bearish Harami (Bearish)

Pattern description: The Bearish Harami is a two-day bearish reversal pattern. A long white candle followed by a small black candle distinguishes this pattern. The second day's black real body must reside within the first day's white real body.

Rules of Recognition

1. An uptrend must be in progress.
2. The first candle is white, reflecting the continuing bullish mood.
3. The second day's candle gaps below the previous close on the opening, trades, and closes within the first day's white real body.
4. The second day is a short day and must be black in colour.

5. The English translation of *harami* is "pregnant." The first white candle depicts the mother candle, while the second short black candle depicts the fetus.

Interpretation: A harami is normally viewed as an "indecision" day. The Western equivalent is an "inside" day. After a strong uptrend (white candle), the bulls are not buying any further on the second day, hence its lower opening and close. This indecision is reflected by its short black candle on the second day. Seen after a strong uptrend or at a high price area, this pattern hints of a market reversal to the downside.

Proper action: Possible bearish reversal. Confirmation is required. Sell if there is a bearish confirmation candle that closes below the low of candles 1 and 2. Otherwise, the uptrend can continue.

Trading the Bullish Harami and Bearish Harami Figure 4.20 and Figure 4.21 show some examples of Bullish Harami and Bearish Harami patterns.

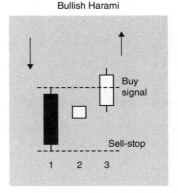

Bullish Harami

The close on candle 3 must exceed the high of candles 1 and 2 to trigger a buy signal. Place sell-stop below the lowest low of candles 1 and 2.

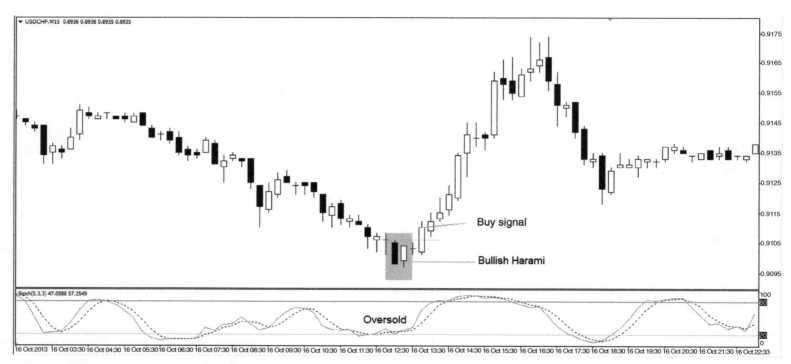

FIGURE 4.20   UsdChf 15-Minute (2013)—Bullish Harami

FIGURE 4.21 UsdJpy 15-Minute (2013)—Bearish Harami

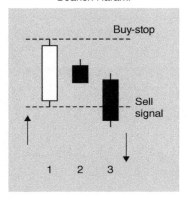

Bearish Harami

The close on candle 3 must exceed the low of candles 1 and 2 to trigger a sell signal. Place buy-stop above the highest high of candles 1 and 2.

Bullish Harami Cross and Bearish Harami Cross

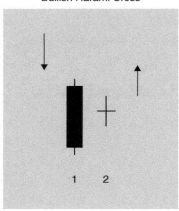

Bullish Harami Cross

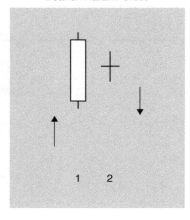

Bearish Harami Cross

Bullish Harami Cross and Bearish Harami Cross pattern descriptions, rules of recognition, interpretations, and proper actions are explained here together with some examples.

Bullish Harami Cross (Bullish)

Pattern description: The Bullish Harami Cross is a two-day bullish reversal pattern. A long black candle followed by a doji distinguishes this pattern. The second day's doji must reside within the first day's white real body.

Rules of Recognition

1. A downtrend must be in progress.
2. The first candle is black, reflecting the continuing bearish mood.
3. The second day's candle is a doji candle. A doji is where the open and close are equal in price.
4. The doji rests within the real body of the first black candle.

Interpretation: The Harami Cross is interpreted in the same way as a harami. It is normally viewed as an "indecision" day. The Western pattern equivalent is an "inside day." After a strong downtrend (black candle) the bears are not selling down any further on the second day, but, instead of a small candle, a doji is formed. Seen after a strong downtrend or at a low price area, a Harami Cross hints of a market reversal to the upside.

Proper action: Possible bullish reversal. Confirmation is required. Buy if there is a bullish confirmation candle that closes above the high of candles 1 and 2. Otherwise, the downtrend can continue.

Bearish Harami Cross (Bearish)

Pattern description: The Bearish Harami Cross is a two-day bearish reversal pattern. A long white candle followed by a doji distinguishes this pattern. The second day's doji must reside within the first day's white real body.

Rules of Recognition

1. An uptrend must be in progress.
2. The first candle is white, reflecting the continuing bullish mood.
3. The second day's candle is a doji candle. A doji is where the open and close are equal in price.
4. The doji rests within the real body of the first white candle.

Interpretation: A Harami Cross is interpreted in the same way as a harami. It is normally viewed as an "indecision" day. The Western pattern equivalent is an "inside day." After a strong uptrend (white candle), the bulls are not buying any further on the second day, hence its lower opening and close. But instead of a short candle on the second day, a doji is formed. Seen after a strong uptrend or at a high price area, a Bearish Harami Cross hints of a market reversal to the downside.

Proper action: Possible bearish reversal. Confirmation is required. Sell if there is a bearish confirmation candle that closes below the low of candles 1 and 2. Otherwise, the uptrend can continue.

Trading the Bullish Harami Cross and Bearish Harami Cross

Figure 4.22 and Figure 4.23 show some examples of Bullish Harami Cross and Bearish Harami Cross patterns.

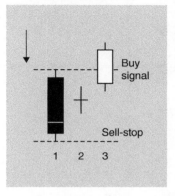

Bullish Harami Cross

The close on candle 3 must exceed the high of candles 1 and 2 to trigger a buy signal. Place sell-stop below the lowest low of candles 1 and 2.

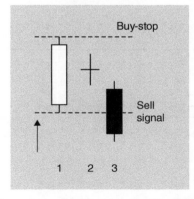

Bearish Harami Cross

The close on candle 3 must exceed the low of candles 1 and 2 to trigger a sell signal. Place buy-stop above the highest high of candles 1 and 2.

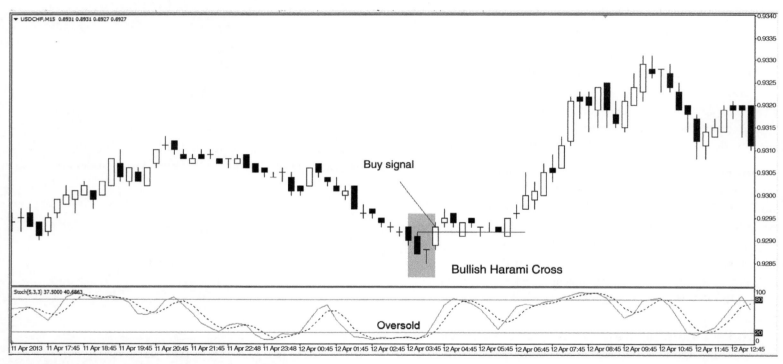

FIGURE 4.22 UsdJpy 15-Minute (2013)—Bullish Harami Cross

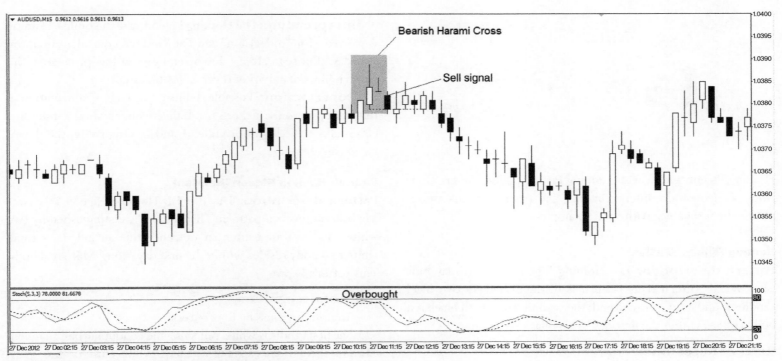

FIGURE 4.23 AudUsd 15-Minute (2013)—Bearish Harami Cross

Homing Pigeon and Bearish Homing Pigeon

Homing Pigeon

Bearish Homing Pigeon

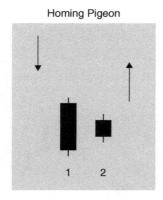
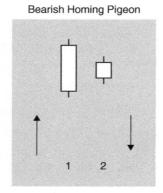

4. Both days' real bodies are black (in a Bullish Harami pattern, the second day's body colour is white).
5. The Japanese name for Homing Pigeon is *shita banare kobato gaeshi*.

Interpretation: The Homing Pigeon, like the Bullish Harami, is viewed as an "indecision" day. The Western equivalent is an "inside day." But seen after a downtrend or at a low price area, this pattern hints of a market reversal to the upside.

Proper action: Possible bullish reversal. Confirmation is required. Buy only if there is a bullish confirmation candle that closes above the high of candles 1 and 2. Otherwise, the downtrend can continue.

Homing Pigeon and Bearish Homing Pigeon pattern descriptions, rules of recognition, interpretations, and proper actions are explained here together with some examples.

Homing Pigeon (Bullish)
Pattern description: The Homing Pigeon is a two-day bullish reversal pattern. This pattern is distinguished by two black candles found after a downtrend; the second day's small black real body resides within the first day's long black real body.

Rules of Recognition
1. A downtrend must be in progress.
2. The first candle is black, reflecting the continuing bearish mood.
3. The second day gaps above the previous close on the opening, trades, and closes within the first day's real body. This small black real body resides inside the previous day's real body.

Bearish Homing Pigeon (Bearish)
Pattern description: The Bearish Homing Pigeon is a two-day bearish reversal pattern. This pattern is distinguished by two white candles found after an uptrend; the second day's small white real body resides within the first day's long white real body. This pattern is rare.

Rules of Recognition
1. An uptrend must be in progress.
2. The first candle is white, reflecting the continuing bullish mood.
3. The second day gaps below the previous close on the opening, trades, and closes within the first day's real body. The colour of the second day is also white. This small real body resides inside the previous day's real body.
4. Both days' real bodies are white. This pattern is similar to a harami pattern but unlike the harami, the second day's body colour is of the same colour as the first.

5. Japanese charting books do not document a bearish version of Homing Pigeon. This version comes from the author, who finds it equally applicable as a bearish equivalent of the Homing Pigeon.

Interpretation: The Bearish Homing Pigeon, like the Bearish Harami, is viewed as an "indecision" day. The Western equivalent is an "inside day." But seen after an uptrend or at a high price area, this pattern hints of a market reversal to the downside.

Proper action: Possible bearish reversal. Confirmation is required. Sell only if there is a bearish confirmation candle that closes below the low of candles 1 and 2. Otherwise, the uptrend can continue.

Trading the Homing Pigeon and the Bearish Homing Pigeon Figure 4.24 and Figure 4.25 show some examples of the Homing Pigeon and the Bearish Homing Pigeon patterns.

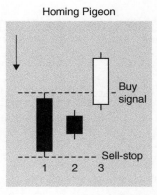

Homing Pigeon

The close of candle 3 must exceed the high of candles 1 and 2 to trigger a buy signal. Place sell-stop below the lowest low of candles 1 and 2.

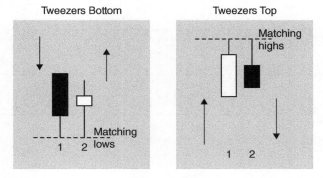

Bearish Homing Pigeon

The close of candle 3 must exceed the low of candles 1 and 2 to trigger a sell signal. Place buy-stop above the highest high of candles 1 and 2.

Tweezers Bottom and Tweezers Top

The Tweezers Bottom and Tweezers Top pattern descriptions, rules of recognition, interpretations, and proper actions are explained here together with some examples.

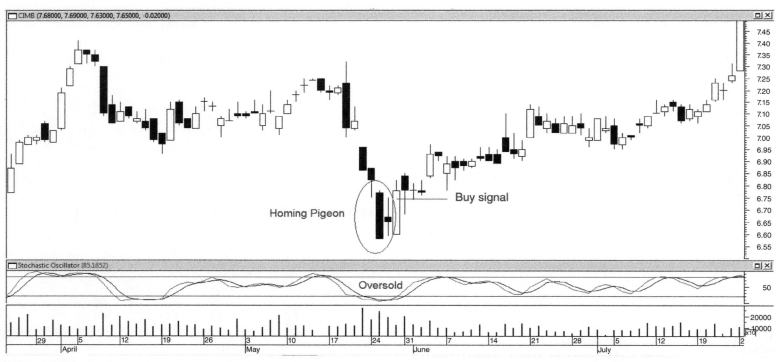

FIGURE 4.24   CIMB Malaysia Daily (2013)—Homing Pigeon

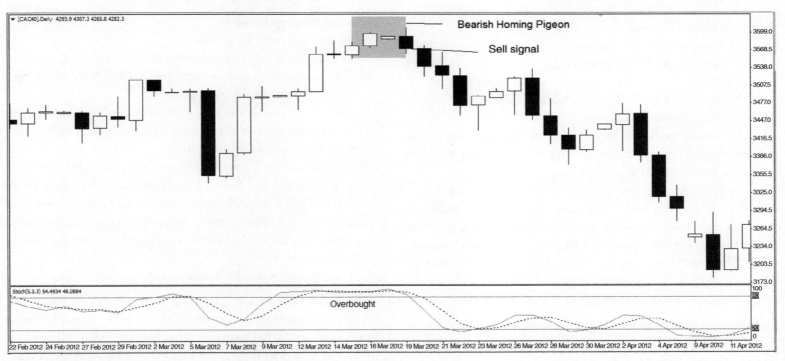

FIGURE 4.25 CAC 40 Daily (2012)—Bearish Homing Pigeon

Tweezers Bottom (Bullish)

Pattern description: The Tweezers Bottom is two-day bullish reversal pattern. Two candles with matching lows distinguish this pattern. The shape of either candle is unimportant.

Rules of Recognition

1. A downtrend must be in progress.
2. The first candle is black, reflecting the continuing bearish mood.
3. The second day candle's low matches the low of the first candle, forming a double bottom.
4. The second candle can be a doji, white, or black candle with or without lower shadows as long as its low is at the same price level as the first candle's low.
5. The first candle is almost always a black candle, but is not a requirement in a Tweezers Bottom formation. It could well be a doji, white, or black candle with or without shadows. The criterion that makes for a Tweezers Bottom is the matching lows of the two candles. Seen after a downtrend, they are potentially bullish reversal signals.
6. The Japanese name for Tweezers Bottom is *kenukizoko*.

Interpretation: The matching lows of the Tweezers Bottom reflect market support. Seen after a downtrend, the Tweezers Bottom can be a major bullish reversal pattern. In identifying a Tweezers formation, the highs and the lows are important and not their real bodies. The Tweezers formation can be multiple candles (more than two).

Proper action: Possible bullish reversal. Buy if there is a bullish confirmation candle that closes above the high of candles 1 and 2. Otherwise, the downtrend can continue.

Tweezers Top (Bearish)

Pattern description: The Tweezers Top is a two-day bearish reversal pattern. Two candles with matching highs distinguish this pattern. The shape of either candle is unimportant.

Rules of Recognition

1. An uptrend must be in progress.
2. The first candle is white, reflecting the continuing bullish mood.
3. The second day candle's high matches the high of the first candle, forming a double top.
4. The second candle can be a doji, white, or black candle with or without upper shadows as long as its high is at the same level as the first candle's high.
5. The first candle is almost always a white candle, but this is not a requirement in a Tweezers Top formation. It could well be a doji, white, or black candle with or without shadows. The criterion that makes for a Tweezers Top is the matching highs of the two candles. Seen after an uptrend, they are potentially bearish reversal signals.
6. The Japanese name for Tweezers Top is *kenukitenjo*.

Interpretation: The matching highs of the Tweezers Top imply market resistance. It reflects the inability of market bulls to drive prices higher than the previous high. Seen after an uptrend, the Tweezers Top can be a major bearish reversal pattern. In identifying a Tweezers formation, the highs and the lows are important and not their real bodies. The Tweezers formation can be multiple candles (more than two).

Proper action: Possible bearish reversal. Sell if there is a bearish confirmation candle that closes below the low of candles 1 and 2. Otherwise, the uptrend can continue.

Trading the Tweezers Bottom and Tweezers Top Figure 4.26 and Figure 4.27 show some examples of the Tweezers Bottom and Tweezers Top patterns.

Tweezers Bottom

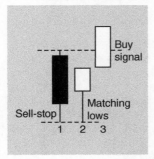

The close on candle 3 must exceed the high of candles 1 and 2 to trigger a buy signal. Place sell-stop below the lowest low of candles 1 and 2.

Tweezers Top

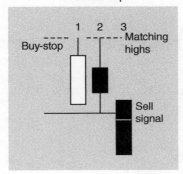

The close on candle 3 must exceed the low of candles 1 and 2 to trigger a sell signal. Place buy-stop above the highest high of candles 1 and 2.

■ Triple Candle stick Patterns

Triple candlestick patterns such as the Doji-Star at the Bottom and Top, Three-River Morning Doji-Star and Three-River Evening Doji-Star, Abandoned Baby Bottom and Top, Three-River Morning Star and Three-River Evening Star, Tri-Star Bottom and Top, Breakaway Three-New-Price Bottom and Top, Bullish Black Three Gaps and Bearish White Three Gaps, Three White Soldiers and Three Black Crows, Advance Block, Deliberation, and Upside Gap Two Crows are discussed here.

Doji-Star at the Bottom and Top

Doji-Star at the Bottom

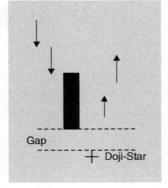

Doji-Star at the Top

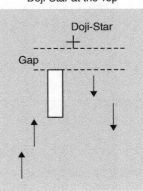

Doji-Star at the Bottom and Top pattern descriptions, rules of recognition, interpretations, and proper actions are explained here together with some examples.

FIGURE 4.26   Dow Jones Industrial Average 4-Hour (2013)—Tweezers Bottom

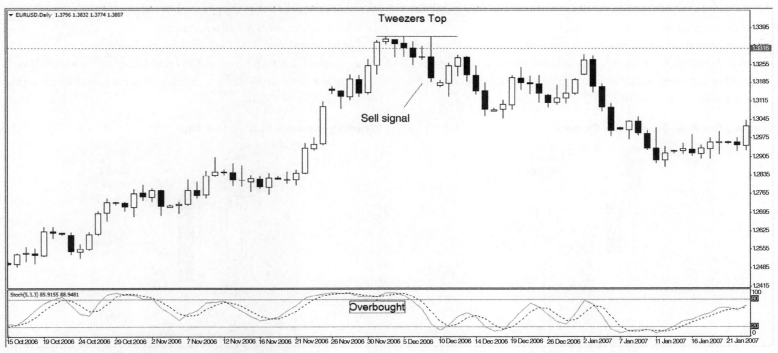

FIGURE 4.27 EurUsd Daily (2013)—Tweezers Top

Doji-Star at the Bottom

Pattern description: The Doji-Star at the Bottom is a doji that gaps below a black candle. It is a warning of a trend change.

Rules of recognition: The first day must be a black candle; the second day is a doji that gaps below the black. The third day's bullish confirmation is a white candle.

Interpretation: The Doji-Star at the Bottom warns of a possible bullish reversal or trend change. But bullish confirmation is required.

Proper action: Wait for a bullish confirmation before acting on a Doji-Star at the Bottom.

Trading the Doji-Star at the Bottom

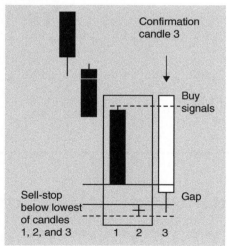

Rules

1. Buy if confirmation candle 3 closes above highest high of candles 1 and 2.
2. In case of a resumption of a downtrend, place sell-stop below the lowest low of candles 1, 2, and 3.

Doji-Star at the Top

Pattern description: The Doji-Star at the Top is a doji that gaps above a white candle. It is a warning of a trend change.

Rules of recognition: The first day must be a white candle; the second day is a doji that gaps above the white. The third day's bearish confirmation is a black candle.

Interpretation: The Doji-Star at the Top warns of a possible bearish reversal or trend change. But bearish confirmation is required.

Proper action: Wait for a bearish confirmation before acting on a Doji-Star at the Top.

Trading the Doji-Star at the Top

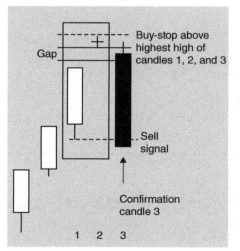

Rules

1. Sell if confirmation candle 3 closes below the lowest low of candles 1 and 2.
2. In case of a resumption of an uptrend, place buy-stop above the highest high of candles 1, 2, and 3.

When a Doji-Star Becomes a Three-River Morning Doji-Star or an Abandoned Baby Bottom In the case of the Doji-Star at the Bottom, the candle subsequent to the doji (i.e., candle) may or may not gap above in forming the white candle.

1. If the opening of the white candle does not gap above the doji, the resulting three-day pattern is called a Three-River Morning Doji-Star. It also qualifies as a Three-River Morning Doji-Star if the open of the white candle gaps above the doji but its lower shadow overlaps the upper shadow of the doji.
2. If the opening of the white candle gaps above the doji and the lower shadow of the white candle does not overlap the upper shadow of the doji, resulting in an "island" being formed between the doji and the white candle, the resulting three-day pattern is called an Abandoned Baby Bottom. Western charting theory calls this pattern an "island reversal bottom."

When a Doji-Star Becomes a Three-River Evening Doji-Star or an Abandoned Baby Top In the case of the Doji-Star at the Top, the candle subsequent to the doji (i.e., candle 3) may or may not gap below in forming the black candle.

1. If the opening of the black candle does not gap below the doji the resulting three-day pattern is called a Three-River Evening Doji-Star. It also qualifies as a Three-River Evening Doji-Star if the open of the black candle gaps below the doji, but its upper shadow overlaps the lower shadow of the doji.
2. If the opening of the black candle gaps below the doji and the upper shadow of the black candle does not overlap the lower shadow of the doji, resulting in an "island" being formed

between the doji and the black candle, the resulting three-day pattern is called an Abandoned Baby Top. Western charting theory names this pattern an "island reversal top."

Three-River Morning Doji-Star and Three-River Evening Doji-Star

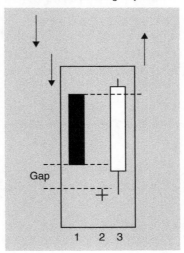

Three-River Morning Doji-Star

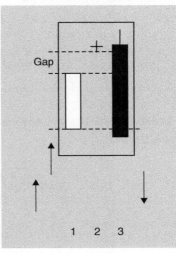

Three-River Evening Doji-Star

Three-River Morning Doji-Star and Three-River Evening Doji-Star pattern descriptions, rules of recognition, interpretations, and proper actions are explained here together with some examples.

Three-River Morning Doji-Star
Pattern Description and Rules of Recognition

1. A Three-River Morning Doji-Star pattern is basically a Doji-Star at the Bottom with bullish confirmation.

2. If the white candle after the doji cannot penetrate the high of the black candle, further confirmation is required via a fourth white candle.

3. Note that the shadows of the doji and the white candle can overlap each other.

Interpretation: Like the Doji-Star at the Bottom, the Three-River Morning Doji-Star represents a major bullish reversal or trend change. But bullish confirmation is required via a fourth candle unless candle 3 can close higher than candles 1 and 2.

Proper action: No confirmation is required if the third candle closes above the highest high of candles 1 and 2. If the third candle's close is still below black candle 1, wait for a bullish confirmation on the fourth candle.

What Constitutes "Confirmation" in the Three-River Morning Doji-Star

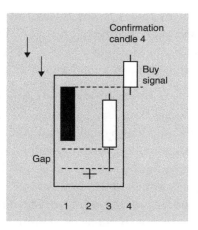

Where confirmation is required via a fourth candle as candle 3 did not close above candles 1 and 2

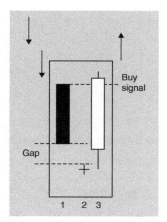

Where no confirmation is required as candle 3 closes higher than candles 1 and 2

Trading the Three-River Morning Doji-Star

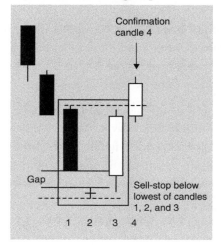

Rules

1. Buy if confirmation candle 4 closes above highest high of candles 1, 2, and 3.
2. In case of a resumption of a downtrend, place sell-stop below the lowest low of candles 1, 2, 3, and 4.

Three-River Evening Doji-Star
Pattern Description and Rules of Recognition

1. A Three-River Evening Doji-Star pattern is basically a Doji-Star at the Top with bearish confirmation.
2. If the black candle (3) after the doji (2) cannot penetrate the low of the white candle (1), further confirmation is required via a fourth white candle.
3. Note that the shadows of the doji and the black candle can overlap each other.

Interpretation: Like the Doji-Star at the Top, the Three-River Evening Doji-Star represents a major bearish reversal or trend change. But bearish confirmation is required via a fourth candle unless candle 3 can close lower than candles 1 and 2.

Proper action: No confirmation is required if the third candle closes below the lowest low of candles 1 and 2. If the third candle's close is still above white candle 1, wait for a bearish confirmation on the fourth candle.

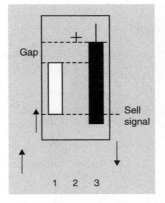

Where no confirmation is required as candle 3 closes
lower than candles 1 and 2

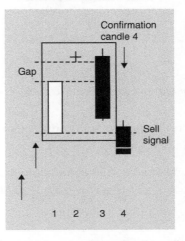

Where confirmation is required via a fourth candle as candle 3
did not close below candles 1 and 2

Abandoned Baby Bottom and Top

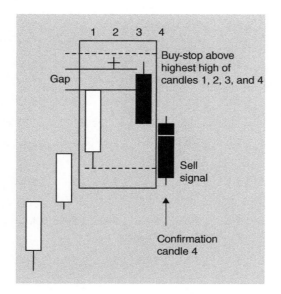

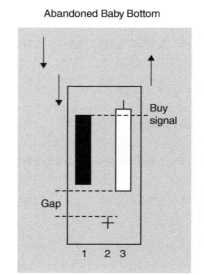

Abandoned Baby Bottom

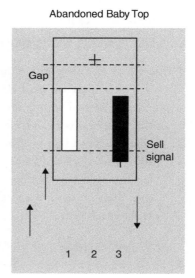

Abandoned Baby Top

Rules

1. Sell if confirmation candle 4 closes below the lowest low of candles 1, 2, and 3.
2. In case of a resumption of an uptrend, place buy-stop above the highest high of candles 1, 2, 3, and 4.

Figure 4.28 and Figure 4.29 show some examples of Three-River Morning and Three-River Evening Doji-Star patterns.

Abandoned Baby Bottom and Abandoned Baby Top pattern descriptions, rules of recognition, interpretations, and proper actions are explained here together with some examples.

Abandoned Baby Bottom
Pattern Description and Rules of Recognition

1. A Three-River Morning Doji-Star pattern becomes an Abandoned Baby Bottom when a gap (or window) occurs between the doji and the third day's white candle.

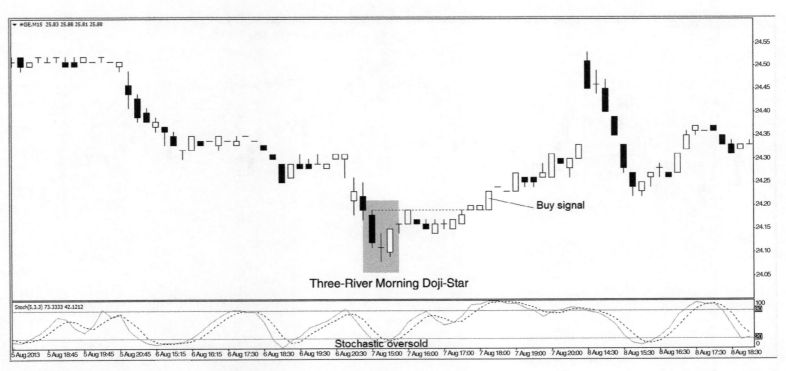

FIGURE 4.28 General Electric 15-Minute (2013)—Three-River Morning Doji-Star

FIGURE 4.29   IBM 5-Minute (2013)—Three-River Evening Doji-Star

2. The lower shadow of the white candle (3) cannot overlap the upper shadow of the doji (2).

Interpretation: Like the Three-River Morning Doji-Star, the Abandoned Baby Bottom represents a major bullish reversal or trend change. But bullish confirmation is required via a fourth candle unless white candle 3 can close higher than candles 1 and 2. This is a rare pattern.

Proper action: No confirmation is required if the third candle closes above the highest high of candles 1 and 2. If the third candle's close is still below black candle 1, wait for a bullish confirmation on the fourth candle.

What Constitutes Confirmation in the Abandoned Baby Bottom

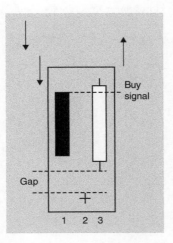

Where no confirmation is required as candle 3 closes higher than candles 1 and 2

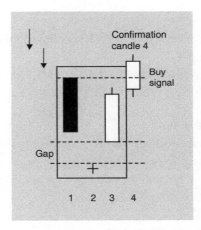

Where confirmation is required via a fourth candle as candle 3 did not close above candles 1 and 2

Trading the Abandoned Baby Bottom

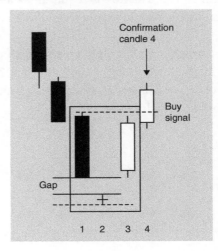

Rules

1. Buy if confirmation candle 4 closes above highest high of candles 1, 2, and 3.
2. In case of a resumption of a downtrend, place sell-stop below the lowest low of candles 1, 2, 3, and 4.

Abandoned Baby Top
Pattern Description and Rules of Recognition

1. A Three-River Evening Doji-Star pattern becomes an Abandoned Baby Top when there is a gap (or window) between the doji and the third day's black candle.
2. The upper shadow of the black candle (3) cannot overlap the lower shadow of the doji (2).

Interpretation: Like the Three-River Evening Doji-Star, the Abandoned Baby Top represents a major bearish reversal or trend change. But bearish confirmation is required via a fourth candle unless black candle 3 closes lower than candles 1 and 2. This is a rare pattern.

Proper action: No confirmation is required if the third candle closes below the lowest low of candles 1 and 2. If the third black candle's close is still above black candle 1, wait for a bearish confirmation on the fourth candle.

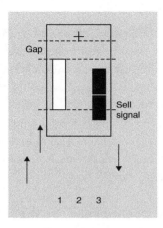

Where no confirmation is required as candle 3
closes lower than candles 1 and 2

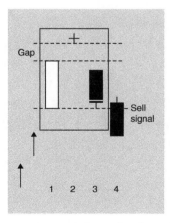

Where confirmation is required via a fourth candle as candle 3
did not close below candles 1 and 2

Trading the Abandoned Baby Top

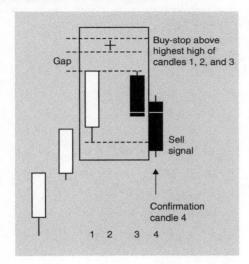

Rules

1. Sell if confirmation candle 4 closes below the lowest low of candles 1, 2, and 3.
2. In case of a resumption of an uptrend, place buy-stop above the highest high of candles 1, 2, 3, and 4.

Figure 4.30 and Figure 4.31 show some examples of Abandoned Baby Top and Abandoned Baby Bottom patterns.

Three-River Morning and Three-River Evening Star

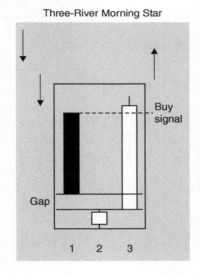

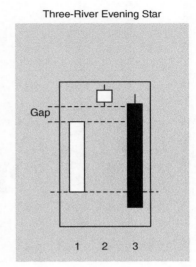

The Three-River Morning Star and Three-River Evening Star pattern descriptions, rules of recognition, interpretations, and proper actions are explained here together with some examples.

Three-River Morning Star

Pattern Description and Rules of Recognition

1. The Three-River Morning Star has a long black candle on the first day.
2. The second day is a Star that gaps below the black candle forming a small Spinning Top. The colour of its real body is unimportant.
3. The third day is likely a long white candle, which triggers a buy signal if it closes above the first and second candle's high.

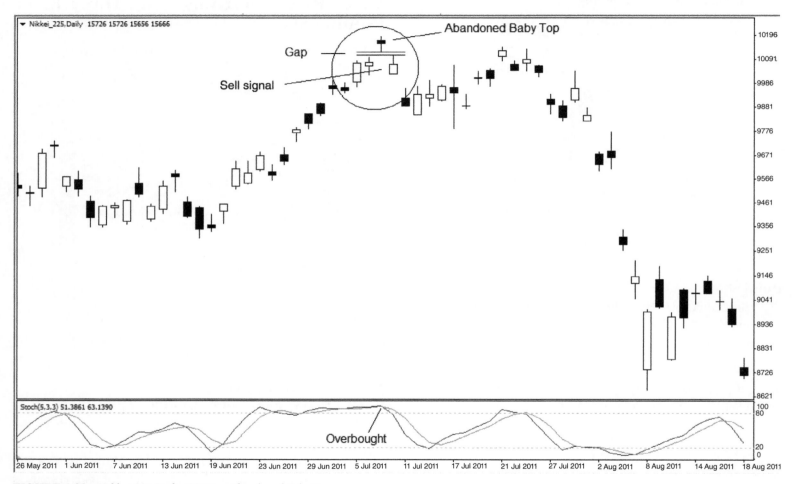

FIGURE 4.30   Nikkei 225 Daily (2011)—Abandoned Baby Top

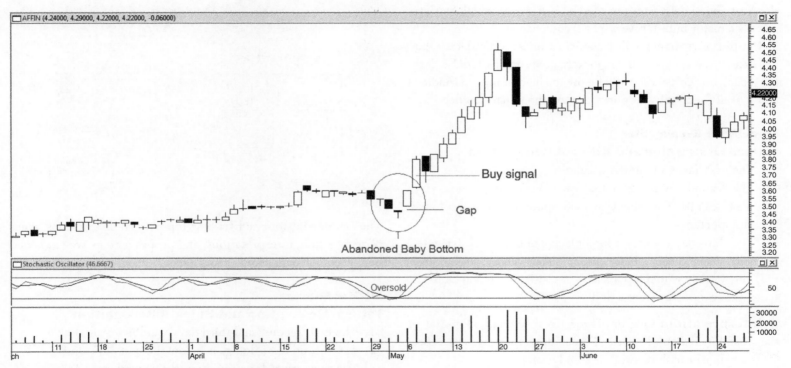

FIGURE 4.31 Affin Malaysia Daily (2013)—Abandoned Baby Bottom

4. This pattern would be called a Three-River Morning Doji-Star if the second day is a doji.

Interpretation: Like the Three-River Morning Doji-Star or the Abandoned Baby Bottom, the Three-River Morning Star represents a major bullish reversal or trend change.

Proper action: No bullish confirmation is required if the third day's candle closes above the highest high of candles 1 and 2. If the third day's candle's close is still below the highest high of candles 1 and 2, wait for a bullish confirmation on the fourth candle.

Three-River Evening Star
Pattern Description and Rules of Recognition
1. The first day is a long white candle.
2. The second day is a Star that gaps above the previous day's white candle. This Star is a small Spinning Top. Its colour is unimportant.
3. The third day is likely a long black candle, which triggers a sell signal if it closes below the first and second candles' lows.
4. This pattern would be called a Three-River Evening Doji-Star if the second day were a doji.

Interpretation: Like the Three-River Evening Doji-Star or the Abandoned Baby Top, the Three-River Evening Star represents a major bearish reversal or trend change.

Proper Action: No bearish confirmation is required if the third day's candle closes below the lowest low of candles 1 and 2. If the third day's candle's close is still above the lowest low of candles 1 and 2, wait for a bearish confirmation on the fourth candle.

Figure 4.32 and Figure 4.33 show some examples of Three-River Morning Star and Three-River Evening Star patterns.

Tri-Star Bottom and Tri-Star Top

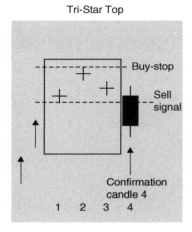

The Tri-Star Bottom and Tri-Star Top pattern descriptions, rules of recognition, interpretations, and proper actions are explained here together with some examples.

Tri-Star Bottom
Pattern Description and Rules of Recognition
1. The first, second, and third days' candles are all doji.
2. The second day's doji gaps below the first day's doji.
3. The third day's doji gaps above the second day's doji.

Interpretation: Spotted after a downtrend, this rare three-day pattern is indicative of market exhaustion.

Proper action: Look for a bullish reversal or trend change. Wait for bullish confirmation via a close above the high of the first day's doji.

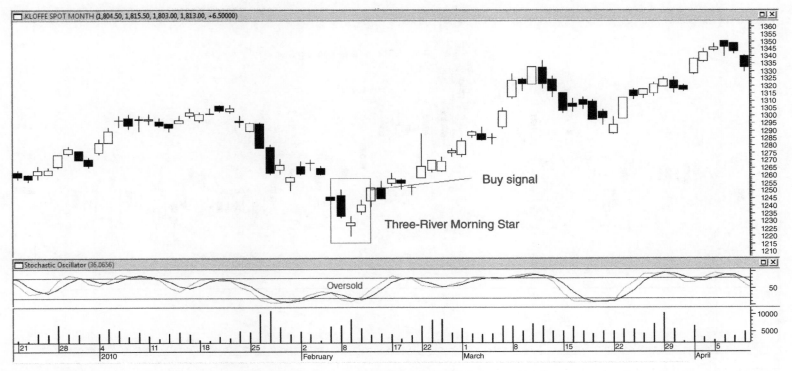

FIGURE 4.32 Kuala Lumpur Composite Index Futures Malaysia Daily (2013)—Three-River Morning Star

FIGURE 4.33   UsdChf 5-Minute (2013)—Three-River Evening Star

Tri-Star Top

Pattern Description and Rules of Recognition

1. The first, second, and third days' candles are all doji.
2. The second day's doji gaps above the first day's doji.
3. The third day's doji gaps below the second day's doji.

Interpretation: Spotted after an uptrend, this rare three-day pattern is indicative of market exhaustion.

Proper action: Look for a bearish reversal or trend change. Wait for bearish confirmation via a close below the low of the first day's doji.

Figure 4.34 and Figure 4.35 show some examples of Tri-Star Bottom and Tri-Star Top patterns.

Breakaway Three-New-Price Bottom and Breakaway Three-New-Price Top

Breakaway Three-New-Price Bottom   Breakaway Three-New-Price Top

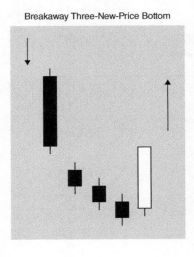 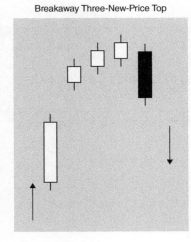

Breakaway Three-New-Price Bottom and Breakaway Three-New-Price Top pattern descriptions, rules of recognition, interpretations, and proper actions are explained here together with some examples.

Breakaway Three-New-Price Bottom (Bullish)

Pattern description: This five-day bullish reversal pattern consists of a down-gap, which is followed by three small candles each making lower lows. The bullish reversal comes on the fifth day through a white candle.

Rules of Recognition

1. A downtrend must be in progress.
2. The first day is a long black candle, reflecting the continuing bearish mood.
3. The second day gaps below the previous day's low and forms a small black candle.
4. The third and fourth days are also small candles making lower lows. They should also make lower highs, but there are no hard and fast rules here as long as the third and fourth candles' high or close is not above the down-gap.
5. Colours of the second, third, and fourth small real bodies need not necessarily be all black although it is preferable.
6. The fifth day is a long white candle that closes above the highest high of the three small real body candles before it.
7. The fifth day's candle need not close above the down-gap.

Interpretation: The Breakaway Three-New-Price Bottom depicts the market's rebound from a grossly oversold situation. The down-gap on the second day implies a sell-off possibly stemming from very bearish news. But there is not much follow-through selling on the third and the fourth day. Although the

FIGURE 4.34 Faber Group Malaysia Daily (2013)—Tri-Star Bottom

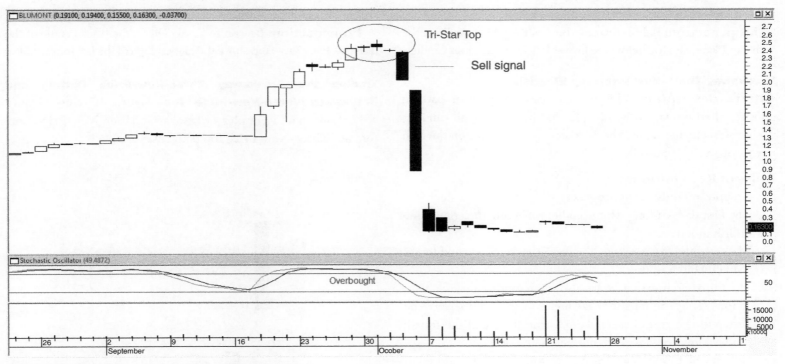

FIGURE 4.35 Belmont Singapore Daily (2013)—Tri-Star Top

market made lower lows, the small real bodies imply the presence of buying support. The fifth day's long white candle reflects the return of the bulls, triggering a trend reversal to the upside. This candle need not fill the down-gap but must close above the highest high of the three small candles before it.

Proper action: Bullish reversal. Buy on the white candle of the fifth day. Place sell-stop below the lowest low of the last four candles.

Breakaway Three-New-Price Top (Bearish)

Pattern description: This five-day bearish reversal pattern consists of an up-gap, which is followed by three small candles, each making higher highs. The bearish reversal comes on the fifth day through a black candle.

Rules of Recognition

1. An uptrend must be in progress.
2. The first day is a long white candle, reflecting the continuing bullish mood.
3. The second day gaps above the previous day's high and forms a small white candle.
4. The third and fourth days are also small candles making higher lows. They should also make higher highs, but there are no hard and fast rules here as long as the third and the fourth candles' lows or closes are not below the up-gap.
5. Colours of the second, third, and fourth small real bodies need not necessarily be all white although it is preferable.
6. The fifth day is a long black candle that closes below the lowest low of the three small real body candles before it.
7. The fifth day's candle need not close below the up-gap.

Interpretation: The Breakaway Three-New-Price Top is the mirror image of the Breakaway Three-New-Price Bottom. It reflects a runaway market that has gotten ahead of its fundamentals. Strong buying triggers the up-gap, which could not be sustained. After three unsuccessful efforts by the bulls to drive prices higher, the market retreats from the lack of follow-through buying, resulting in a collapse coming from an increase in supply.

Proper action: Bearish reversal. Sell on the black candle of the fifth day. Place buy-stop above the highest high of the last four candles.

Trading the Breakaway Three-New-Price Bottom and Breakaway Three-New-Price Top Figure 4.36 and Figure 4.37 show some examples of breakaway Three-New-Price Bottom and Three-New-Price Top patterns.

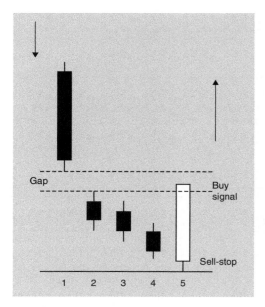

The close of candle 5 must exceed the highest high of candles 2, 3, and 4 to trigger a buy signal. Place sell-stop below the lowest low of candles 2, 3, 4, and 5.

FIGURE 4.36 Silver Daily (2010)—Breakaway Three-New-Price Bottom

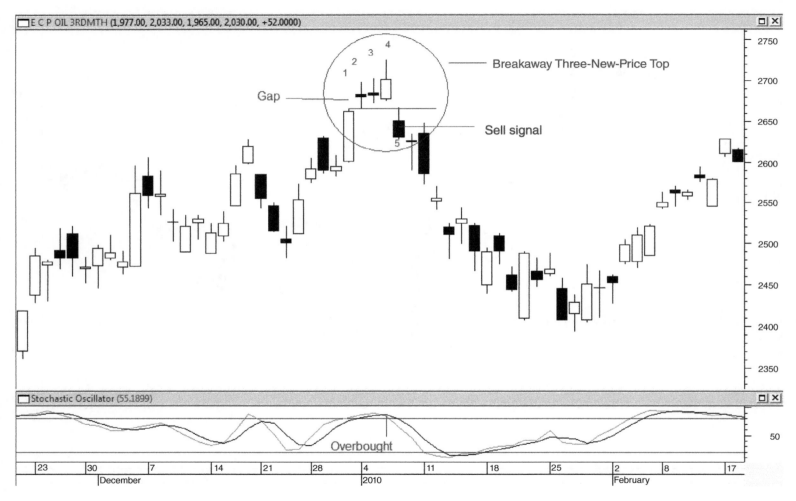

E C P OIL 3RDMTH (1,977.00, 2,033.00, 1,965.00, 2,030.00, +52.0000)

Breakaway Three-New-Price Top

Gap

Sell signal

Stochastic Oscillator (55.1899)

Overbought

50

FIGURE 4.37   Crude Palm Oil Daily (2010)—Breakaway Three-New-Price Top

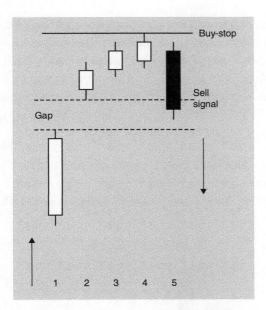

The close of candle 5 must exceed the lowest low of candles 2, 3, and 4 to trigger a sell signal. Place buy-stop above the highest high of candles 2, 3, 4, and 5.

Bullish Black Three Gaps and Bearish White Three Gaps

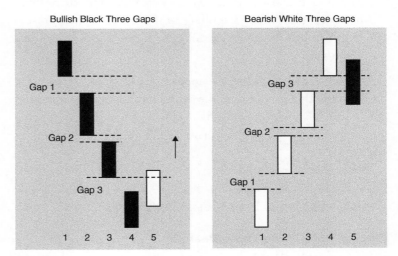

Bullish Black Three Gaps and Bearish White Three Gaps pattern descriptions, rules of recognition, interpretations, and proper actions are explained next, together with some examples.

Bullish Black Three Gaps (Bullish)

Pattern description: This is a four-day bullish reversal pattern and is distinguished by four black candles gapping away from one another in a downtrend.

Rules of Recognition

1. A downtrend must be in progress.
2. Four black candles gapping away from one another appear consecutively in a downtrend.

3. The fifth is a white candle that makes a U-turn and closes the down-gap created by the fourth black candle.
4. The fourth and the fifth candles can form bullish reversal patterns like Bullish Engulfing or Fred Tam's White Inside Out Up, but the criterion must be a close above the third down-gap.

Interpretation: After the appearance of three down-gaps, the Japanese trader considers the downtrend as having exhausted itself. The next white candle that closes above the last (third) down-gap is the bullish reversal signal. No confirmation is required.

Proper action: Bullish reversal. No confirmation is required. Buy if the fifth white candle fills the third down-gap. Place a sell-stop below the lowest low of candles 3, 4, and 5.

Bearish White Three Gaps (Bearish)

Pattern description: This is a four-day bearish reversal pattern and is distinguished by four white candles gapping away from one another in an uptrend.

Rules of Recognition

1. An uptrend must be in progress.
2. Four white candles gapping away from one another appear consecutively in an uptrend.
3. The fifth is a black candle that makes a U-turn and closes the up-gap created by the fourth white candle.
4. The fourth and fifth candles can form bearish reversal patterns like Bearish Engulfing or Fred Tam's Black Inside Out Down, but the criterion must be a close below the third up-gap.

Interpretation: After the appearance of three up-gaps, the Japanese trader considers the uptrend as having exhausted itself. The next black candle that closes below the last (third) up-gap is the bearish reversal signal. No confirmation is required.

Proper action: Bearish reversal. No confirmation is required. Sell if the fifth black candle fills the third up-gap. Place a buy-stop above the highest high of candles 3, 4, and 5.

Trading the Bullish Black Three Gaps and the Bearish White Three Gaps
Figure 4.38 and Figure 4.39 show some examples of the Bullish Black Three Gaps and Bearish White Three Gaps patterns.

Bullish Black Three Gaps

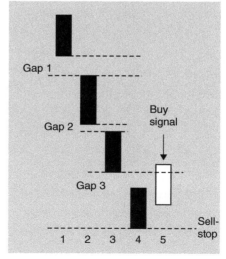

The close of white candle 5 must fill gap 3 and close above the close of candle 3. Place sell-stop below the lowest low of candles 3, 4, and 5.

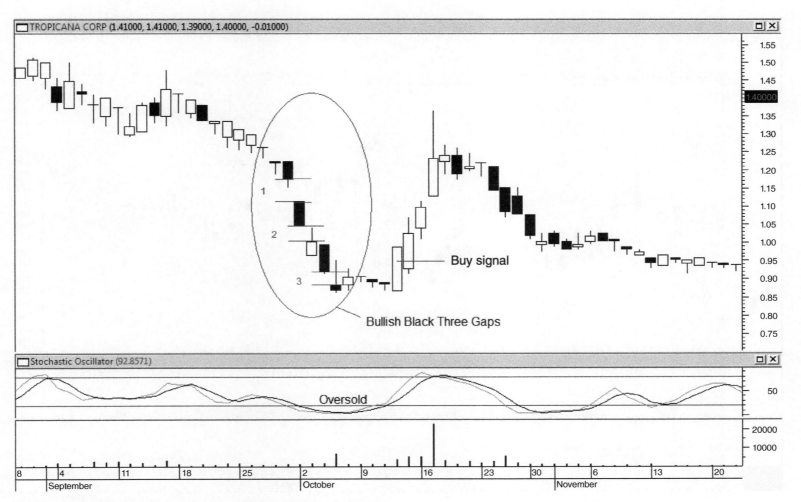

FIGURE 4.38   Tropicana Malaysia Daily (1999)—Bullish Black Three Gaps

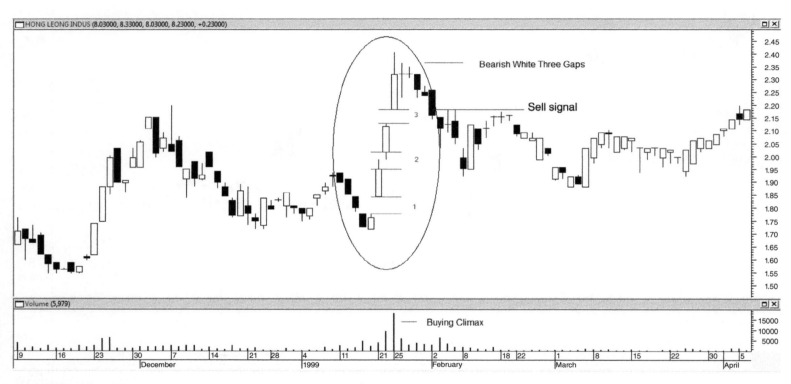

FIGURE 4.39 Hong Leong Industries Malaysia Daily (1999)—Bearish White Three Gaps

Bearish White Three Gaps

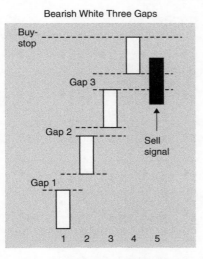

The close of black candle 5 must fill gap 3 and close below the close of candle 3. Place buy-stop above the highest high of candles 3, 4, and 5.

Three White Soldiers and Three Black Crows

Three White Soldiers

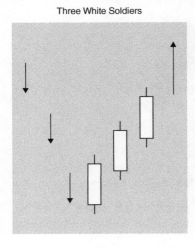

Three Black Crows

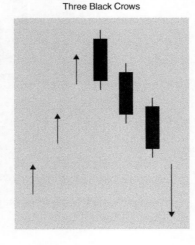

Three White Soldiers and Three Black Crows pattern descriptions, rules of recognition, interpretations, and proper actions are explained here together with some examples.

Three White Soldiers (Bullish)

Pattern description: The Three White Soldiers is made up of three white candles with consecutively higher closes. In a low price area or after a series of stable prices, it confirms renewed strength ahead.

Rules of Recognition

1. A downtrend must be in progress.
2. This is followed by a trend reversal with the formation of three white candles, each with a higher close.
3. Each subsequent candle should open within the previous session's white real body but this overlap is not a rule. An open at or a little higher than the previous session's real body is also valid.
4. Each of the white candles must close at or near its highs.
5. It is sometimes known as the Three Advancing White Soldiers. Its Japanese name is *aka sanpei*.

Interpretation: The Three White Soldiers is representative of a trend reversal, especially if seen after a sharp downtrend or at a low price area. The three successive higher highs and higher lows made in a step-like fashion reflect a bullish market ahead.

Proper action: Bullish reversal. Buy on third white candle. Place sell-stop below the lowest low of the last three candles.

Three Black Crows (Bearish)

Pattern description: The Three Black Crows is made up of three black candles with consecutively lower closes. This is a top reversal pattern if seen after an extended rally or at a high price area.

Rules of Recognition

1. An uptrend must be in progress.
2. This is followed by a trend reversal with the formation of three black candles, each with a lower close.
3. Each subsequent candle should open within the previous session's black real body, but this overlap is not a rule. An open at or a little lower than the previous session's real body is also valid.
4. Each of the black candles must close at or near its lows.
5. Its Japanese name is *sanba garasu*.

Interpretation: The Three Black Crows is the mirror image of the Three White Soldiers. It forewarns of lower prices and is a sign of weakness ahead. The three black candles imply strong selling by the bears.

Proper action: Bearish reversal. Sell on third black candle. Place buy-stop above the highest high of the last three black candles.

Trading the Three White Soldiers and Three Black Crows

Figure 4.40 and Figure 4.41 show some examples of Three White Soldiers and Three Black Crows patterns.

BASIC CANDLESTICK TECHNIQUES

Three White Soldiers

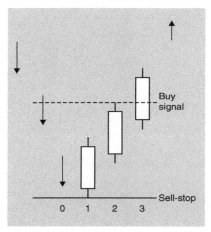

Buy on candle 3. Place sell-stop below the lowest low of candles 1 and 0.

Three Black Crows

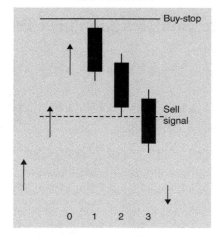

Sell on candle 3. Place buy-stop above the highest high of candles 1 and 0.

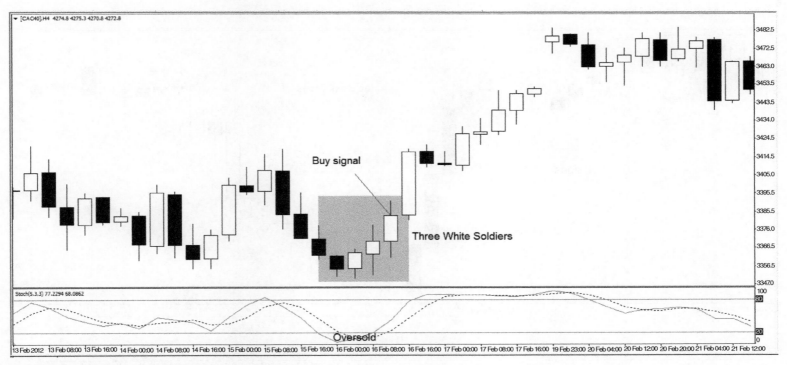

Buy signal

Three White Soldiers

Oversold

FIGURE 4.40 CAC 40 4-Hour (2013)—Three White Soldiers

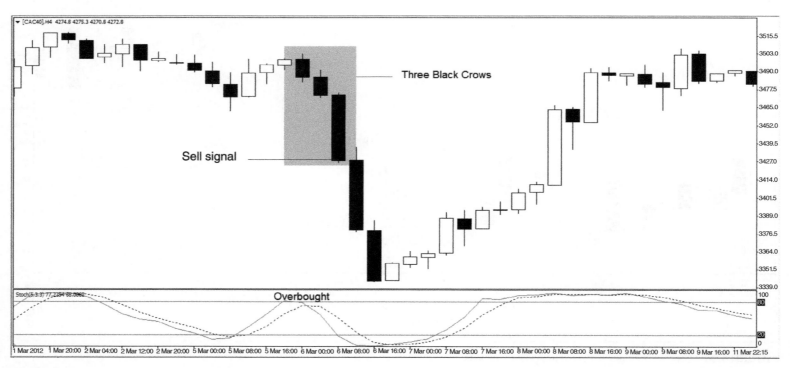

FIGURE 4.41 CAC 40 4-Hour (2013)—Three Black Crows

Advance Block

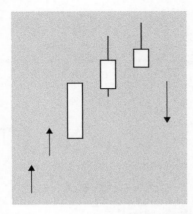

Advance Block pattern description, rules of recognition, interpretation, and proper action are explained here together with some examples.

Advance Block (Bearish)

Pattern description: The Advance Block is a derivative of the Three White Soldiers pattern. The Advance Block is made up of three white candles but the weak closes on the second and third candle put the rally under threat of a reversal. The long upper shadows and smaller real bodies on the second and third candles hint of strong resistance. Found after a strong uptrend or a high price area, the Advance Block signals a bearish reversal.

Rules of Recognition

1. An uptrend must be in progress.

2. Three white candles are sighted, each with a higher close.
3. Each subsequent candle should open within the previous session's white real body, but this overlap is not a rule. An open at or a little higher than the previous session's real body is also valid.
4. But unlike the Three White Soldiers, where each of the white candles closes at or near its highs, the second and third candles display long upper shadows and small real bodies. Longer upper shadows on the two latter candles imply a weakening of the bulls' strength.
5. The Japanese name for Advance Block is *saki zumari*.

Interpretation: The Advance Block is reflective of an over-extended rally. The long upper shadows and small real bodies on the second or third candle imply a weakening of buying power. Found after a rally or at a high price area, the Advance Block results in a reversal to the downside. Bulls should protect their long positions by taking some profits. The Advance Block is normally a short-term top reversal pattern. After a short correction, the prior uptrend resumes. But in some instances, it can trigger a major decline.

Proper action: Bearish reversal. Sell and take profits on the third candle. Conservative traders should wait for confirmation via a fourth candle that closes below the lowest low of candles 2 and 3 before selling. Place buy-stop above the highest high of the last three candles.

Trading the Advance Block   Figure 4.42 shows an example of an Advance Block pattern.

FIGURE 4.42 Apple 15-Minute (2013)—Advance Block

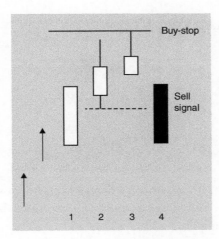

Aggressive traders sell on candle 3. Conservative traders sell if fourth candle closes below the lowest low of candles 2 and 3. Place buy-stop above the highest high of candles 1, 2, and 3.

Deliberation

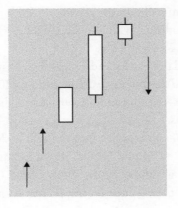

Deliberation pattern description, rules of recognition, interpretation, and proper action are explained here together with some examples.

Deliberation (Bearish)

Pattern description: The Deliberation or Stalled pattern is also a derivative of the Three White Soldiers pattern. The Deliberation pattern is made up of three white candles but has a long white candle on the second candle followed by a small real body (Spinning Top) on the third candle. Like the Advance Block, the Deliberation pattern hints of an exhaustion of the bulls' strength. The small Spinning Top on the third candle reflects this exhaustion. Found after an uptrend or at a high price area, the Deliberation pattern signals a bearish reversal.

Rules of Recognition

1. An uptrend must be in progress.
2. Three white candles are sighted, each with a higher close.
3. The first and second candles have long white candles.
4. The third candle has a small real body (Spinning Top), which can either gap above the second candle (in which case it is called a Star) or rests just beside the close of the second long white candle.
5. The Japanese name for Deliberation is *aka sansei shian boshi*.

Interpretation: The Deliberation or Stalled pattern is indicative of market exhaustion from an excessively strong second day. The Spinning Top on the third day depicts "uncertainty." The bulls are undecided on buying further, hence its pattern name, Deliberation. Found after a rally or at a high price area, the Deliberation pattern results in a reversal to the downside. Bulls should protect their long positions by taking some profits. The Deliberation pattern is normally viewed as a short-term top reversal pattern. After a short correction, the prior uptrend resumes. But in some instances, it can trigger a major decline.

Proper action: Bearish reversal. Sell and take profits on the third candle. Conservative traders should wait for confirmation via a fourth candle that closes below the lowest low of candles 2 and 3 before selling. Place buy-stop above the highest high of the last three candles.

Trading the Deliberation Pattern   Figure 4.43 shows an example of the Deliberation pattern.

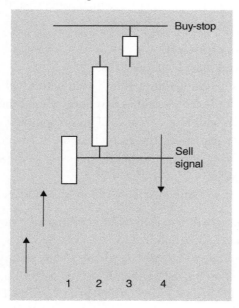

Aggressive traders sell on candle 3. Conservative traders sell if fourth candle closes below the lowest low of candles 2 and 3. Place buy-stop above the highest high of candles 1, 2, and 3.

Upside Gap Two Crows

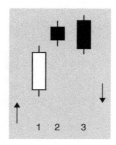

Upside Gap Two Crows pattern description, rules of recognition, interpretation, and proper action are explained here together with some examples.

Upside Gap Two Crows (Bearish)

Pattern description: Two black candles that gap above a long white candle in an uptrend distinguishes this three-day bearish reversal pattern.

Rules of Recognition:

1. An uptrend must be in progress.
2. The first candle is white, reflecting the continuing bullish mood.
3. The second day's black candle gaps above on the opening, but sellers prevail setting up a small Spinning Top.
4. The third day's black candle opens above the second candle's open and closes beneath the second candle's close. The third candle may penetrate back into the real body of the first day's white candle equal to or below its midpoint.
5. This pattern is similar to the Dark Cloud Cover if the third black candle closes into the midpoint of the first white candle, closing the up-gap.

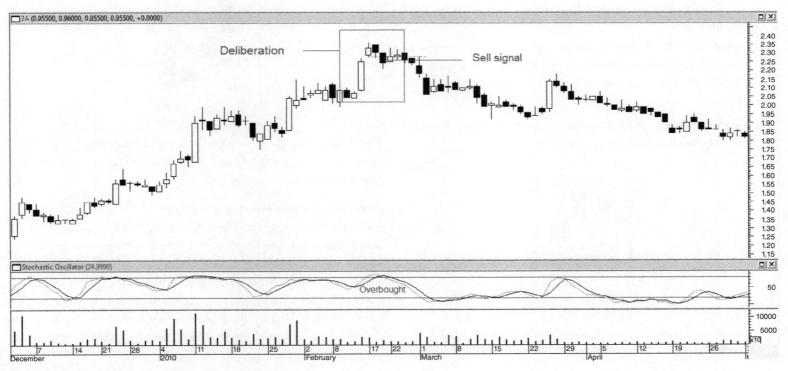

FIGURE 4.43 3A Malaysia Daily (2010)—Deliberation

Interpretation: The Upside Gap Two Crows can be interpreted as a market under selling pressure. What appears to be a gapping play on the second candle fizzles out when sellers take over on the third candle. The selling pressure is strong enough to cause a close at or below the midpoint of the first white candle.

Proper action: Possible bearish reversal. Confirmation is required. Sell if there is a bearish confirmation where candle 4 closes below the low of candles 2 and 3. Otherwise, the uptrend can continue.

Trading the Upside Gap Two Crows Figure 4.44 shows an example of the Upside Gap Two Crows pattern.

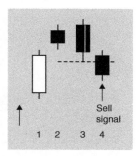

The close on candle 4 must exceed the low of candles 2 and 3 to trigger a sell signal. Place buy-stop above the highest high of candles 2 and 3.

■ Multiple Candlestick Patterns

Multiple candlestick patterns such as the Concealing Baby Swallow, Ladder Bottom, Tower Bottoms and Tower Tops, and Eight-to-Ten New Record Lows and Highs are discussed here.

Concealing Baby Swallow

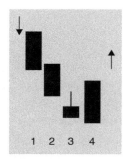

The Concealing Baby Swallow pattern description, rules of recognition, interpretation, and proper action are explained here together with some examples.

Concealing Baby Swallow (Bullish)

Pattern description: The Concealing Baby Swallow is made up of four black candles in a downtrend with consecutive lower closes. Like the Ladder Bottom (discussed next), it reflects an oversold situation after a strong sell-off and represents a bottom reversal pattern if seen after an extended decline or at a low price area. It differs slightly from the Ladder Bottom in the shape of the third and fourth candles, but otherwise they represent an oversold market and have bullish implications.

Rules of Recognition

1. A downtrend must be in progress.
2. The first two black candles are Black Marubozu days.
3. The third candle gaps down but rebounds intra-day to pierce back into the body of the second day before closing as a Black Inverted Hammer.

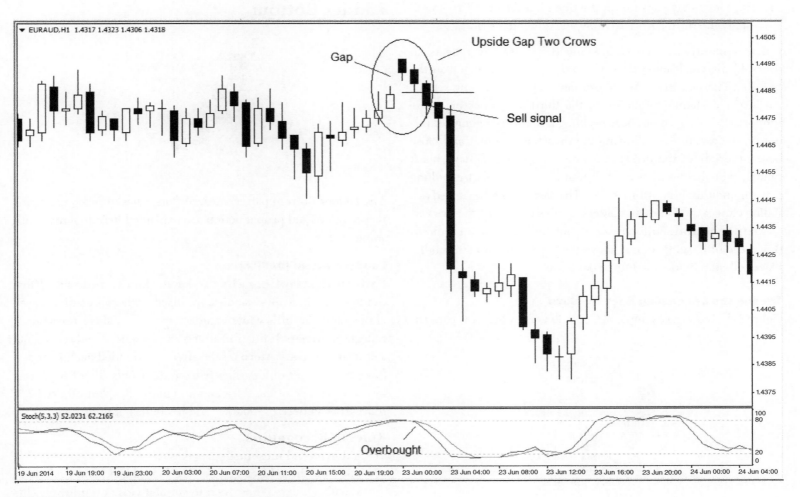

FIGURE 4.44 EurUsd Hourly (2014)—Upside Gap Two Crows

4. The fourth day gaps up on the open but falls back to engulf totally the third day's real body, including the shadow.

Interpretation: The Concealing Baby Swallow reflects an oversold market leading to a rebound (or trend change) on the fifth day. The two Black Marubozu days represent strong selling. An Inverted Hammer follows on the third day, reflecting some support after two days of heavy selling. But strong selling continues on the fourth day following the Inverted Hammer and close below the low of the Inverted Hammer. This fourth day's black candle, though viewed as bearish, can be akin to a last engulfing pattern, indicating a bottom is near. This last day is also viewed as a selling climax, where weak holders are flushed out of the market.

Proper action: Bullish reversal, but confirmation is required. Buy if the fifth candle closes above the high of the fourth candle. Place sell-stop below the fourth day's low.

Trading the Concealing Baby Swallow

Figure 4.45 shows an example of Concealing Baby Swallow pattern.

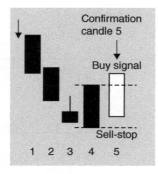

The close on candle 5 must exceed the high of candle 4 to trigger a buy signal. Place sell-stop below the low of candle 4.

Ladder Bottom

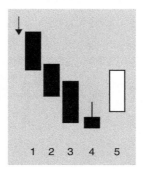

The Ladder Bottom pattern description, rules of recognition, interpretation, and proper action are explained here together with some examples.

Ladder Bottom (Bullish)

Pattern description: The Ladder Bottom is made up of five candles. The first four candles are black with consecutive lower closes, and the fifth white candle triggers a bullish reversal. It reflects an oversold situation after a strong sell-off and represents a bottom reversal pattern if seen after an extended decline or at a low price area. It differs slightly from the Concealing Baby Swallow in the shape of the third and fourth candles, but otherwise it represents an oversold market and has bullish implications.

Rules of Recognition

1. A downtrend must be in progress.
2. The first three black candles are long, black, and preferably Marubozu days. They open lower and close even lower. This pattern is somewhat like a Three Black Crows pattern, except that Three Black Crows is a bearish reversal pattern because it is located after an uptrend whereas these three black candles

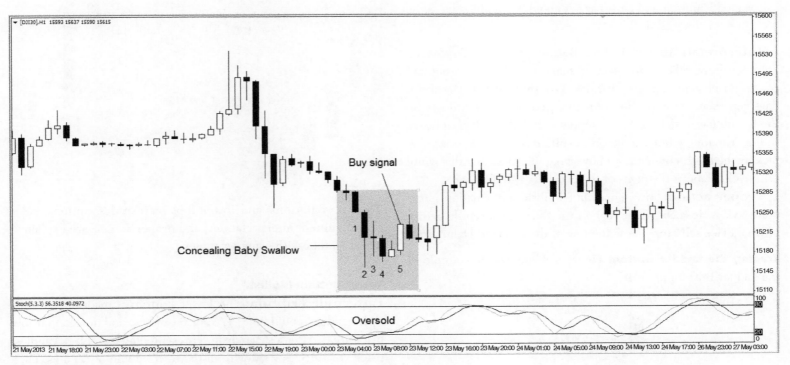

FIGURE 4.45 Dow Jones Industrial Average Hourly (2013)—Concealing Baby Swallow

are foretelling an end to a downtrend as they are found after a downtrend.

3. The fourth candle is a black Inverted Hammer.
4. The fifth candle preferably opens above the body of the Inverted Hammer and closes as a long white candle. This is the confirmation candle.

Interpretation: The Ladder Bottom, like the Concealing Baby Swallow, reflects an oversold market leading to a rebound (or trend change) on the fifth day. The three Black Marubozu days represent strong selling. An Inverted Hammer follows on the fourth day, reflecting some support after three days of heavy selling. The long white candle on the fifth day signals a counterattack by the bulls, confirming a buy signal. It is best that this white candle close above the highs of the previous two days.

Proper action: Buy signal, but bullish confirmation is required via a close above the high of the third black candle before buying. Place sell-stop below the low of the Inverted Hammer.

Trading the Ladder Bottom Figure 4.46 shows an example of the Ladder Bottom pattern.

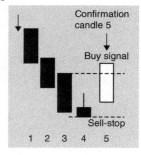

The close on candle 5 must exceed the highest high of candles 3 and 4 to trigger a buy signal. Place sell-stop below the low of candle 4.

Tower Bottom and Tower Top

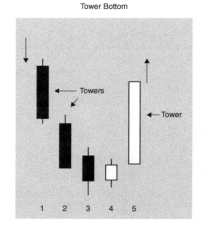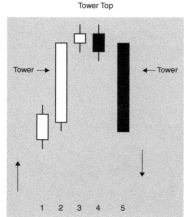

The Tower Bottoms and Tower Tops pattern descriptions, rules of recognition, interpretations, and proper actions are explained here together with some examples.

Tower Bottom (Bullish)

Pattern description: The Tower Bottom is made up of multiple candles (could be 3, 4, 5, or 6 candles) and develops at low price areas. After a sharp drop represented by long black candles, price volatility slows down on the next couple of candles. Then the market makes a turnaround and swing upward in one or two long candles. The characteristic that makes for a Tower Bottom is the long black candle on the way down and the long white candle on the way up. The long candles or long columns look like towers—hence their name. A Tower Bottom is a bullish reversal pattern.

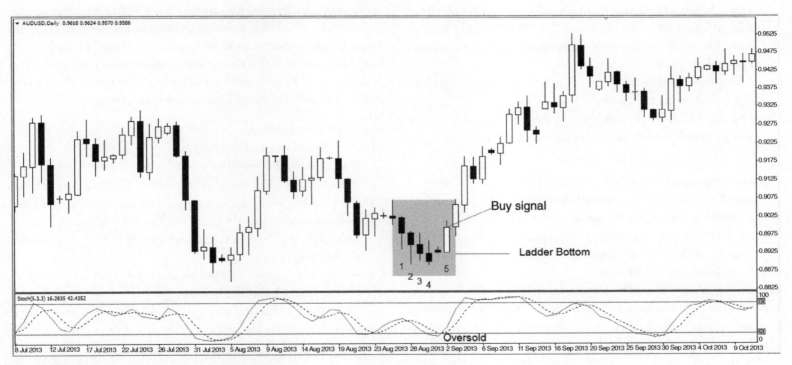

FIGURE 4.46 AudUsd Daily (2013)—Ladder Bottom

Rules of Recognition

1. A downtrend must be in progress.
2. The first candle must be a long black candle, preferably a Marubozu day. The market is weak but is getting oversold.
3. This is followed by a short consolidation consisting of a multiple of small white or black candles (like Spinning Tops or doji). The small candles imply a pause in selling pressure and a possible bottom.
4. A long white candle forms on the right reversing the psychology from bearish to bullish.
5. The tall black candle on the left is called the left tower while the tall white candle on the right is called the right tower.

Interpretation: The Tower Bottom is a bullish reversal pattern. Long towers on the left and right, of different colours, reveal strong sell-offs but countered by equally strong buying. The long white candle or tall column on the right is a significant candle, and as long as the low of this white candle is not violated on the downside, the market is poised for a trend reversal upwards. The low of a long white candle acts as a support area in the event of a pullback. Stops can be placed just below this support area or below the low of the previous candle.

Proper action: Buy signal. However, bullish confirmation is required via a close above the highest high of the previous two candles. Place sell-stop below the low of the long white candle that makes the right tower or the low of the candle before it.

Tower Top (Bearish)

Pattern description: The Tower Top is the mirror image of the Tower Bottom. It is made up of multiple candles (could be 3, 4, 5, or 6 candles) and develops at high price areas. After a sharp rally represented by long white candles, price volatility drops on the next couple of candles, forming a potential market top. Then the market makes a turnaround and swing downward in one or two long black candles. The characteristic that makes for a Tower Top is the long candle or tower formed on the way up and on the way down. A Tower Top is a bearish reversal pattern.

Rules of Recognition

1. An uptrend must be in progress.
2. The first candle must be a long white candle, preferably a Marubozu day. The market is strong but is getting overbought.
3. This is followed by a short consolidation consisting of a multiple of small white or black candles (like Spinning Tops or doji). The small candles imply a pause in buying. The market deliberates.
4. A long black candle forms on the right, reversing the psychology from bullish to bearish.
5. The tall white candle on the left is called the left tower while the tall black candle on the right is called the right tower.

Interpretation: The Tower Top is a bearish reversal pattern. Long towers on the left and right, of different colours, reveal strong buying but are countered by equally strong selling. The long black candle or tall column on the right is a significant candle, and as long as the high of this black candle is not violated on the upside, the market is poised for a trend reversal downward.

The high of a long black candle acts as a resistance area in the event of a rebound. Stops should be placed just above this resistance area or above the high of the previous candle.

Proper action: Sell signal. However, bearish confirmation is required via a close below the lowest low of the two preceding candles. Place buy-stop above the high of the long black candle that makes the right tower or the high of the candle before it.

Trading the Tower Bottom and Tower Top Figure 4.47 and Figure 4.48 show some examples of the Tower Bottom and Tower Top patterns.

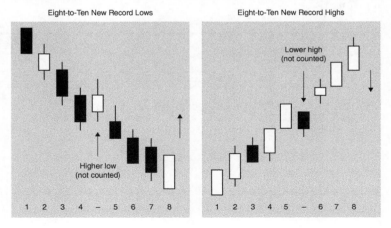

Tower Top

The close on candle 5 must exceed the lowest low of candles 3 and 4 to trigger a sell signal. Place buy-stop above the highest high of candles 4 and 5.

Eight-to-Ten New Record Lows and Highs

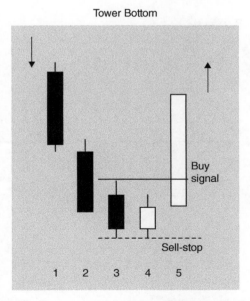

Tower Bottom

The close on candle 5 must exceed the highest high of candles 3 and 4 to trigger a buy signal. Place sell-stop below the lowest low of candles 4 and 5.

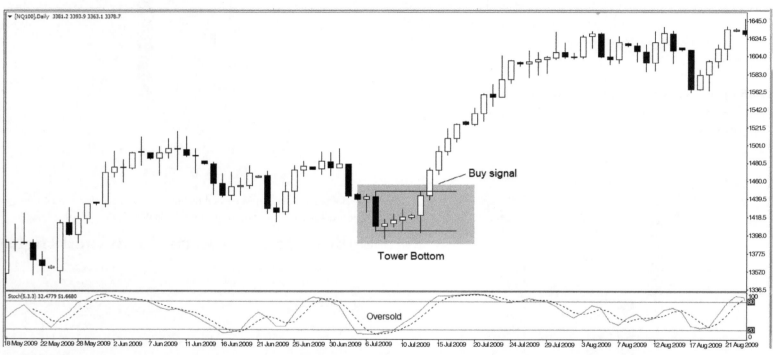

FIGURE 4.47 Nasdaq 100 Daily (2009)—Tower Bottom

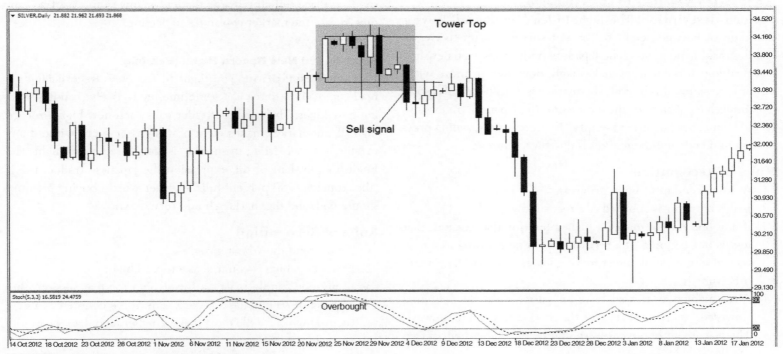

FIGURE 4.48 Silver Daily (2013)—Tower Top

The Eight-to-Ten New Record Lows and Highs pattern descriptions, rules of recognition, interpretations, and proper actions are explained next, together with some examples.

Eight-to-Ten New Record Lows (Bullish)

Pattern description: The Eight-to-Ten New Record Lows is made up of between eight to ten but sometimes up to twelve candles making new lows. The Japanese trader calls each new low a record low. If the market makes eight new lows or more without any meaningful rebound, the market is considered oversold. The English equivalent of the expression the Japanese traders use is "the stomach is 80 percent empty." In other words, selling pressure should end, and the market is due for a rebound.

Rules of Recognition

1. A downtrend must be in progress.
2. Every new low is counted as a record low.
3. If any one candle makes a higher low for that session, that low is not counted as a record low. To be counted as a new record low, a candle must make a lower low than the candle preceding it.
4. After eight new record lows buy-stops must be tightened (lowered) as one prepares for the market to reverse upward.
5. The placement of buy-stops should be the higher high of two candles back.
6. A buy signal will be triggered when a bullish white candle closes above the high of the two candles before it.

Interpretation: The Eight-to-Ten New Record Lows is a bullish reversal pattern. After about eight to ten new price lows, selling pressure eases. The bears are exhausted and the market is considered oversold. After eight to ten new lows, look for a bullish white candle to emerge.

Proper action: Buy signal. However, bullish confirmation is required via a close above the highest high of the previous two candles. Place sell-stop below the lowest low of the last two candles in case the market continues to decline.

Eight-to-Ten New Record Highs (Bearish)

Pattern description: The Eight-to-Ten New Record Highs is made up of eight to ten and sometimes up to twelve candles making new highs. The Japanese trader calls each new high a record high. If the market makes eight new highs or more without any meaningful correction, the market is considered overbought. The English equivalent of the expression the Japanese traders use is "the stomach is 80 percent full." In other words, buying pressure should end, and the market should turn down.

Rules of Recognition

1. An uptrend must be in progress.
2. Every new high is counted as a record high.
3. If any one candle makes a lower high for that session, that high is not counted as a record high. To be counted as a new record high, a candle must make a higher high than the candle preceding it.
4. After eight new record highs, sell-stops must be tightened (raised) as one prepares for the market to reverse downward.
5. The placement of sell-stops should be the lower low of two candles back.
6. A sell signal will be triggered when a bearish black candle closes below the low of the two candles before it.

Interpretation: The Eight-to-Ten New Record Highs is a bearish reversal pattern. After about eight to ten new price highs, buying pressure should end. The bulls are exhausted, and the market is considered overbought. After eight to ten new highs, look for a bearish black candle to liquidate longs and selling is suggested.

Proper action: Sell signal. However, bearish confirmation is required via a close below the lowest low of the previous two candles. Place the buy-stop above the highest high of the last two candles in case the market continues to rally.

Trading the Eight-to-Ten New Record Lows and Highs Figure 4.49 and Figure 4.50 show some examples of Eight-to-Ten New Record Lows and Highs patterns.

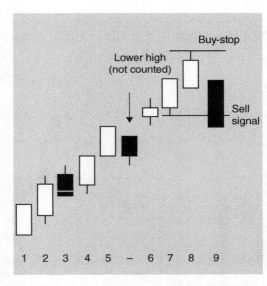

The close on candle 9 must exceed the lowest low of candles 8 and 7 to trigger a sell signal. Place buy-stop above the highest high of candles 8 and 9.

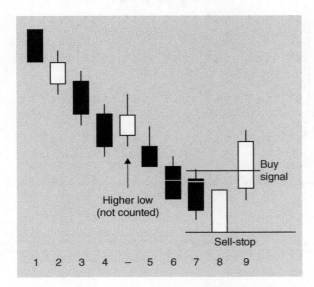

The close on candle 9 must exceed the highest high of candles 8 and 7 to trigger a buy signal. Place sell-stop below the lowest low of candles 8 and 9.

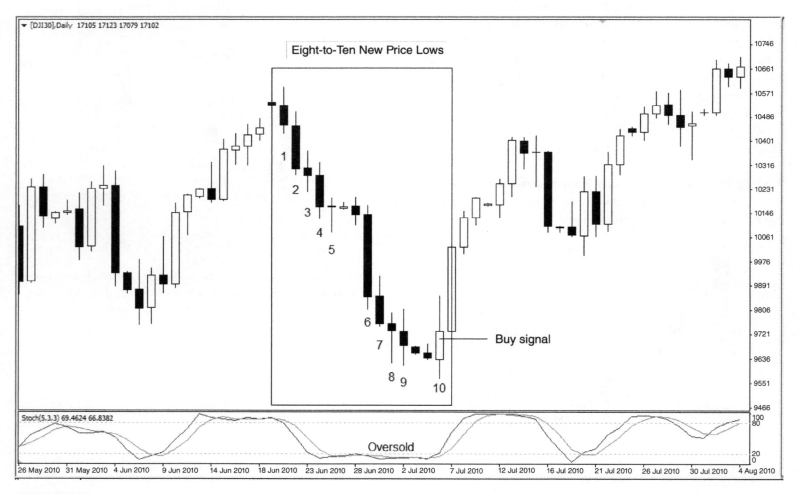

FIGURE 4.49 Dow Jones Industrial Average Daily (2010)—Eight-to-Ten New Record Lows

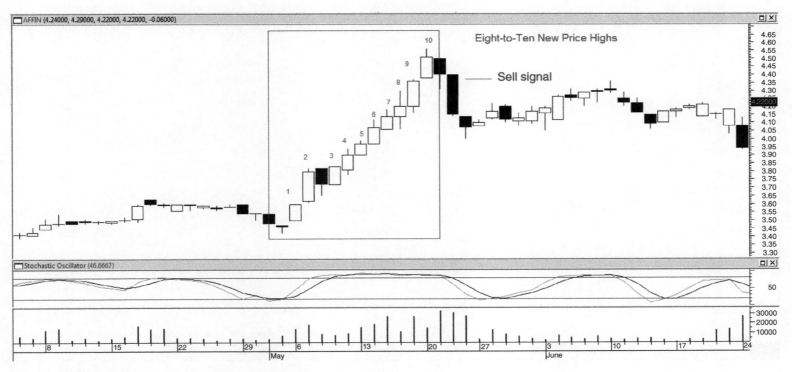

FIGURE 4.50 Affin Malaysia Daily (2013)—Eight-to-Ten New Record Highs

CHAPTER 5

Continuation Patterns

■ Introduction

As we have seen in Chapter 4 on reversal patterns, the Japanese candlestick technique has many more reversal patterns than Western classical charting theory.

This book covers 53 reversal patterns, but in Western charting theory the number of reversal patterns documented is considerably less. Japanese candlestick patterns clearly give us more clues for spotting market reversals.

While reversal patterns warn us of a trend change or market reversal, continuation patterns tell us that the market is consolidating and taking a rest, after which it is expected to move or to resume its prior trend.

No stock or market moves up in a straight line without pulling back. These periods of pullback are normally due to profit taking. There will be periods when the market will get overbought after which it stages a pullback or correction, even if it is to continue with its prior trend. Conversely, a market in a downtrend will not plunge straight down without a rebound. Even if the market is to fall further, a brief rebound usually takes place before resuming its downtrend.

Continuation patterns therefore represent temporary pauses in the existing trend. In this chapter, I will be looking at a number of continuation patterns. There are, however, fewer continuation patterns in Japanese candlestick theory than there are reversal patterns.

Continuation patterns fall broadly into these categories:

■ Double Candlestick Patterns

Double candlestick patterns such as the Separating Lines, Kicking pattern, On-Neck pattern, In-Neck pattern, and Thrusting Line are discussed here:

Separating Lines

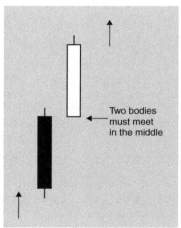

Bullish Separating Lines

Two bodies must meet in the middle

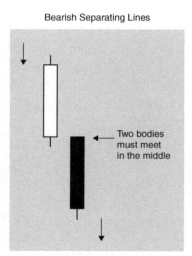

Bearish Separating Lines

Two bodies must meet in the middle

Bullish Separating Lines and Bearish Separating Lines pattern descriptions, rules of recognition, interpretations, and proper actions are explained next, together with some examples.

Bullish Separating Lines (Bullish)

■ **Pattern description:** The Bullish Separating Line is made up of two opposite-coloured candles. The first is a black candle that is followed by a white candle. One characteristic is that the white candle is a Belt-Hold candle (where the open is also the low). The second characteristic is that the first candle's open is at the same price as the second candle's open.

Rules of Recognition

1. An uptrend must be in progress.
2. The first day is a black candle.
3. The second day is a White Belt-Hold candle. A White Belt-Hold candle is one that opens at the low and rallies to close near the high but not necessarily at its high.
4. The open of the first black candle is at the same price as the open of the second white candle.
5. The Japanese name for Separating Line is *ikichigaisen*, which means "lines that move in opposite directions." They are also known as Dividing (*furiwake*) Lines.

- **Interpretation:** The Bullish Separating Line is viewed as bullish despite the appearance of the first black candle. The first black candle gives the impression that the uptrend is under siege. However, the next day's candle gaps higher to open at the previous black candle's open. This up-gap on the second day together with a close higher than the previous high shows that the bulls have regained control, and the uptrend continues.

- **Proper action:** Bullish continuation signal. Place sell-stop below the low of the black candle.

Bearish Separating Lines (Bearish)

- **Pattern description:** The Bearish Separating Line is made up of two opposite-coloured candles. The first is a white candle that is followed by a black candle. The black candle must be

a black Belt-Hold candle (where the open is also the high). Second, the first candle's open must be the same price as the second candle's open, but the second black candle makes a new low.

Rules of Recognition

1. A downtrend must be in progress.
2. The first day is a white candle.
3. The second day is a Black Belt-Hold candle. A Black Belt-Hold candle is one that opens at the high and falls to close near the low but not necessarily at its low.
4. The open of the first white candle is at the same price as the open of the second black candle.
5. The Japanese name for Separating Line is *ikichigaisen*, which means "lines that move in opposite directions." They are also known as Dividing (*furiwake*) Lines.

- **Interpretation:** The Bearish Separating Line is viewed as bearish despite the appearance of the first white candle. The first white candle gives the impression of a counterattack by the bulls. However, the next day's candle gaps lower to open at the previous white candle's open. The second day's down-gap and lower closes show that the bears are still in control of the downtrend.

- **Proper action:** Bearish continuation signal. Place buy-stop above the high of the white candle.

Trading the Bullish Separating Lines and Bearish Separating Lines
Figure 5.1 and Figure 5.2 show some examples of Bullish and Bearish Separating Lines patterns.

FIGURE 5.1 Dow Jones Industrial Average 5-Minute (2014)—Bullish Separating Lines

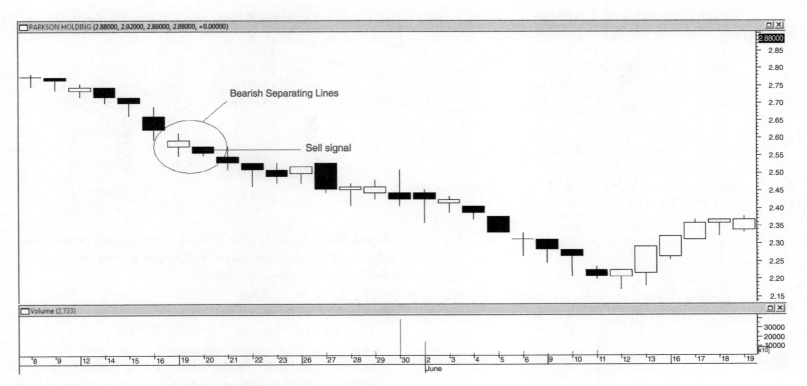

FIGURE 5.2 Parkson Holdings Malaysia Daily (2014)—Bearish Separating Lines

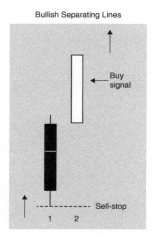

Bullish Separating Lines

The close on candle 2 must exceed the high of candle 1 to trigger a buy signal. Place sell-stop below the low of candle 1.

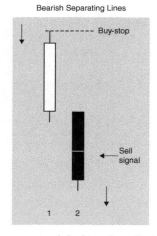

Bearish Separating Lines

The close of candle 2 must exceed the low of candle 1 to trigger a sell signal. Place buy-stop above the high of candle 1.

Kicking Pattern

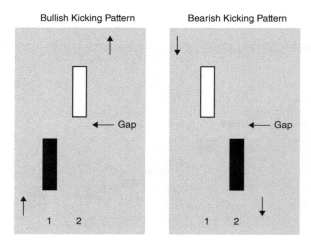

Bullish Kicking and Bearish Kicking pattern descriptions, rules of recognition, interpretations, and proper actions are explained next, together with some examples.

Bullish Kicking Pattern (Bullish)

- **Pattern description:** The Bullish Kicking pattern is nearly identical to the Bullish Separating Lines except for a gap between the black and the white candle. The first day is a Marubozu Black Candle that is followed by a Marubozu White Candle. A Marubozu Candle is one where there are no upper or lower shadows.

  One way of analysing the next direction is to compare the length of the real body of the two candles. The market should move in the direction of the longer of the two candles.

This implies that the Bullish Kicking pattern would be a top reversal pattern if the Marubozu White Candle is shorter than the Marubozu Black Candle.

Rules of Recognition

1. An uptrend must be in progress.
2. The first day is a Marubozu Black Candle.
3. The second day is a Marubozu White Candle.
4. An up-gap is formed between the black and the white candle.
5. Existence of shadows are also acceptable, not necessarily Marubozus.

- **Interpretation:** The Bullish Kicking pattern is viewed as bullish despite the appearance of the first black candle. The first black candle gives the impression that the uptrend is under siege. But the next day's candle gaps higher to open above the previous black candle's open. This up-gap on the second day together with a close higher than the previous high shows that the bulls have regained control and the uptrend continues.

- **Proper action:** Bullish continuation signal. Maintain long position. Place sell-stop below the low of the black candle.

Bearish Kicking Pattern (Bearish)

- **Pattern description:** The Bearish Kicking pattern is nearly identical to the Bearish Separating Lines except for a gap between the white and the black candle. The first day is a Marubozu White Candle that is followed by a Marubozu Black Candle. A Marubozu Candle is one where there are no upper or lower shadows.

One way of analysing the next direction is to compare the length of the real body of the two candles. The market should move in the direction of the longer of the two candles.

This implies that the Bearish Kicking pattern would be a bottom reversal pattern if the Marubozu Black Candle is shorter than the Marubozu White Candle.

Rules of Recognition

1. A downtrend must be in progress.
2. The first day is a Marubozu White Candle.
3. The second day is a Marubozu Black Candle.
4. A down-gap is formed between the white and the black candle.
5. Existence of shadows are also acceptable, not necessarily Marubozus.

- **Interpretation:** The Bearish Kicking pattern is viewed as bearish despite the appearance of the first white candle. The first white candle gives the impression of a counterattack by the bulls. However, the next day's candle gaps lower to open below the previous white candle's open. This down-gap on the second day, together with a close lower than the previous low, shows that the bears have regained control, and the downtrend continues.

- **Proper action:** Bearish continuation signal. Maintain short position. Place buy-stop above the high of the white candle.

Trading the Bullish Kicking and Bearish Kicking Pattern

Figure 5.3 and Figure 5.4 show some examples of Bullish Kicking and Bearish Kicking patterns.

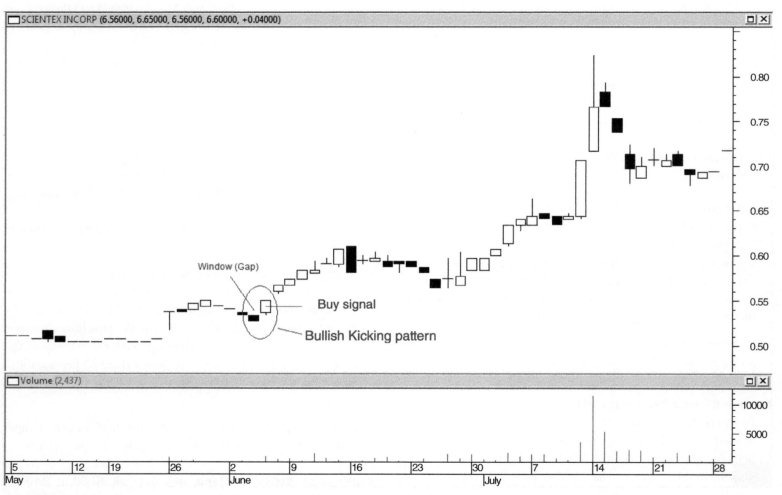

FIGURE 5.3 Scientex Malaysia Daily—Bullish Kicking pattern

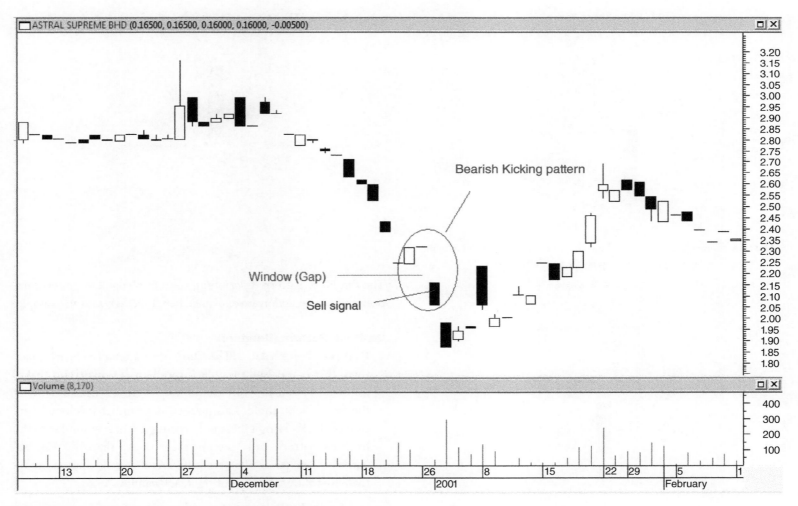

FIGURE 5.4 Astral Supreme Daily (2000)—Bearish Kicking pattern

Bullish Kicking Pattern

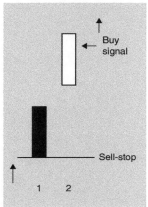

Buy signal

Sell-stop

1   2

The close on candle 2 must exceed the high of candle 1 to trigger a further buy signal. Place sell-stop below the low of candle 1.

Bearish Kicking Pattern

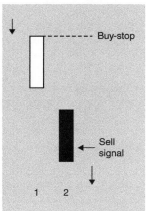

Buy-stop

Sell signal

1   2

The close of candle 2 must exceed the low of candle 1 to trigger a further sell signal. Place buy-stop above the high of candle 1.

On-Neck Pattern

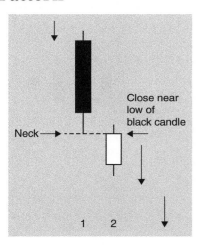

Close near low of black candle

Neck

1   2

The On-Neck Pattern description, rules of recognition, interpretation, and proper action are explained here together with an example.

On-Neck Pattern (Bearish)

- **Pattern description:** The On-Neck pattern is a bearish pattern. It is comprised of a black candle in a downtrend that is followed by a small white candle whose close is near the low of the first black candle. This pattern is an underdeveloped version of the Piercing Line and Thrusting Line. It is similar to the In-Neck pattern and Meeting Lines. Note that they can become bottom reversal patterns if there is a confirmation candle that rises above the high of the black candle.

Rules of Recognition

1. A downtrend must be in progress.

2. The first day is a long black candle.
3. The second day is a small white candle that closes at the low of the first day's black candle.

- **Interpretation:** The On-Neck pattern is viewed as a bearish continuation pattern because the second day's small white candle only manages to close at the low of the black candle. The bears are still in control, and the market should continue to move lower if the low of the white candle is broken.

- **Proper action:** Bearish continuation signal. Maintain short position. Confirmation is required to further sell. Place buy-stop above the high of the black candle.

Trading the On-Neck Pattern Figure 5.5 shows an example of an On-Neck pattern.

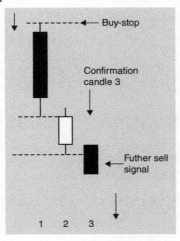

The close of candle 3 must exceed the low of candle 2 to trigger a further sell signal. Place buy-stop above the high of candle 1.

In-Neck Pattern

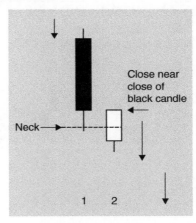

In-Neck pattern description, rules of recognition, interpretation and proper action are explained here together with an example:

In-Neck Pattern (Bearish)

- **Pattern description:** The In-Neck pattern is a bearish pattern. It is comprised of a black candle in a downtrend that is followed by a Short Closing Bozu White Candle whose close is near or just inside the close of the first black candle. It is called In-Neck because of the white candle's close above the low (also known as the neck) of the first black candle. This pattern is an underdeveloped version of the Piercing Line and Thrusting Line. It is similar to the On-Neck pattern and Meeting Lines. Note that they can become bottom reversal patterns if there is a confirmation candle that rises above the high of the black candle.

Rules of Recognition

1. A downtrend must be in progress.

FIGURE 5.5   IJM Daily (2000)—On-Neck pattern

2. The first day is a long black candle.

3. The second day is a white candle that opens below the first day's low but closes into and above the low of the first day. They may even close into the real body of the black candle.

- **Interpretation:** The In-Neck pattern is viewed as a bearish continuation pattern because the second day's white candle only manages to close at the close of the black candle. The bears are still in control, and the market should continue to move lower if the low of the white candle is broken.

- **Proper action:** Bearish continuation signal. Maintain short position. Confirmation is required to further sell. Place buy-stop above the high of the black candle.

Trading the In-Neck Pattern Figure 5.6 shows an example of an In-Neck pattern.

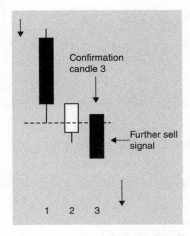

The close of candle 3 must exceed the low of candle 2 to trigger a further sell signal. Place buy-stop above the high of candle 1.

Thrusting Line

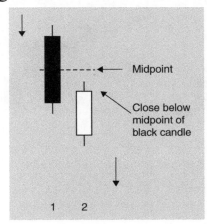

The Thrusting Line pattern description, rules of recognition, interpretation, and proper action are explained next, together with an example.

Thrusting Line (Bearish)

- **Pattern description:** The Thrusting Line can be both a bullish or bearish pattern. It becomes a bearish pattern if there is no bullish confirmation. It is comprised of a black candle in a downtrend that is followed by a white candle that closes into but just below the midpoint of the black's real body. The Thrusting Line is an underdeveloped version of the Piercing Line.

  - If there is bullish confirmation via a close above the high of the last two candles, it becomes a bullish reversal pattern.

  - The Thrusting Line will also become a bullish reversal pattern if two of these patterns appear within a few days of each other, in which case it is called a Double Thrusting Line pattern.

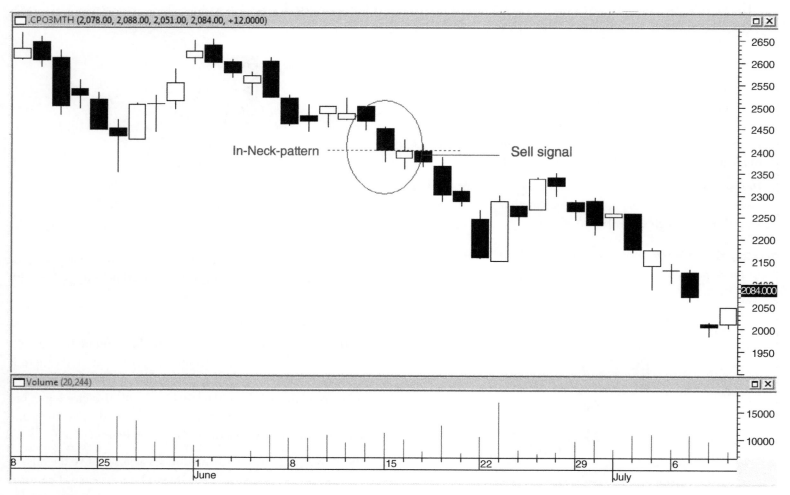

FIGURE 5.6   Crude Palm Oil Futures Daily (2014)—In-Neck pattern

Rules of Recognition
1. A downtrend must be in progress.
2. The first day is a long black candle.
3. The second day is a white candle that opens below the first day's low but closes into but not above the midpoint of the black candle's real body.

- **Interpretation:** The Thrusting Line is a bearish continuation pattern because, like the On-Neck and In-Neck patterns, the Thrusting Line represents the failure of the bulls to stage a successful counterattack. The bears are still in control, and the market should continue to move lower if the low of the white candle is broken.

- **Proper action:** Bearish continuation signal. Maintain short position. Confirmation is required to further sell. Place buy-stop above the high of the black candle.

Trading the Thrusting Line Figure 5.7 shows an example of a Thrusting Line Pattern.

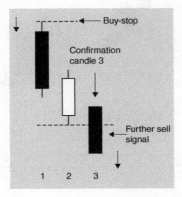

The close of candle 3 must exceed the low of candle 2 to trigger a further sell signal. Place buy-stop above the high of candle 1.

■ Multiple Candlestick Patterns

Multiple candlestick patterns such as the Rising Three and Falling Three Methods, Mat Hold, Windows, Tasuki Upside and Downside Gaps, Gapping Side-by-Side White Lines, and High-Price and Low-Price Gapping Plays are discussed here.

Rising Three Methods and Falling Three Methods

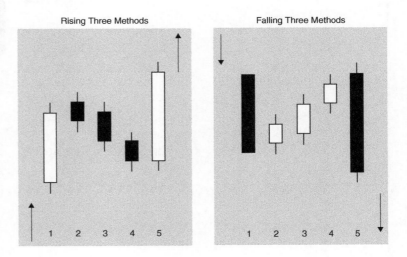

The Rising Three Methods and Falling Three Methods pattern descriptions, rules of recognition, interpretations, and proper actions are explained here together with some examples.

FIGURE 5.7 U.S. Dollar Index Daily (2009)—Thrusting Line

Rising Three Methods (Bullish)

Pattern description: The Rising Three Methods is a bullish continuation pattern that depicts a market at rest. It is comprised of five candles, one long white candle followed by three small black candles and another white candle. It represents a temporary pause in the current trend after a rally. The period of correction or rest is likely to be three days (hence the name *san-poh* or "three methods" in Sakata's Five Methods) after which the prior trend continues. Though the number three is a significant number in traditional Japanese candlestick theory, there is no hard and fast rule here that the correction has to take three days. It can be from one to five days, but three is the most common number. This pattern is equivalent to the Western Bullish Flag.

Rules of Recognition

1. An uptrend must be in progress.
2. The first day is a long white candle.
3. The second, third, and fourth days are composed of smaller candles that go against the main (up)trend. Their lower prices represent profit taking. These candles may be white or black candles but are likely to be black. The three candles must reside within the range of the first white candle.
4. The fifth day is a long white candle, reflecting a strong day, breaking out of the consolidation, and closing above the first white candle's close.
5. Volume falls during the correction on the second to the fourth day but rises significantly on the fifth day, on breakout.

- **Interpretation:** The Rising Three Methods is a bullish continuation pattern that is part of Sakata's Five Methods. After a

rally, profit taking sets in, resulting in a minor correction—but not a trend change. It represents a market at rest. Volume drops significantly during this rest period, implying weak sellers. After the fourth day, buyers resurface to take the market higher for an uptrend continuation.

- **Proper action:** Bullish continuation signal. Maintain long position. Further buy if the close of the fifth white candle exceeds the highest high of the last four candles. Place sell-stop below the lowest low of the last two candles.

Falling Three Methods (Bearish)

- **Pattern description:** The Falling Three Methods is a bearish continuation pattern. It is comprised of five candles, one long black candle followed by three small white candles and another black candle. It represents a temporary pause in the current trend after a period of decline. The market makes a brief rebound, likely to be three days (hence the name *san-poh* or "three methods" in Sakata's Five Methods), after which the prior downtrend continues. Though the number three is a significant number in traditional Japanese candlestick theory, there is no hard and fast rule here that the rebound has to take three days. It can be from one to five days, but three is the most common number. This pattern is equivalent to the Western Bearish Flag.

Rules of Recognition

1. A downtrend must be in progress.
2. The first day is a long black candle.

3. The second, third, and fourth days are composed of smaller candles that go against the main (down) trend. Their higher prices represent bargain hunting. These candles may be white or black candles but are likely to be white. The three candles must reside within the range of the first black candle.

4. The fifth day is a long black candle, reflecting a weak day, breaking out of the consolidation and closing below the first black candle's close.

5. Volume falls during the rebound on the second to the fourth days but rises significantly on the fifth day, on breakdown.

- **Interpretation:** The Falling Three Methods is a bearish continuation pattern that is part of Sakata's Five Methods. After a decline bargain hunting surfaces, resulting in a minor rally—but not a trend change. It represents a market at rest. Volume drops significantly during this rest period, implying weak buyers. After the fourth day, sellers resurface to sell-down the market lower for a downtrend continuation.

- **Proper action:** Bearish continuation signal. Maintain short position. Further sell if the close of the fifth black candle exceeds the lowest low of the last four candles. Place buy-stop above the highest high of the last two candles.

Trading the Rising Three Methods and the Falling Three Methods Figure 5.8 and Figure 5.9 show some examples of Rising Three Methods and Falling Three Methods patterns.

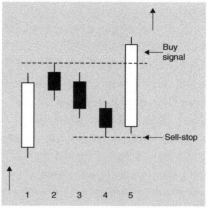

The close of candle 5 must exceed the highest high of the last four candles 1 to 4 to buy. Place sell-stop below the lowest low of candles 4 and 5.

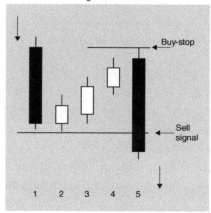

The close of candle 5 must exceed the lowest low of the last four candles 1 to 4 to sell. Place buy-stop above the highest high of candles 4 and 5.

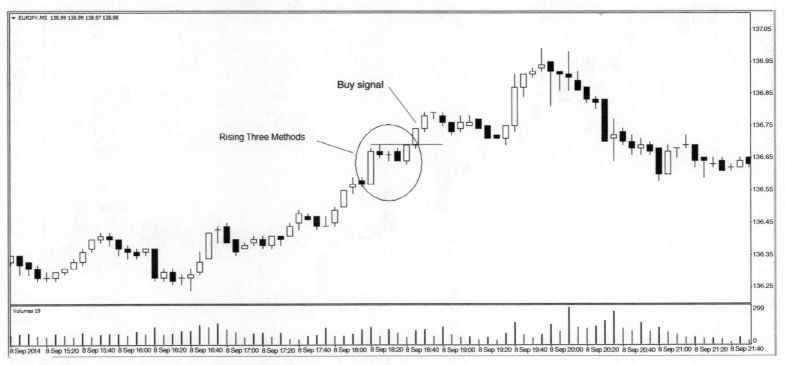

FIGURE 5.8 EurJpy 5-Minute (2014)—Rising Three Methods

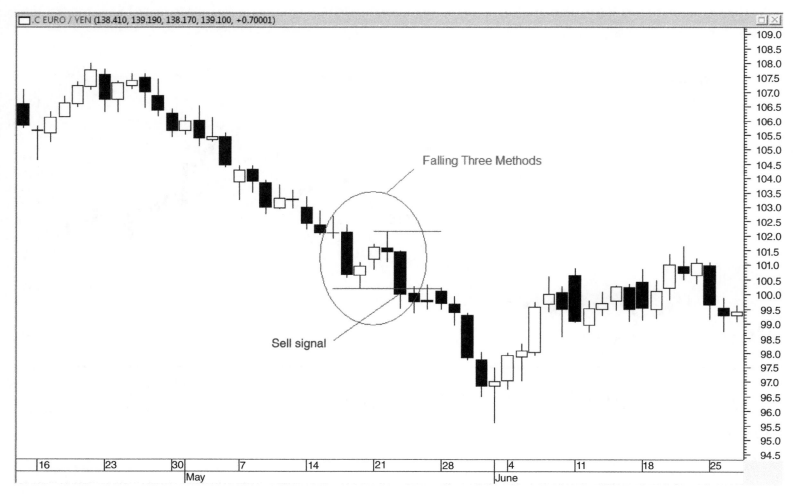

FIGURE 5.9 EurJpy Daily (2012)—Falling Three Methods

Mat Hold Pattern

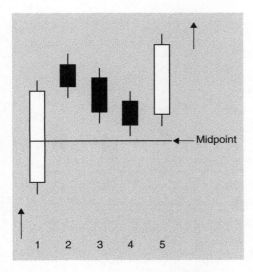

The Mat Hold pattern description, rules of recognition, interpretation and proper action are explained next, together with an example.

Mat Hold Pattern (Bullish)

■ **Pattern description:** The Mat Hold pattern is a bullish continuation pattern that is quite like the Rising Three Methods. The difference in the Mat Hold is where the second candle gaps above the first white candle and closes with the gap unfilled. The third candle comes down to fill the gap and closes into the first white candle. The first three days pattern will therefore look like an Upside Gap Two Crows but with the third candle penetrating back into the

body of the first long white day. The fourth candle closes even lower but above the midpoint of the first day's white real body. The pullback here is not as severe as the Rising Three Methods. This pattern has similarities to the Western Bullish Flag.

Rules of Recognition

1. An uptrend must be in progress.
2. The first day is a long white candle.
3. The second day gaps up but with a lower close (black candle). This gap is unfilled on the second day.
4. The third day comes down, covers the gap, and penetrates into the real body of the first white candle.
5. The fourth day closes even lower but above the midpoint of the first white candle.
6. The fifth day is a long white candle that closes above the second day's high. It still qualifies as a breakout even with a lower close as long as it closes above the highest high of the last two candles and volume rises significantly.
7. Volume falls during the correction on the second to the fourth days but rises significantly on the fifth day, on breakout.

■ **Interpretation:** The Mat Hold pattern is a bullish continuation pattern that is similar to the Rising Three Methods and is part of Sakata's Five Methods. It is more bullish than the Rising Three Methods because the correction days are less severe. They do not fall below the midpoint of the first white candle. This dip is a result of profit taking and not a trend change. It represents a market at rest. Volume drops significantly during this rest period, but the uptrend resumes on the fifth day as buyers resurface.

- **Proper action:** Bullish continuation signal. Maintain long position. Further buy if the close of the fifth white candle exceeds the highest high of the last four candles. Place sell-stop below the lowest low of the last two candles.

Trading the Mat Hold Pattern Figure 5.10 shows an example of a Mat Hold pattern.

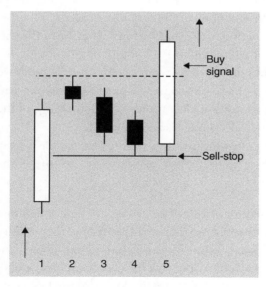

Further buy if the close of candle 5 exceeds
the highest high of the last four candles 1 to 4.
Place sell-stop below the lowest low of candles 4 and 5.

■ Windows (Gaps)

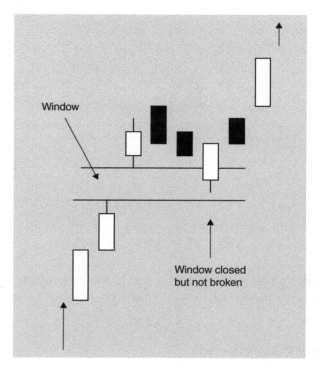

Window in an Uptrend—Window not broken

There are several continuation patterns that come with gaps, which the Japanese refer to as windows.

In my first book, *Maximising Stock Market Profit*, I defined a gap as "an area in a chart where no transactions are done."

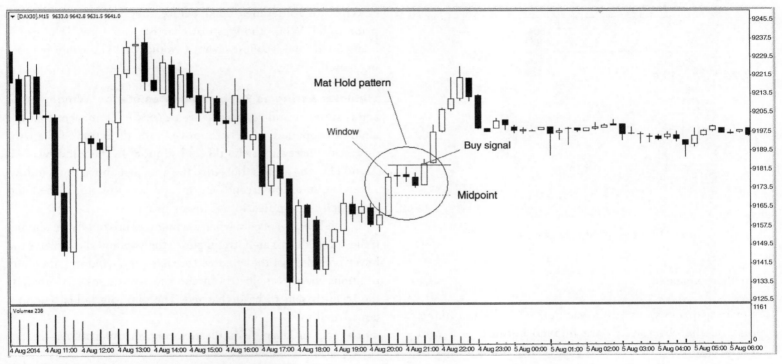

FIGURE 5.10 Dax 30 15-Minute (2014)—Mat Hold pattern

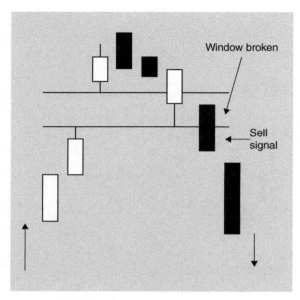

Trend Change—Window broken (violated)

I further explained:

A price gap is essentially a vacuum or a discontinuous point on the chart. Gaps are formed because of a void in buy/sell orders or due to an overwhelming influx of buy/sell orders. In an uptrend, for example, prices open above the highest price of the previous day, leaving an up-gap or an open space on the chart that is not filled during the day. In a downtrend, prices open below yesterday's low, leaving a down-gap that is not filled during the down day.

Upside gaps are signs of market strength while down gaps are signs of market weakness. Both represent potential power in the move that follows.

Gaps are sometimes filled before they continue with their prior trend. While the Western chartist would say, "The gap is being filled," the Japanese chartist would say, "The window is being closed."

Windows Acting as Support and Resistance Windows also act as support and resistance areas. A rallying market that has a window opened is likely to move in the direction of the window. Any corrections should find support in the window area. A good buying area is therefore the area just above the window. Likewise, in a downtrend, an opened window not closed and exceeded is an indication of lower prices.

A trend change occurs when a window is broken. For example, if the correction of an uptrend closes the window and violates the lower boundary of the window (breaking the window), then buy positions should be closed out and short positions instituted, as the trend is said to have changed. The opposite holds true in a downtrend.

The various Japanese candlestick continuation patterns that involve gaps or windows are:

Pattern Names

- Tasuki Upside Gap
- Tasuki Downside Gap
- Up-Gap Side-by-Side White Lines

- Down-Gap Side-by-Side White Lines
- High Price Gapping Plays
- Low Price Gapping Plays

Tasuki Upside and Downside Gaps

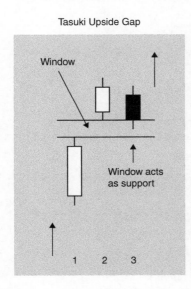

Tasuki Upside Gap

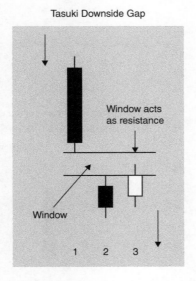

Tasuki Downside Gap

Tasuki Upside and Downside Gaps pattern descriptions, rules of recognition, interpretations, and proper actions are explained here together with some examples.

Tasuki Upside Gap (Bullish)

- **Pattern description:** The Tasuki Upside Gap consists of a white candle that gaps up and closes higher than a previous long white candle. This is followed by a black candle opening inside the white's body and closing below the white's body. The window may be closed but must not be violated (broken) on the downside. If so, selling pressure is deemed to be strong, and this bullish pattern will be negated.

Rules of Recognition

1. An uptrend must be in progress.
2. The first day is a long white candle.
3. The second day is a small white candle that gaps up on the open and closes higher.
4. The third day is a small black candle that opens within the body of the second candle and closes below it.
5. The window (or gap) may be closed (filled) by the black candle on the third day but must not be violated on the downside.

- **Interpretation:** The Tasuki Upside Gap is a bullish continuation pattern. The correction on the third day did not close the window, implying sellers are weak. Japanese candlestick theory calls for a buy on the third day's black candle.

- **Proper action:** Bullish continuation signal. Maintain long position. Although Japanese candlestick theory calls for a buy on the third day, we suggest bullish confirmation via a close on the fourth day that is higher than the highest high of the previous two candles. Place sell-stop below the window.

Tasuki Downside Gap (Bearish)

- **Pattern description:** The Tasuki Downside Gap consists of a small black candle that gaps below and closes lower than a previous Long Black Candle. This is followed by a small white candle opening inside the black's body and closes above the black's body. The window may be closed but must not be violated (broken) on the upside. If so, buying momentum is deemed to be strong, and this bearish pattern will be negated.

Rules of Recognition
1. A downtrend must be in progress.
2. The first day is a long black candle.
3. The second day is a small black candle that gaps below on the open and closes lower.
4. The third day is a small white candle that opens within the body of the second candle and closes above it.
5. The window (or gap) may be closed (filled) by the white candle on the third day but must not be violated on the upside.

■ **Interpretation:** The Tasuki Downside Gap is a bearish continuation pattern. The rally on the third day did not close the window, implying buyers are weak. Japanese candlestick theory calls for a sell on the third day's white candle.

■ **Proper action:** Bearish continuation signal. Maintain short position. Although Japanese candlestick theory calls for a sell on the third day, we suggest bearish confirmation via a close on the fourth day that is lower than the lowest low of the previous two candles. Place buy-stop above the window.

Trading the Tasuki Upside and Downside Gaps Figure 5.11 and Figure 5.12 show some examples of Tasuki Upside and Downside Gaps patterns.

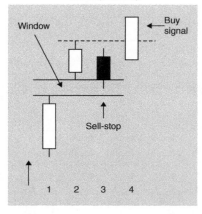

Further buy if the close of candle 4 exceeds the highest high of candles 2 and 3. Place sell-stop below the window.

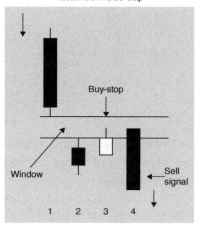

Further sell if the close of candle 4 exceeds the lowest low of candles 2 and 3. Place buy-stop above the window.

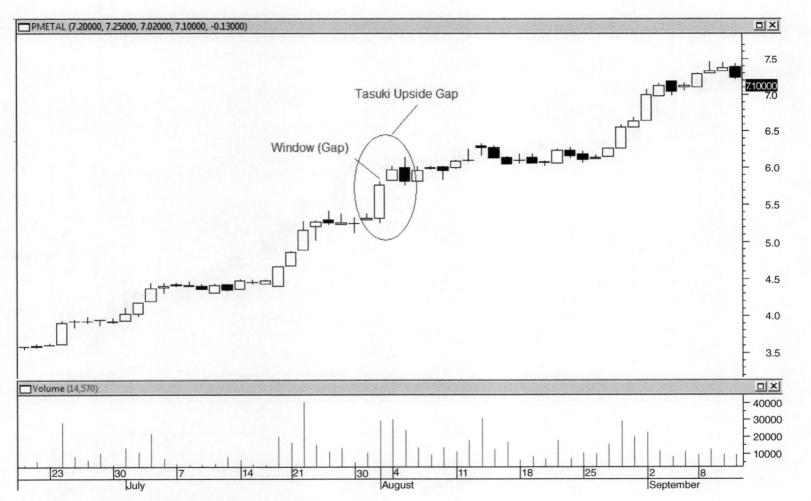

FIGURE 5.11   Press Metal Malaysia Daily (2014)—Tasuki Upside Gap

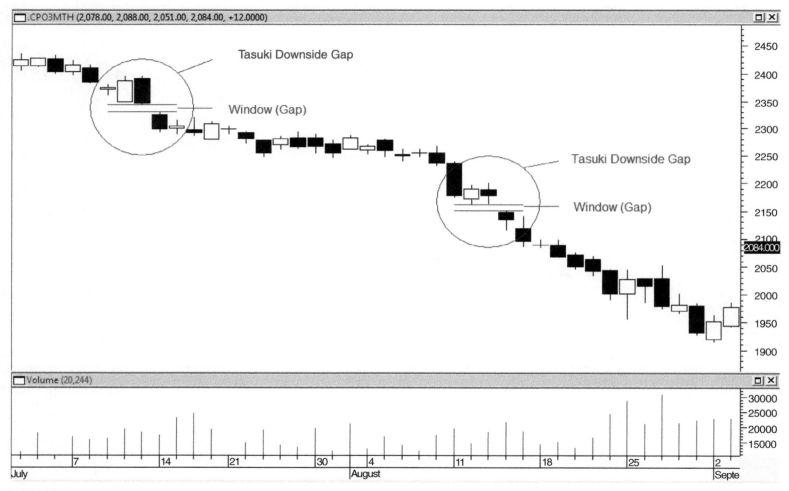

FIGURE 5.12 Crude Palm Oil Futures Daily (2014)—Tasuki Downside Gap

Gapping Side-by-Side White Lines

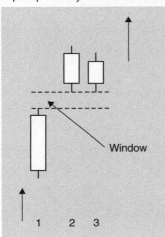

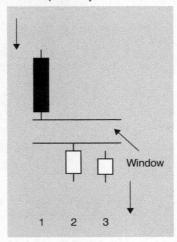

Up-Gap and Down-Gap Side-by-Side White Lines pattern descriptions, rules of recognition, interpretations, and proper actions are explained next, together with some examples.

Up-Gap Side-by-Side White Lines (Bullish)

- **Pattern description:** The Up-Gap Side-by-Side White Lines is a bullish continuation pattern. This pattern consists of two white candles of similar sizes with about the same open gapping above a long white candle. Gapping side-by-side white lines are rare.

Rules of Recognition

1. An uptrend must be in progress.
2. The first day is a long white candle.
3. Two consecutive small white candles of about the same size gap above the long white candle.

4. The window (or gap) is not closed.
5. An upside breakout should occur within the next few candles on stronger volume.

- **Interpretation:** The two white candles that lie side-by-side with one another imply some profit taking but are yet well supported by the bulls. The inability of the bears to close the window and violate it implies bullish support. Japanese candlestick theory calls for a buy if the window is not violated on the downside. But I prefer an establishment of a higher close before further buying.

- **Proper action:** Bullish continuation signal. Maintain long position. Further buy above the highest high of the second and third candles but place sell-stop below the window.

Down-Gap Side-by-Side White Lines (Bearish)

- **Pattern description:** The Down-Gap Side-by-Side White Lines is a bearish continuation pattern. This pattern consists of two white candles of similar sizes with about the same open gapping below a long black candle. Breaking a new low is recommended before further selling in this bearish scenario. Gapping side-by-side white lines are rare.

Rules of Recognition

1. A downtrend must be in progress.
2. The first day is a long black candle.
3. Two consecutive small white candles of about the same size gap below the black candle.
4. The window (or gap) is not closed.
5. A downside breakout should occur within the next few candles on stronger volume.

- **Interpretation:** The two white candles that lie side-by-side with one another are viewed as short covering or bargain hunting. Once they are over, the bearish trend continues. Japanese candlestick theory calls for a sell if the window is not violated on the upside. But I prefer an establishment of a lower close before further selling.

- **Proper action:** Bearish continuation signal. Maintain short position. Bearish confirmation is suggested by further selling only upon the break of the lowest low of the two white candles. Place buy-stop above the window.

Trading the Up-Gap and Down-Gap Side-by-Side White Lines Figure 5.13 and Figure 5.14 show some examples of Up-Gap and Down-Gap Side-by-Side White Lines patterns.

BASIC CANDLESTICK TECHNIQUES

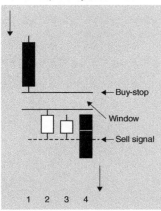

Down-Gap Side-by-Side White Lines

Further sell if the close of candle 4 exceeds the lowest low of candles 2 and 3. Place buy-stop above the window.

High-Price and Low-Price Gapping Plays

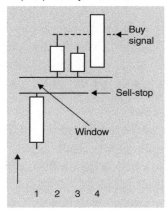

Up-Gap Side-by-Side White Lines

Further buy if the close of candle 4 exceeds the highest high of candles 2 and 3. Place sell-stop below the window.

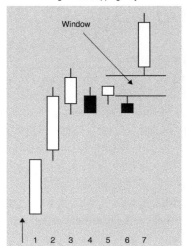

High-Price Gapping Play

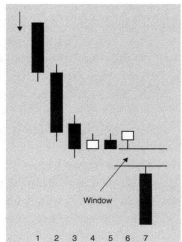

Low-Price Gapping Play

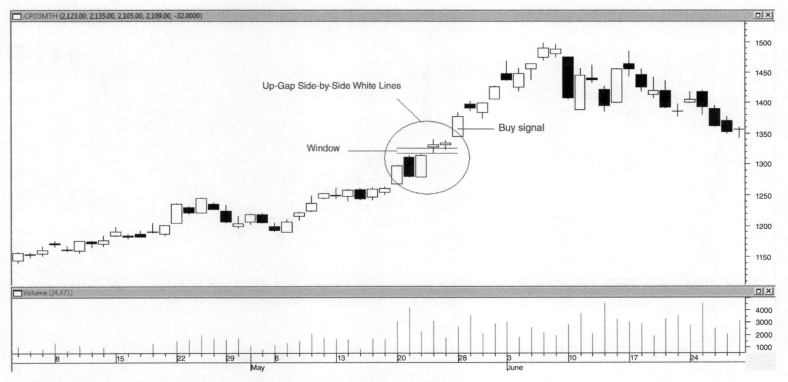

FIGURE 5.13 Crude Palm Lio Futures Daily (2002)—Up-Gap Side-by-Side White Lines

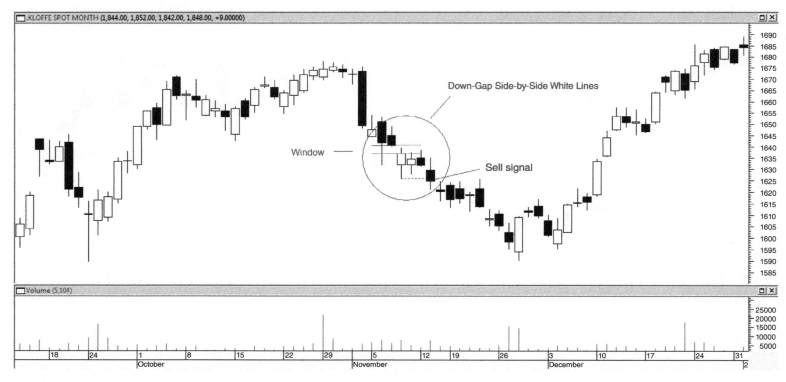

FIGURE 5.14 Kuala Lumpur Composite Index Futures Daily (2012)—Down-Gap Side-by-Side White Lines

The High-Price and Low-Price pattern descriptions, rules of recognition, interpretations, and proper actions are explained next, together with some examples.

High-Price Gapping Play (Bullish)

- **Pattern description:** The High-Price Gapping Play is a bullish continuation pattern. After a rally, the market consolidates its gains with a few small body candles. The market then makes an up-gap (or opens a window), and breaks out of the consolidation for an uptrend continuation. The High-Price Gapping Play is equivalent to the Western Bullish Pennant Breakout.

Rules of Recognition

1. An uptrend must be in progress.
2. The first day is a long white candle.
3. This is followed by a series of candles with small real bodies, indicating a market consolidation.
4. The long white candle gaps up and breaks out of the consolidation to continue its prior trend.
5. The window (or gap) is not closed. Volume is significantly higher on the breakout candle.

- **Interpretation:** After a rally, profit taking usually sets in, which is represented by a group of small candles. This consolidation should not last more than a week and represents the market taking a breather. Soon the bulls resurface to take prices higher, as they still see value in the market. Japanese candlestick theory calls for a buy on the breakout day.

- **Proper action:** Bullish continuation signal. Maintain long position. The gapping day is a buy day. Confirmation is in the

form of higher volume on the breakout day, and the close is usually above the highest high of the consolidation candles. Place sell-stop below the window.

Low-Price Gapping Play (Bearish)

- **Pattern description:** The Low-Price Gapping Play is a bearish continuation pattern. After a decline, the market consolidates for a few sessions. The market then makes a down-gap (or opens a window), and breaks out of the consolidation for a downtrend continuation. The Low-Price Gapping Play is equivalent to the Western Bearish Pennant Breakout.

Rules of Recognition

1. A downtrend must be in progress.
2. The first day is a long black candle.
3. This is followed by a series of candles with small real bodies, indicating a market consolidation.
4. A long black candle gaps down and breaks out of the consolidation to continue its downtrend.
5. The window (or gap) is not closed. Volume is significantly higher on the breakout candle.

- **Interpretation:** After a decline, bargain hunting usually surfaces; this is represented by a group of small candles moving in a sideways direction. This consolidation should not last more than a week and represents the market taking a rest after a sell-off. Soon the bears re-emerge to continue selling, as they believe the market is still overvalued. Japanese candlestick theory calls for a sell on the breakout day.

- **Proper action:** Bearish continuation signal. Maintain short position. The gapping day is a sell day. Confirmation is in the form of higher volume on the breakout day, and the close is usually below the lowest low of the consolidation candles. Place buy-stop above the window.

Trading the High-Price and Low-Price Gapping Plays Figure 5.15 to Figure 5.17 show some examples of High-Price and Low-Price Gapping Play patterns.

High-Price Gapping Play

Window

Buy signal

Sell-stop

1 2 3 4 5 6 7

Further buy if the close of candle 7 exceeds the highest high of candles 3 to 6. Place sell-stop below the window.

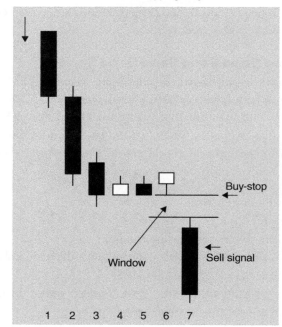

Low-Price Gapping Play

Buy-stop

Window

Sell signal

1 2 3 4 5 6 7

Further sell if the close of candle 7 exceeds the lowest low of candles 3 to 6. Place buy-stop above the window.

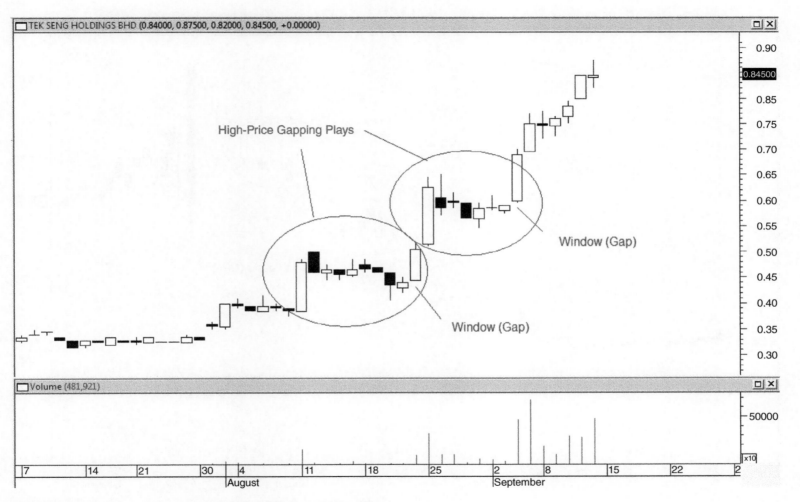

FIGURE 5.15   Tek Seng Malaysia Daily (2014)—High-Price Gapping Plays

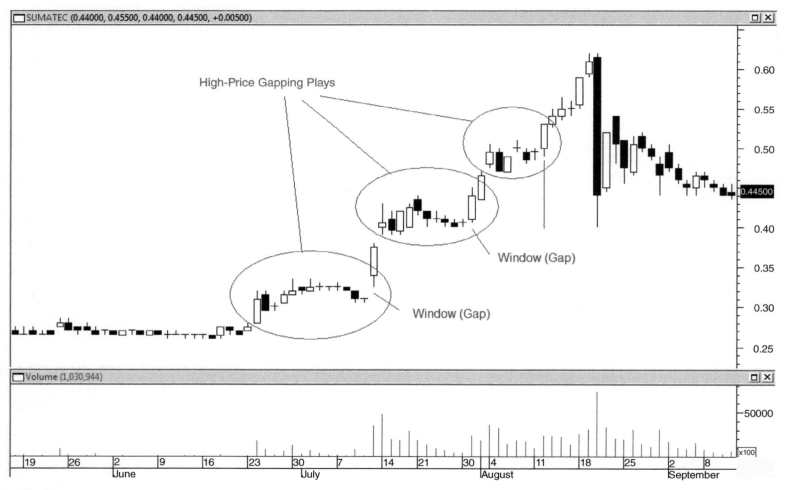

FIGURE 5.16   Sumatec Malaysia Daily (2014)—High-Price Gapping Plays

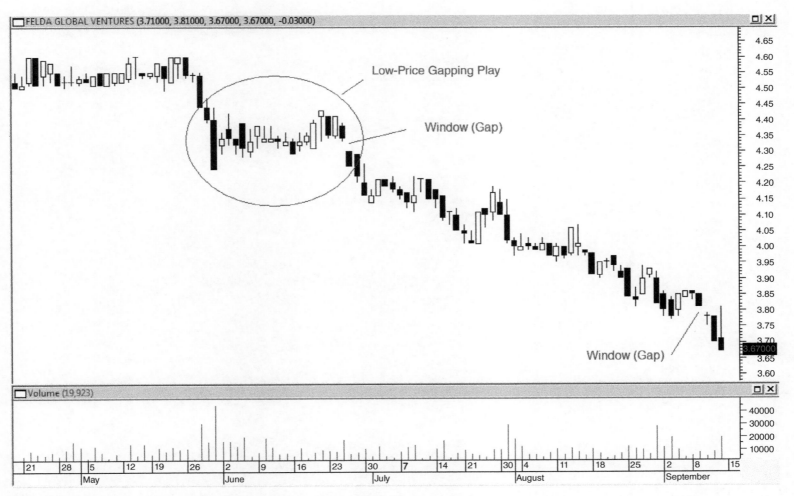

FIGURE 5.17 Felda Global Ventures Malaysia (2014)—Low-Price Gapping Play

CHAPTER 6

Summarizing Part I

Part I of this book has been devoted to describing the most common candlestick patterns. So far I have described:

1. Ten single black and white candles, seven doji, four in the umbrella group
2. Fifty-three reversal patterns
3. Fourteen continuation patterns

But this is not an exhaustive list of patterns available in candlestick literature. There are many more patterns, some of them abstract ones that a normal trader will not find useful or encounter.

Alternatively, they may be covered by another pattern. For example the Stick Sandwich is an abstract pattern. However, this pattern is sufficiently covered by a similar pattern called Tweezers Bottom. The Anaume is another example of an abstract pattern, but it bears some resemblance to an Inverted Hammer confirmation pattern.

The trader must understand that even with the large number of patterns in candlestick analysis, there is no necessity to know an all-encompassing list. I believe that the many patterns covered in this book are detailed enough to make you a better-equipped candlestick trader.

Can One Trade the Market and Profit Just by Applying Candlestick Chart Analysis?

Yes, because the candlestick technique is a standalone technique. A trader can make money just by using pure candlestick chart analysis because Japanese candlestick theory is best applied in trading fast-moving markets and is excellent in catching market turning points. Knowledge of the many types of reversal patterns gives you an edge over other traders. Similarly, knowledge of continuation patterns gives you that additional edge as to when to hold on to a position, add to new positions, and where to place your stops.

But using pure candlestick chart analysis can result in a high number of false signals. There are times when the candle signals fail. Therefore, to increase the chances of making a correct trade one should augment candlesticks with other techniques to filter out false signals. Knowing when to take a candlestick signal and when to ignore one will determine the extent of a trader's success.

Candlestick Chart Analysis Is Best Used in Conjunction with Technical Indicators

Test results and experience have shown that whilst the candlestick technique is a valuable trading tool, using it as a standalone may not give the desired result for many traders.

One must understand that candlestick patterns do not work all the time. Some patterns may fail some of the time for various reasons. One example of failure is when a bearish candle pattern signals a sell in an uptrend. This sell signal in a bullish scenario is a weak sell signal and should not be taken, as the market can soon revert back to an uptrend to reach a higher high.

Conversely, a bullish candle pattern may not give the desired result after buying because the primary trend is down. A buy signal in a downtrend is considered a weak buy signal, and the market may soon revert back into a downtrend.

Another reason for failure is when signals are triggered in a sideways trend. Candles do not work best in sideway trends. As such, if one applies indiscriminately, for example, a buy-and-hold strategy following the occurrence of a candlestick pattern, the trade may or may not show a profit over the next 5 to 10 days or in the following weeks.

Jack Schwager in his book *Schwager on Futures—Technical Analysis* revealed some tests by Bruce Babcock, the editor and publisher of *Commodity Traders Consumers Report*, which showed that the results were much better if one had applied some kind of filter to sieve out false signals. In his test, he used the momentum indicator to assure that the trade was consistent with the short-term trend direction.

Schwager's conclusions on candlestick analysis are as follows:

1. The Bruce Babcock tests revealed that a simplistic interpretation of candlestick patterns is not profitable. In other words, blindly following candlestick patterns is not an effective methodology.
2. If the trader takes into account the context in which specific candlesticks occur (i.e., by looking at other prevailing patterns, both candlestick and classical and at the overall trend)

before buying or selling, then candlestick chart analysis will produce better results.

3. Besides applying the candlestick technique, a trader should incorporate money management strategies to produce better results.

■ Conclusion

From the results of the Bruce Babcock tests as well as from my experience, my conclusion is that candlestick-charting analysis should be used in conjunction with trend analysis.

In other words, the trader should take a candlestick signal that is in the direction of the primary trend and ignore (or give less weight to) a candlestick signal that is counter to this trend.

To define a trend, use Western classical charting techniques like trend line analysis, support, and resistance. Once the primary trend is determined, you should use candlestick analysis to trade in the direction of this trend and to ignore (or give less weight to) candlestick signals counter to this defined trend.

Another way to define a trend is by applying the moving average over price. Yet another way is by using Western oscillators like momentum, relative strength index, moving average convergence divergence, commodity channel index, directional movement index, stochastic, Elliott wave theory, and so on. The use of Western technical indicators to help define a trend is discussed in Part II of this book.

Once the main trend of the market is determined, be it the short-term, intermediate, medium, or long-term, the trader should then execute trades by taking candlestick signals that are in the direction of the defined trend.

Summarising, the trader starts by:

1. Identifying the primary trend (by asking the question: Is the trend bullish or bearish?).
2. Trade in the direction of this trend.

This will improve your percentage of winning trades and reduce your percentage of losing trades. It is important not to go against the primary trend.

In Part II, I will be looking at how to apply Western technical indicators to help you define whether the primary trend is bullish or bearish and then apply candle patterns to execute trades in the direction of this trend. This concept of using Western technical indicators to confirm a candle signal is known as candlestick filtering or the Rule of Multiple Techniques.

ADVANCED CANDLESTICK TECHNIQUES

CHAPTER 7

Filtering with Western Indicators

Candlestick chart analysis can be used as a standalone technique in trading the markets. But profitability improves when candlestick analysis is used in conjunction with Western classical charting and with oscillator analysis.

"Candlestick methods, by themselves, are a valuable trading tool," says Steve Nison, in his book, *Japanese Candlestick Charting Techniques*. "But candlestick techniques become even more powerfully significant if they confirm a Western technical signal."[1]

This method of looking for confirmation from different technical indicators is called filtering or the Rule of Multiple Techniques. Arthur Sklarew in his book *Techniques of a Professional Commodity Chart Analyst* emphasises this principle, which says that "the more technical indicators that assemble at the same price area, the greater the chance of an accurate forecast."[2]

---

[1] Steve Nison, *Japanese Candlestick Charting Techniques: A Contemporary Guide to the Ancient Investment Techniques of the Far East* (Paramus, NJ: New York Institute of Finance, 1991).

[2] Arthur Sklarew, *Techniques of a Professional Commodity Chart Analyst* (Brightwaters, NY: Windsor Books, 1980).

■ Using Filtering or the Rule of Multiple Techniques

1. Define the trend. You can use trend lines, moving averages, or oscillators to help you define the trend. There are only three classifications of a trend: up, down, and sideways. An uptrend is also known as a bullish trend and a downtrend is known as a bearish trend.
2. Trade in the direction of this trend.

■ Scenario 1: In the Case of a Bull Market or Bullish Trend

1. If the trend is bullish, look for bullish candlestick patterns to enter the market on the *buy* or *long* side for both stocks and futures.
2. If the trend remains bullish, maintain *buy* or *long* positions on both stocks and futures. One should ignore candlestick sell signals. At most, use candlestick sell patterns to close longs *but do not enter short positions* until the trend line, oscillators, or moving average turn bearish.

■ Scenario 2: In the Case of a Bear Market or Bearish Trend

1. If the trend is bearish, look for bearish candlestick patterns to enter the market on the *sell* or *short* side for both stocks and futures.

2. If the trend remains bearish, maintain *short* positions in futures but *stay out (this is because in Malaysia short selling is prohibited)* of stocks. One should ignore candlestick buy signals. At most, use candlestick buy patterns to cover short positions *but do not enter* long *positions* on stocks and futures until the trend line, oscillators, or moving average turn bullish.

■ Scenario 3: In the Case of Overbought or Oversold Situations

1. If the market is overbought, look for bearish reversal candle patterns to exit your trades.
2. If the market is oversold, look for bullish candle reversal patterns to enter your trades.

On the questions of using daily, weekly, or monthly candle charts, future traders should use daily and weekly charts to determine the direction of the trend. Next, use the shorter-term charts like the 30-minute and 15-minute charts to trigger buy or sell signals, but only if they are in line with the direction of the longer-term charts.

For Malaysian stock market traders, you should use weekly and monthly candle charts to determine the direction of the trend. Next, use daily charts to trigger buy or sell signals. Hourly charts may even be used to provide earlier signals, but these signals must be in the direction of the longer-term trend.

This technique of using three time-frame charts (daily, weekly, and monthly) to screen your signals is called Triple Screening. More details are available in the author's second book,

Understanding KLCI Stock Index Futures, or in *High Probability Trading* by Marcel Link.

■ Filtering with Moving Averages

The moving average is one of the oldest and most popular tools used by technicians. Its strength is as a trend-following device that offers the technician the ability to catch major moves.

The objective of a moving average is to smooth out daily fluctuations of prices to make it easier to view the underlying trend. If the slope of the moving average is pointing upward, it shows that market players are bullish about the market. If the slope of the moving average is down, it shows players are bearish.

If market players continue to be bullish, then the moving average will continue to rise. But because this line is an average of a body of data, this line naturally lags behind price. Therefore, in a bullish market, prices will soon rise above the moving average. Putting it another way, if prices are trending above the moving average, the market is bullish.

On the other hand, if players are bearish, the moving average will fall. And when this bearishness continues, prices will soon fall below the moving average. Another way of saying this is, "If price is trending below the moving average, the market is bearish." It is the interplay between price and the moving average that generates buy or sell signals.

The Simple Moving Average

This is the average of all the current closing prices against past price movements. Every period carries equal weight.

Formula for 3-day moving average = (Closing price of Day 1) + (Closing price of Day 2) + (Closing price of Day 3) divided by 3.

The result would be plotted as the first average. To create a moving average, the calculation is repeated and a new value plotted. This step is repeated to establish another moving average of longer term, for example, eight days.

The Weighted Moving Average

A different weight is given to each price used to compute the average. Usually the most recent prices are weighted more heavily than earlier prices. How the data is weighted is a matter of preference.

The Exponential Moving Average

The exponential moving average includes all prior prices used in the database. The last period carries the most weight, and smaller weights are assigned to each of the past prices.

Interpretation

The moving average can be used to define a trend. Once the market trend is defined, candlestick patterns can be used to time market entry and exit.

The Single Moving Average Crossover Method   When the closing price rises above the moving average, the market is in a bullish trend (*buy*). When the closing price falls below the moving average, the market is in a bearish trend (*sell*).

Rule

> Closing Price > M.A. = Trend Bullish = Buy
> Closing Price > M.A. = Trend Bearish = Sell

When close is above the moving average, it is known as the Golden Cross.

When close is below the moving average, it is known as the Dead Cross.

The parameter that I used to define a trend is 50-SMA.

The Dual Moving Average Crossover Method When the short-term moving average rises above the long-term moving average, a bullish reversal is signalled (*buy*). When the long-term moving average falls below the short-term moving average, a bearish reversal is signalled (*sell*).

Rule

> Shorter M.A. > Longer M.A. = Trend Bullish = Buy
> Shorter M.A. < Longer M.A. = Trend Bearish = Sell

When the shorter moving average is above the longer moving average, it is also known as the Golden Cross. When the shorter moving average is below the longer moving average, it is also known as the Dead Cross.

Proper Action

Applying Candlesticks with Moving Averages

- **At Golden Cross.** Look for bullish candlestick patterns like the Hammer, Inverted Hammer, Bullish Engulfing, Piercing Line, Morning Star, Doji-Star confirmations, and so on to establish buy or long positions.

- **At Dead Cross.** Look for bearish candlestick patterns like the Shooting Star, Hanging Man, Bearish Engulfing, Dark Cloud Cover, Evening Star, Doji-Star confirmations, and so on to establish sell or short positions.

Using the Rule of Multiple Techniques

- **In case of bullish trend (Close > M.A.).** Look for bullish candlestick patterns to buy or go long. If trend remains bullish, maintain longs. Ignore candlestick sell signals or at most close longs but do not short.

- **In case of bearish trend (Close < M.A.).** Look for bearish candlestick patterns to sell or go short. If trend remains bearish, maintain shorts. Ignore candlestick buy signals or at most cover shorts but do not go long.

Figure 7.1 and Figure 7.2 show some examples of filtering with moving average and candle patterns at Golden and Dead Cross.

■ Filtering with MACD (Moving Average Convergence Divergence)

MACD or Moving Average Convergence Divergence is a popular indicator developed by Gerald Appel as a trend indicator. It is best used to determine the direction of a trend, and the idea here is to trade only in the direction of the MACD.

The MACD has two lines. The first MACD line makes use of the difference between two exponential moving averages (usually the 12-day and 26-day), and it employs a second exponential moving average (usually a 9-day) of the actual MACD line as a signal line.

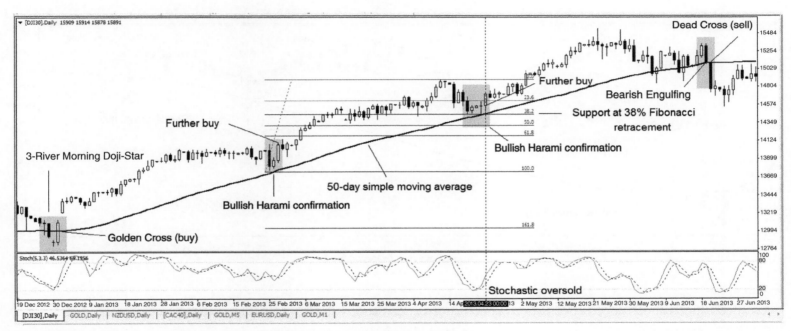

FIGURE 7.1 Dow Jones Industrial Average Daily (2013)—Filtering with moving average

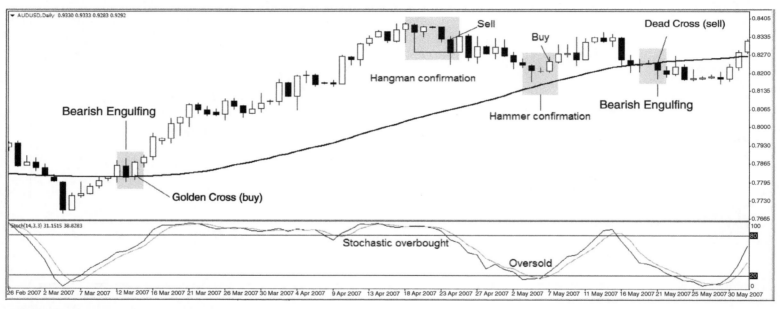

FIGURE 7.2   AudUsd Daily (2007)—Look for candle patterns at "golden" and at "dead" cross

The formula for MACD: The MACD line is the difference between two exponential averages (EMA), as shown here.

$$MACD = EMA1 - EMA2$$

The signal line will be an exponential moving average of the actual MACD line.

The number of days used is usually 12 and 26 days for the MACD line and a 9-day EMA for the signal line.

The MACD can also be plotted as a histogram that can be applied to determine the psychology of the players. An extreme reading on the histogram can signal an overbought or an oversold market. Drawn as an oscillator, the crossing of the zero line is used to trigger buy/sell signals. The other use of the MACD is to spot trend reversal through the concept of bull or bear divergence.

Interpretation

1. A buy signal is generated when the (fast) MACD line crossed above the (slower) signal line.
2. A sell signal is generated when the MACD line crosses below the signal line.
3. I use the parameters 5, 34, 5 for more timely crossings. These parameters have been popularized by Dr. Bill Williams. He also makes use of the MACD histogram to distinguish between Elliott's Wave 3 and Wave 5. Wave 3s tend to have the most extreme oscillator histogram reading while Wave 5's histogram is less extreme, producing a divergence.

Proper Action

Applying Candlesticks with MACD

- **MACD buy signal:** Look for bullish reversal patterns like the Hammer, Piercing Line, Bullish Engulfing, Morning Star, and so on to *buy*.

- **MACD sell signal:** Look for bullish reversal patterns like the Shooting Star, Doji-Star, Evening Star, Bearish Engulfing, Dark Cloud Cover, and so on to *sell*.

Using the Rule of Multiple Techniques

- **In case of bullish trend (MACD > signal).** Look for bullish candlestick patterns to buy or go long. If trend remains bullish, maintain longs. Ignore candlestick sell signals or at most close longs but do not short.

- **In case of bearish trend (MACD < signal).** Look for bearish candlestick patterns to sell or go short. If trend remains bearish, maintain shorts. Ignore candlestick buy signals or at most cover shorts but do not go long.

Figure 7.3 and Figure 7.4 show some examples of filtering with MACD and different MACD parameters that give differing timing signals.

■ Filtering with Relative Strength Index

The relative strength index (RSI) was developed in 1978 by J. Welles Wilder Jr. as an oscillator that graphically shows the internal strength of price advances to price declines over a specified

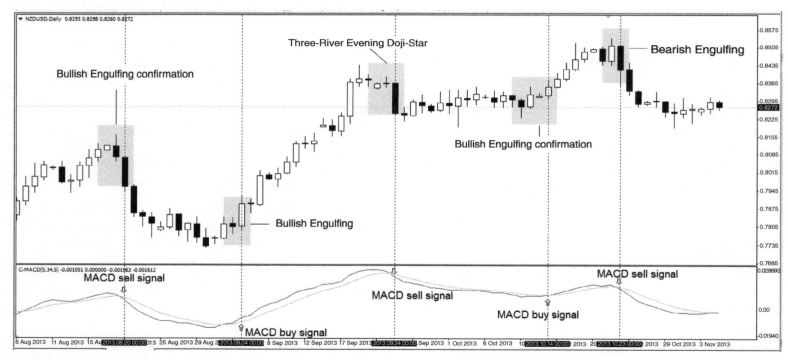

FIGURE 7.3 NzdUsd Daily (2007)—Filtering with MACD

This example shows that MACD (5,34,5) is more timely than MACD(12,26,9)

FIGURE 7.4 NzdUsd Daily (2011)—Different MACD parameters give differing timing signals

period. It creates a value that oscillates between 0 and 100 percent. Fourteen days is the most popular period.

The formula used is dependent only on closing price and is computed as follows:

$$RSI = 100 - (100/(1 + (AV. \text{ up price change} - AV. \text{ down price change})))$$

*AV. = Average

Interpretation

1. It is an overbought indicator when it approaches over 70 percent; the market is regarded as oversold when the RSI reads less than 30 percent.
2. Look for divergence. When prices make a new high and the RSI fails to make a similar move, there is bearish divergence, and this is potentially bearish. A bullish divergence occurs when prices make a new low, but the RSI does not. Divergences are more meaningful when the RSI oscillator readings are in overbought or oversold regions.
3. Crossing of the 50 level.

   If RSI > 50 = Trend Bullish = Buy
   If RSI < 50 = Trend Bearish = Sell

Proper Action

Applying Candlesticks with RSI

- **Above 70%.** Look for the Tweezers Top, Bearish Meeting Line, Bearish Harami, Doji-Star, Three-River Evening Star, Shooting Stars, and so on to sell. Market overbought.

- **Below 30%.** Look for the Tweezers Bottom, Bullish Harami, Doji-Star, Three-River Morning Star, Hammers, Inverted Hammers, and so on to buy. Market oversold.

- **RSI > 50.** Look for bullish candlestick patterns like the Hammer, Piercing Line, Bullish Engulfing, Morning Star, and so on to *buy*.

- **RSI < 50.** Look for bearish candlestick patterns like the Shooting Star, Doji-Star, Evening Star, Engulfing Bearish, Dark Cloud Cover, and so on to *sell*.

Using the Rule of Multiple Techniques

- **In case of bullish trend (RSI > 50).** Look for bullish candlestick patterns to buy or go long. If trend remains bullish, maintain longs. Ignore candlestick sell signals or at most close longs but do not short.

- **In case of bearish trend (RSI < 50).** Look for bearish candlestick patterns to sell or go short. If trend remains bearish, maintain shorts. Ignore candlestick buy signals or at most cover shorts but do not go long.

Figure 7.5 and Figure 7.6 show some examples of filtering with RSI and reversal patterns at overbought and oversold areas.

■ Filtering with Stochastic

The Stochastic Oscillator, developed by George Lane, compares the latest closing price with the total range of price action for a specific period. Lane uses five days. The values are between 0 and 100 percent. This indicator will prevent you from buying at

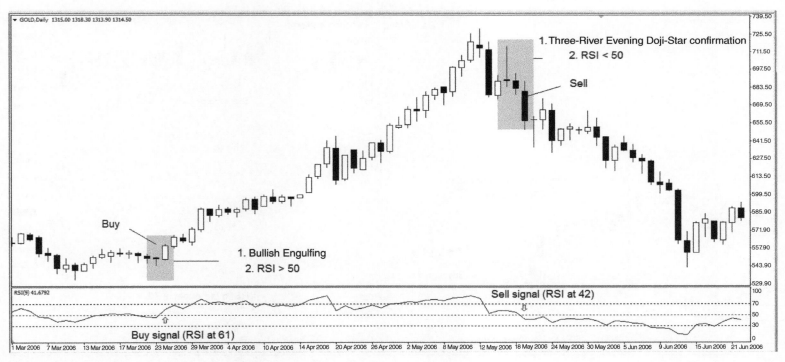

FIGURE 7.5 Gold Daily (2006)—Filtering with RSI (buy > 50; sell < 50)

FIGURE 7.6 Gold Hourly (2013)—Look for reversal patterns at overbought and oversold areas

the top and selling at the bottom of the market, as it is usually a forward measurement. It is used to trigger buy/sell signals as well as to detect periods where the market is either overbought or oversold.

Formulas require the raw or fast %K (number of time intervals) to be slowed internally by taking a moving average of the last three-day %K and the calculation of %D, which is smoothed again by using a three-day moving average of the slow %K.

%K (FAST)

$$= \frac{(\text{Current close}) - (\text{Lowest low of X period})}{(\text{Highest high of X period}) - (\text{Lowest low of X period})} \times 100$$

%K (SLOW)

$$= \frac{(\%K \text{ FAST 1} + \%K \text{ FAST 2} + \%K \text{ FAST 3})}{3}$$

$$\%D = \frac{(\%K \text{ SLOW 1} + \%K \text{ SLOW 2} + \%K \text{ SLOW 3})}{3}$$

Where X = user-defined period. For short-term trend identification, I use 14 days.

Interpretation

1. The market is overbought when the stochastic reading is over 80 percent and oversold below 20 percent.
2. Stochastic buy/sell rules:

   %K > %D = Trend Bullish = Buy
   %K < %D = Trend Bearish = Sell

3. Divergence occurs when the stochastic indicator diverges from price action. If price has gone up and the stochastic fails to exceed its previous corresponding high, this is indicative of a bearish divergence. On the other hand, if price has gone down and stochastic fails to make a new low, we have a bullish divergence. Divergences warn of an imminent trend reversal.

Proper Action

Applying Candlesticks with Stochastic

- **Stochastic > 80% (overbought).** Look for the Shooting Star, doji, Dark Cloud Cover, Hangman, Engulfing Bearish, Harami Line or Cross, Evening Star, and so on to sell or go short.

- **Stochastic < 20% (oversold).** Look for Tweezers Bottom, Hammer, doji, Engulfing Bullish, Morning Star, and so on to buy or go long.

Using the Rule of Multiple Techniques

- **In case of bullish trend (%K > %D).** Look for bullish candlestick patterns to buy or go long. If trend remains bullish, maintain longs. Ignore candlestick sell signals or at most close longs but do not short.

- **In case of bearish trend (%K < %D).** Look for bearish candlestick patterns to sell or go short. If trend remains bearish, maintain shorts. Ignore candlestick buy signals or at most cover shorts but do not go long.

Figure 7.7 shows an example of filtering with stochastic.

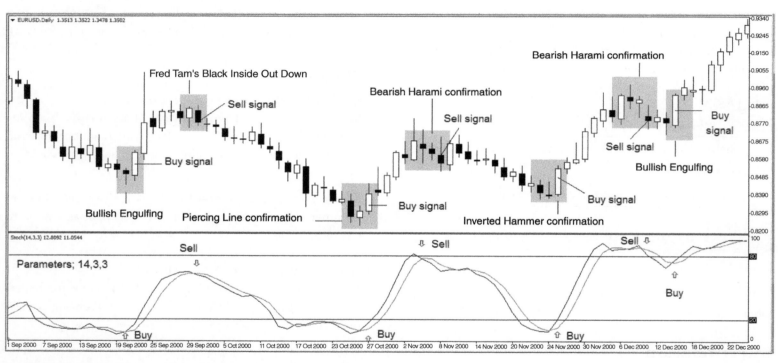

FIGURE 7.7 EurUsd Daily (2000)—Filtering with stochastic (buy if %K>%D) (sell if %K<%D)

■ Filtering with Momentum

Momentum is the most basic application of oscillator analysis. It is based on the concept that price movements do not progress at a constant rate at all times and that an increase in rate of movement shows the strength of the trend.

Momentum is used to monitor price movement by making direct comparisons between current and past prices on a continuing basis.

To construct a 10-day momentum line, simply subtract the closing price 10 days ago from the last closing price. The positive or negative value is then plotted against a zero line.

The formula is:

$$Momentum = ((\text{Closing price today}) - (\text{closing price of } n \text{ number of days ago}))$$

Where n = User-defined period. For short-term trend identification, I use 10 days.

Interpretation

The Momentum line oscillates around the zero line. Extremes in either direction warn of oversold and overbought situations. Signals are given by the crossings of the zero line in the direction of the trend.

Rule

Momentum > 0 = Trend Bullish = Buy
Momentum < 0 = Trend Bearish = Sell

Proper Action

Applying Candlesticks with Momentum

If momentum > 0. Look for Bullish Engulfing, Piercing Line, Morning Star, Hammer, Inverted Hammer confirmation, and so on to *buy*.

If momentum < 0. Look for Bearish Engulfing, Three Crows, Evening Star, Shooting Star, Hanging Man confirmation, and so on to *sell*.

Using the Rule of Multiple Techniques

In case of bullish trend (momentum > 0). Look for bullish candlestick patterns to buy or go long. If trend remains bullish, maintain longs. Ignore candlestick sell signals or at most close longs but do not short.

In case of bearish trend (momentum < 0). Look for bearish candlestick patterns to sell or go short. If trend remains bearish, maintain shorts. Ignore candlestick buy signals or at most cover shorts but do not go long.

Figure 7.8 and Figure 7.9 show some examples of filtering with momentum and candle patterns at momentum crossover points.

■ Filtering with Williams' Percentage Retracement

The Williams' Percentage Retracement (%R) was developed by Larry Williams. This oscillator closely resembles the Stochastic Oscillator. It is commonly used as a tool to indicate when to buy

FIGURE 7.8 AudUsd Daily (2013)—Filtering with Momentum (buy if momentum>0) (sell if momentum<0)

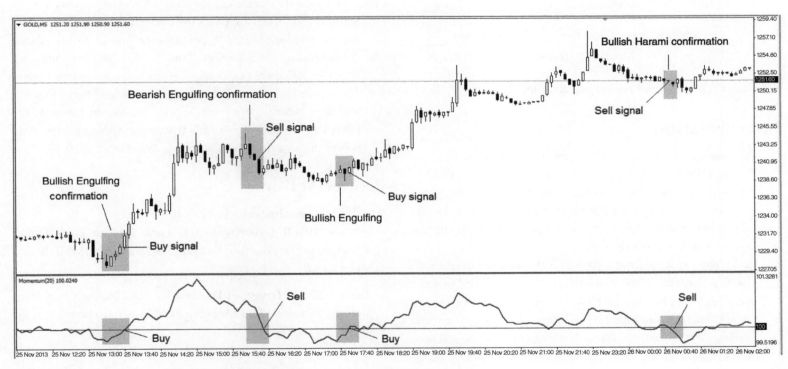

FIGURE 7.9   Gold 5-Minute (2013)—Look for candle patterns at momentum crossover points

on dips in a bull market and when to sell on rallies in a bear market. The short-term period is usually nine days. Williams' %R is plotted on a scale between 0 and 100.

Larry Williams' formula is:

$$\%R = \frac{(\text{Highest high of X period}) - (\text{Current close})}{(\text{Highest high of X period}) - (\text{Lowest low of X period})}$$

Where X = User-defined period, usually nine days.

Interpretation

1. The analysis of the %R is very similar to that of the Stochastic Oscillator except that %R is upside-down and the stochastic has internal smoothing. As such, readings in the range of 80 to 100 percent indicate that the market is oversold, while readings in the 0 to 20 percent range suggest that the market is overbought.

2. However, in some software, the %R is the inverse of Williams'. This was done to remain consistent with the standard practice that a high number for an oscillator indicates an overbought market and a lower number indicates an oversold market. Readings in the range of 80 to 100 percent in some software therefore indicate that the market is overbought while readings in the 0 to 20 percent range suggest that the market is oversold.

3. As with all overbought/oversold indicators, it is best to wait for the security's price to change direction before placing your trades. For example, if an overbought/oversold indicator (such as the Stochastic Oscillator or Williams' %R) is showing an overbought condition, it is wise to wait for the security's price to turn down before selling the security. It is not unusual for overbought/oversold indicators to remain in an overbought/oversold condition for a long time period as the security's price continues to climb/fall. Selling simply because the security appears overbought may take you out of the security long before its price shows signs of deterioration.

4. An interesting phenomenon of the %R indicator is its uncanny ability to anticipate a reversal in the underlying security's price. The indicator almost always forms a peak and turns down a few days before the security's price peaks and turns down. Likewise, %R usually creates a trough and turns up a few days before the security's price turns up. (See Figure 7.10.)

Proper Action

Applying Candlesticks with %R

- **Above 20%R (overbought).** Look for the Dark Cloud Cover, Engulfing Bearish, Evening Star, Shooting Star, doji, and so on to *sell*.

- **Below 80%R (oversold).** Look for the Hammer, Engulfing Bullish, Piercing Line, Morning Star, Inverted Hammer, doji, and so on to *buy*.

■ Filtering with Directional Movement Index

The Directional Movement Index (DMI) system, developed by J. Welles Wilder Jr., deals with the trending quality of a market and provides timely buy or sell signals for longer-term investors. It is

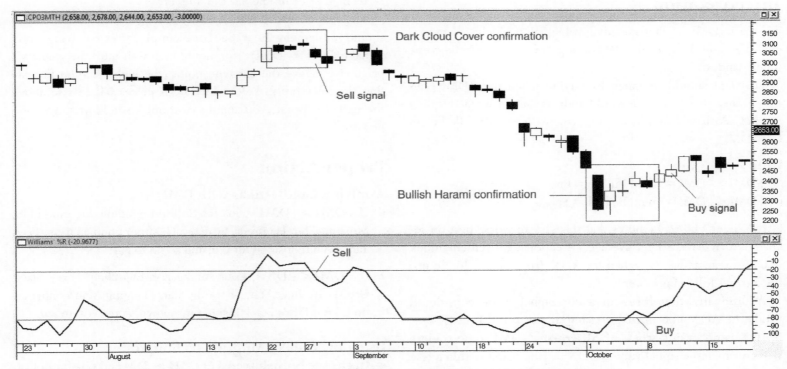

FIGURE 7.10 Crude Palm Oil Daily (2013)—Filtering with %R (look for reversal patterns at overbought/oversold areas)

explained thoroughly in his book *New Concepts in Technical Trading Systems*.

Interpretation

The basic DMI trading system involves plotting the 14-period +DMI and the 14-period –DMI on top of each other in the same inner window.

Positions should be taken by buying when the +DMI rises above the –DMI as this would indicate an upward-trending market. Positions should be sold when the +DMI falls below the –DMI.

Rule

+DMI > –DMI = Trend Bullish = Buy
+DMI < –DMI = Trend Bearish = Sell

In Wilder's book, he notes that this system works best on securities that have a high average Directional Movement Index (ADX) value, above 25. When the ADX drops below 20, do not use a trend-following system.

Additionally, therefore, for a buy signal to be considered valid, the ADX line must be rising at the time of crossover. If ADX is not rising when +DMI crosses –DMI some traders will consider the signal valid if ADX begins rising within a few bars. Preliminary exit signals can be interpreted if ADX begins declining or if +DMI and –DMI cross again in the opposite direction.

The Extreme Point Rule This rule is designed to prevent whipsaws and reduce the number of false trades. The extreme point rule requires that on the day the +DMI and –DMI cross, you note the "extreme" price. If you are long, the extreme price is the low price of the day the lines cross. If you are short, the extreme price is the high price on the day the lines cross.

The extreme point is then used as a trigger point at which you should implement the trade. For example, after receiving a buy signal (+DMI > –DMI), you should then wait until the security's price rises above the extreme point (the high price on the day that the lines cross) before buying. If prices fail to rise above the extreme point, you should continue to hold your existing position.

Proper Action

Applying Candlesticks with DMI

- **If +DMI > –DMI.** Look for Bullish Engulfing, Piercing Line, Morning Star, Hammer, Inverted Hammer confirmation, Fred Tam's White Inside Out Up, and so on to *buy*.

- **If +DMI < –DMI.** Look for Bearish Engulfing, Three Black Crows, Evening Star, Shooting Star, Hanging Man confirmation, Fred Tam's Black Inside Out Down, and so on to *sell*.

Using the Rule of Multiple Techniques

- **In case of bullish trend (+DMI >–DMI).** Look for bullish candlestick patterns to buy or go long. If trend remains bullish, maintain longs. Ignore candlestick sell signals or at most close longs but do not short.

- **In case of bearish trend (+DMI <–DMI).** Look for bearish candlestick patterns to sell or go short. If trend remains bearish, maintain shorts. Ignore candlestick buy signals or at most cover shorts but do not go long.

Figure 7.11 shows an example of reversal patterns at DMI crossover points.

■ Filtering with Commodity Channel Index

Developed by Donald Lambert, the Commodity Channel Index (CCI) is calculated by first determining the difference between the mean price of a commodity and the average of the means over the time period chosen. This difference is then compared to the average difference over the time period (this factors in the commodity's own inherent volatility). The result is then multiplied by a constant that is designed to adjust the CCI so that it fits into a "normal" trading range of $+/-100$.

Interpretation

While the CCI was originally designed for commodities, the indicator also works very well with stocks and futures.

There are three ways of interpreting the CCI:

1. **Looking for divergences.**
   A popular method of analyzing the CCI is to look for divergences in which the underlying security is making new highs while the CCI is failing to surpass its previous highs. This classic divergence is usually followed by a correction in the security's price.

2. **As an overbought/oversold indicator.**
   The CCI usually oscillates between $+/-100$. Readings outside this range imply an overbought/oversold condition.

3. **As a signal indicator.**
   CCI > 0 = Bullish Trend = Buy
   CCI < 0 = Bearish Trend = Sell

Proper Action

Applying Candlesticks with CCI

■ **CCI > 100 (overbought).** Look for bearish reversal patterns like the Shooting Star, Doji-Star, Evening Star, Bearish Engulfing, Dark Cloud Cover, and so on to *sell*.

■ **CCI < 100 (oversold).** Look for bullish reversal patterns like the Hammer, Piercing Line, doji, Bullish Engulfing, Morning Star, and so on to *buy*.

Using the Rule of Multiple Techniques

■ **In case of bullish trend (CCI > 0).** Look for bullish candlestick patterns to buy or go long. If trend remains bullish, maintain longs. Ignore candlestick sell signals or at most close longs but do not short.

■ **In case of bearish trend (CCI < 0).** Look for bearish candlestick patterns to sell or go short. If trend remains bearish, maintain shorts. Ignore candlestick buy signals or at most cover shorts but do not go long.

Figure 7.12 shows an example of reversal patterns at overbought/oversold areas in CCI.

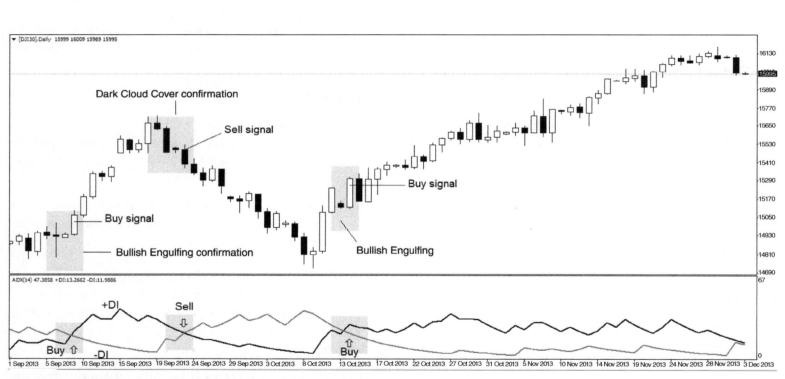

FIGURE 7.11　Dow Jones Industrial Average Daily (2013)—Look for reversal patterns at DMI crossover points

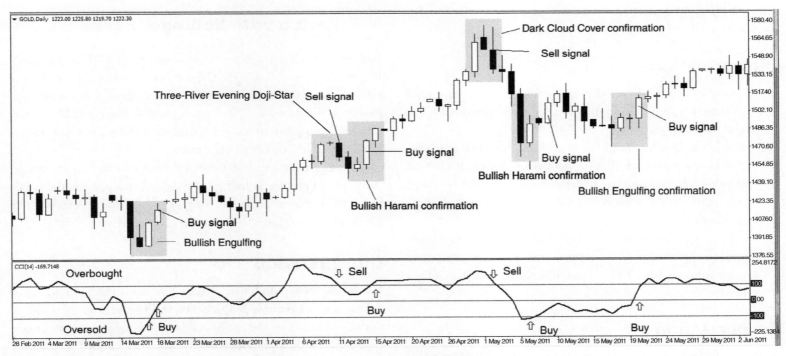

FIGURE 7.12 Gold Daily (2011)—Look for reversal patterns at overbought/oversold areas in CCI

■ Filtering with Volume

The greater the volume, the greater the force behind the move. Volume measures the intensity of a price move and is therefore used to confirm a move or breakout.

Interpretation

1. As long as volume increases, the current price trend should continue; if volume declines as a price trend progresses, the trend may not continue.
2. Volume can also be useful for confirming tops and bottoms. As price rises, volume should gradually increase. If after an extended rally volume suddenly spikes up, it could be a sign of the market's exhaustion. This phenomenon is called a *buying climax*.
3. Conversely, if after an extended decline volume suddenly increases by an unusually large amount, the market may be bottoming out. This phenomenon is called a *selling climax*.

Proper Action

- **When volume spikes up and price is up.** Look for bearish single candlestick patterns like the Shooting Star, doji, Hanging Man, Doji-Star, and so on to indicate a top.

- **When volume spikes up and price is down.** Look for bullish single candlestick patterns like the Hammer, Inverted Hammer, doji, Doji-Star, and so on to indicate a bottom.

Figure 7.13 shows an example of reversal patterns when volume is unusually large.

■ Filtering with Bollinger Bands

Bollinger Bands are a type of envelope developed by John Bollinger, founder of Bollinger Capital Management. This indicator refers to bands plotted above and below a simple moving average, usually a 20-day period. The bands plotted above and below this moving average are moving standard deviations. Their purpose is to measure the volatility of the market.

By using standard deviations rather than a fixed percentage, the bands adjust for volatility. During volatile periods the bands move further away from the average, while during market lulls the bands move closer to the average.

Interpretation

When displaying Bollinger Bands, you are prompted to enter the number of periods in the bands and the number of standard deviations between the bands and the moving average. Bollinger recommends default values of "20" for the number of periods, "simple" for the moving average method and "2" deviations. He notes that periods of less than 10 do not appear to work very well.

Because the spacing between Bollinger Bands is based on the standard deviation of the security, the bands widen when the security becomes more volatile, and contract when the security becomes less volatile.

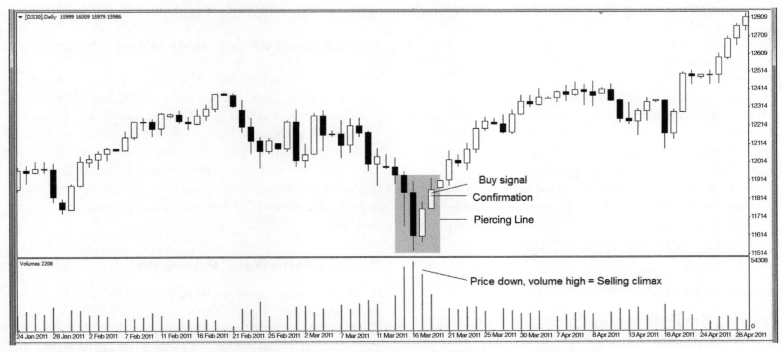

FIGURE 7.13 Dow Jones Industrial Average Daily (2011)—Look for reversal patterns when volume is unusually large

Bollinger notes the following characteristics of Bollinger Bands:

1. The bands narrow after a quiet period in the market. They will expand rapidly as the market becomes more volatile. Then rapid price moves usually occur.
2. When price moves outside the upper band, this is a sign of great strength, and a continuation of the uptrend is implied.
3. When price moves outside the lower band, this is a sign of great weakness, and a continuation of the downtrend is implied.
4. A sharp move outside the bands followed by an immediate retracement of the move is a sign of exhaustion.
5. Bottoms/tops made outside the bands followed by bottoms/tops made inside the bands call for reversals in the trend.
6. A move originating at one band tends to go all the way to the other band. This is useful in projecting price targets.

Proper Action

Applying Candlesticks with Bollinger Bands

- **Outside the upper band and re-enters band**. Look for bearish reversal patterns like the Doji-Star, Evening Star, Bearish Engulfing, Bearish Harami, Dark Cloud Cover, and so on to *sell*.

- **Outside the lower band and re-enters band**. Look for bullish reversal patterns like the Bullish Engulfing, Piercing Line, Morning Star, Bullish Harami, and so on to *buy*.

Figure 7.14 and Figure 7.15 show some examples of market exhaustion and reversal patterns if price moves outside and re-enters Bollinger Bands.

■ Filtering with Elliott Wave Theory

An accountant, Ralph Nelson Elliott, discovered the Wave Principle, more popularly known as the Elliott Wave Principle. The study of this principle requires many years before one can apply it reasonably well to predict the stock and futures markets. This section merely introduces the basic ideas of the Wave Principle and how it can be used in conjunction with candlestick techniques. Students keen on this subject should refer to the *Elliott Wave Principle* by A. J. Frost and Robert Prechter Jr.

Basics of the Wave Principle

R. N. Elliott discovered the Wave Principle at the turn of the twentieth century. He pointed out that in a bull market there should be a series of five waves known as Waves 1, 2, 3, 4, and 5. The bear market waves, on the other hand, should be made up of three waves, known as Waves a, b, and c, to form a complete cycle of eight waves.

Waves 1, 3, and 5 are called *impulse* waves, and Waves 2 and 4 *corrective* waves. Wave 2 corrects Wave 1, Wave 4 corrects Wave 3, and the entire sequence of Waves 1, 2, 3, 4, and 5 is corrected by the sequence Waves a, b, and c.

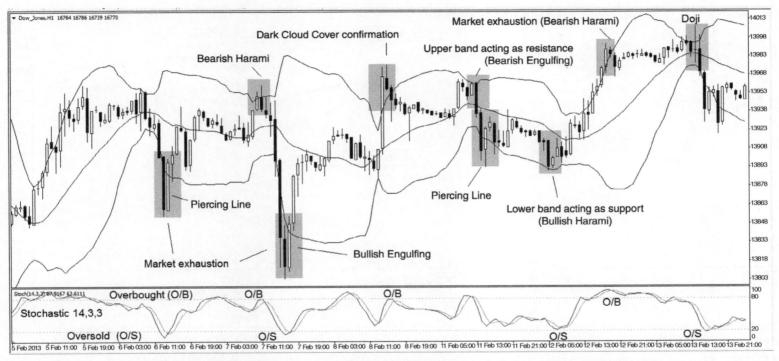

FIGURE 7.14 Dow Jones Industrial Average Daily (2013)—Market exhaustion if price moves outside and re-enters Bollinger Band

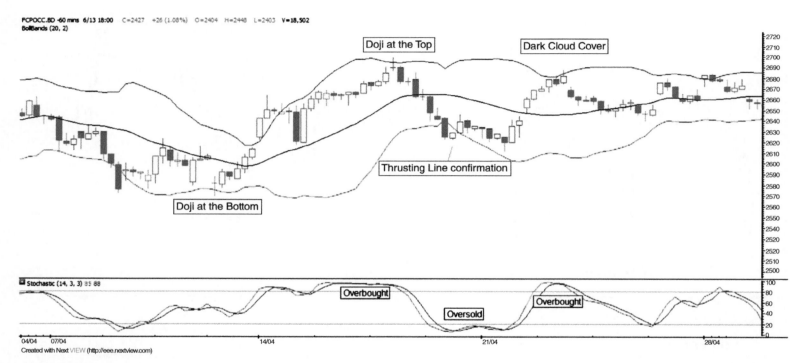

FIGURE 7.15 Crude Palm Oil Daily (2014)—Look for reversal patterns when price moves outside and re-enters Bollinger Band. Oscillators like Stochastic can help spot overbought and oversold areas.

Next, each impulse wave—1, 3, and 5—is further divided into five waves of a lesser degree that in turn can be subdivided into waves of an even lesser degree. The same goes for corrective Waves 2 and 4, which are subdivided into three, Waves a, b, and c.

The division goes on and on. Elliott categorises nine different degrees of wave magnitude, ranging from the Grand Super-Cycle spanning two hundred years to a subminute degree covering only a few hours.

Elliott Wave: The Basic Pattern

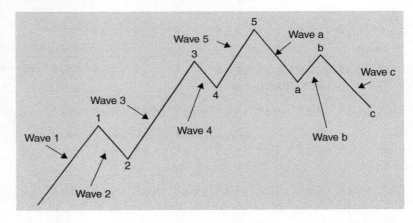

Figure 7.16 and Figure 7.17 show some examples on how to combine candlesticks with the Wave Principle.

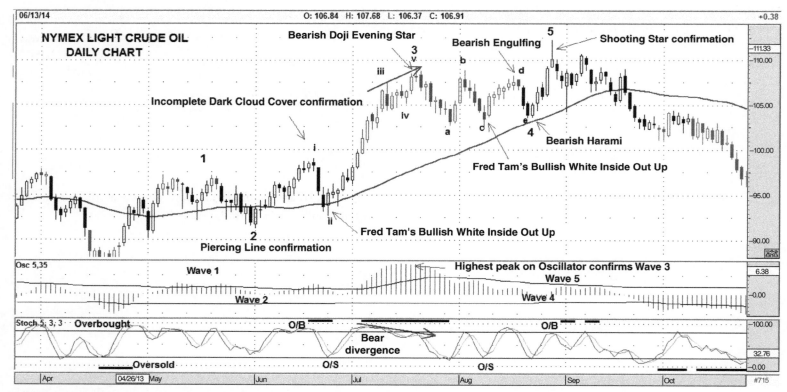

FIGURE 7.16 NYMEX Light Crude Oil Daily (2014)—Ride Wave 3 and sell on divergence and cross below displaced moving average

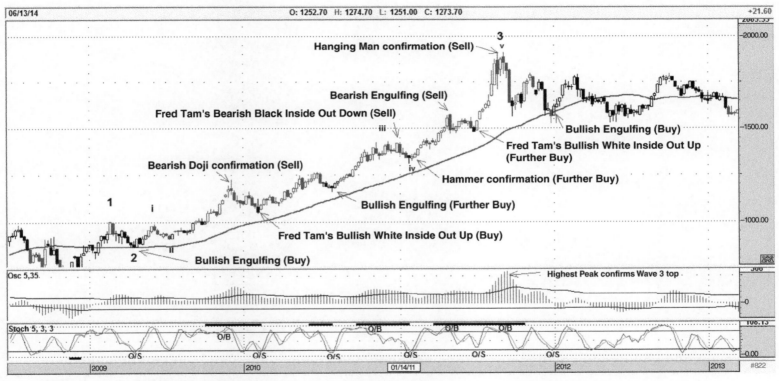

FIGURE 7.17   Gold Weekly (2009–2013)—Filtering with the Wave Principle (use MACD oscillator to spot top of Wave 3)

CHAPTER 8

P.I. System Trader

Candlestick patterns can be easy to identify at times, but at others they can be ambivalent.

The following example highlights the difficulty in identifying certain candle patterns. On this diagram, it is easy to spot the common two-day reversal pattern, the Bearish Engulfing, which calls for a sell signal on candle 4.

But the next diagram shows no obvious reversal patterns. Traders, especially those new to the candlestick technique, may not be able to spot a trend reversal in this example. Here is where my P.I. System Trader can help you spot buy or sell signals not apparent with the candlestick technique.

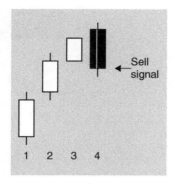

There is no problem in identifying a sell signal in this example. The Bearish Engulfing pattern clearly calls for a sell. One would sell on candle 4.

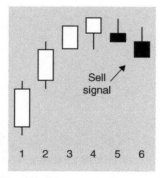

This sell signal is not so clear-cut, but with the help of the P.I. System Trader, a sell signal is automatically flagged out even if you fail to identify a candle pattern.

The P.I. System Trader Mimics Candlesticks

The P.I. System Trader, which I developed in 1998, will greatly alleviate the frustrations of a trader who sometimes finds it difficult to identify a particular candle reversal pattern. The P.I. System Trader essentially mimics the candlestick reversal patterns such that the timing of its buy or sell signals tends to coincide with that of candlestick patterns.

With the help of P.I. System Trader, you will not miss out on any reversal signals because they mimic candlestick reversal patterns. Note that the P.I. System Trader picks up candlestick reversal signals and not continuation signals. Having a system that can pick up reversal patterns as soon as the market turns is important because winning in the markets is all about buying low and selling high.

Using the Rule of Multiple Techniques

Using the P.I. System Trader as a standalone can give rise to false signals. To filter as many of these false signals as possible, I would recommend you use the 50-day simple moving average indicator or any of the oscillators mentioned in this book. The weekly P.I. System Trader can also be used to filter out false P.I. System Trader daily signals.

Figure 8.1 shows an example of P.I. System Trader that mimics candlesticks.

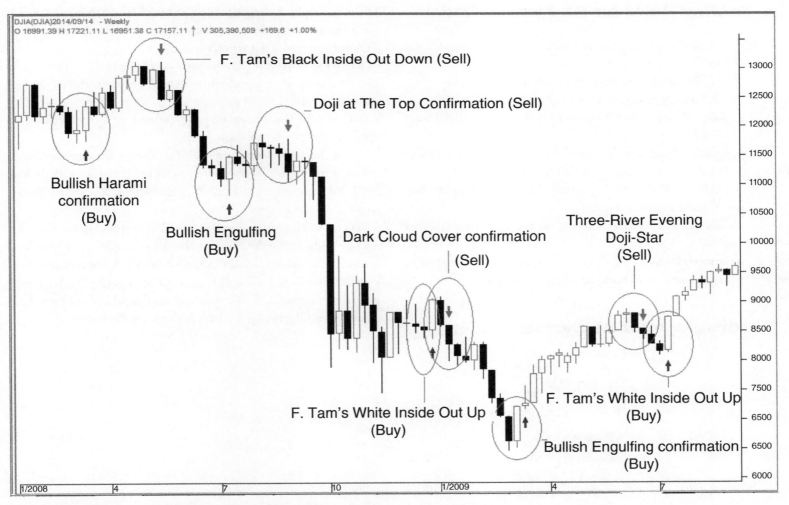

Figure content labels:

DJIA(DJIA)2014/09/14 - Weekly
O 16991.39 H 17221.11 L 16951.38 C 17157.11 ↑ V 305,390,509 +169.6 +1.00%

F. Tam's Black Inside Out Down (Sell)

Doji at The Top Confirmation (Sell)

Bullish Harami
confirmation
(Buy)

Bullish Engulfing
(Buy)

Dark Cloud Cover confirmation
(Sell)

Three-River Evening
Doji-Star
(Sell)

F. Tam's White Inside Out Up
(Buy)

F. Tam's White Inside Out Up
(Buy)

Bullish Engulfing confirmation
(Buy)

FIGURE 8.1   Dow Jones Industrial Average Weekly (2009)—P.I. System Trader mimics candlesticks

■ Trading Rules for P.I. System Trader

Step 1: Check out the 50-day moving average indicator for the longer-term trend.

Step 2: If the 50-day moving average indicator is bullish (Figure 8.2 and Figure 8.3), then:

  a. Take all buy signals (arrows) on the P.I. System Trader (Daily).

  b. Ignore all sell signals (arrows) on the P.I. System Trader (Daily) or close longs but do not short.

Step 2A: If the 50-day moving average indicator is bearish (Figure 8.2 and Figure 8.3), then:

  a. Take all sell signals (arrows) on the P.I. System Trader (Daily).

  b. Ignore all buy signals (arrows) on the P.I. System Trader (Daily) or cover shorts but do not turn long.

■ Advantages of P.I. System Trader

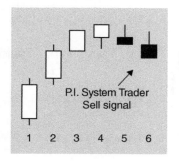

P.I. System Trader
Sell signal

In the example at the beginning of the chapter, this sell signal is not obvious if based on candlestick patterns, but the P.I. System Trader triggered a sell signal on candle 6.

With the help of the P.I. System Trader, the trader will not miss out on any reversal signals just because candle patterns did not show up clearly.

P.I. System Trader can be programmed into any software by applying the previous simple rules.

Note: Instead of using the 50-day moving average system to define trend in Step 1, the trader could use trend lines, daily RSI, DMI, Momentum, MACD, CCI, or the weekly P.I. System Trader to filter out false signals.

Then switch to Step 2 and use the P.I. System Trader daily signals to trade in the direction of the defined trend. The idea here is not to rely on candlesticks alone or the P.I. System Trader daily signals to execute trades. This concept of applying Western indicators in conjunction with Japanese candlesticks to spot reversals is known as filtering or the Rule of Multiple Techniques.

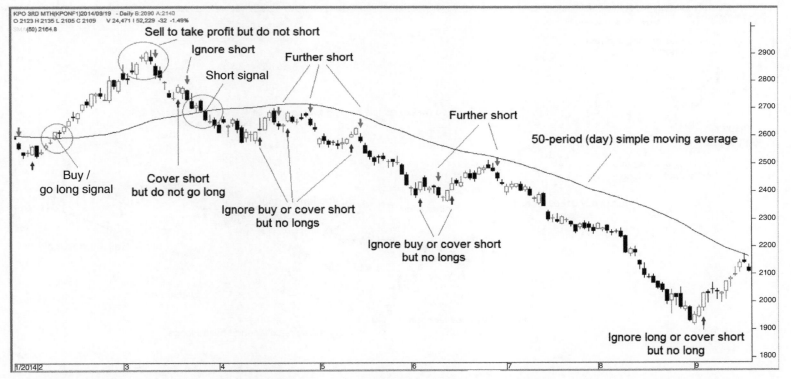

FIGURE 8.2 Hang Seng Index Daily (2014)—Take all P.I. System Trader buy signals when trend is bullish. Ignore sell signals or at most close longs but do not short.

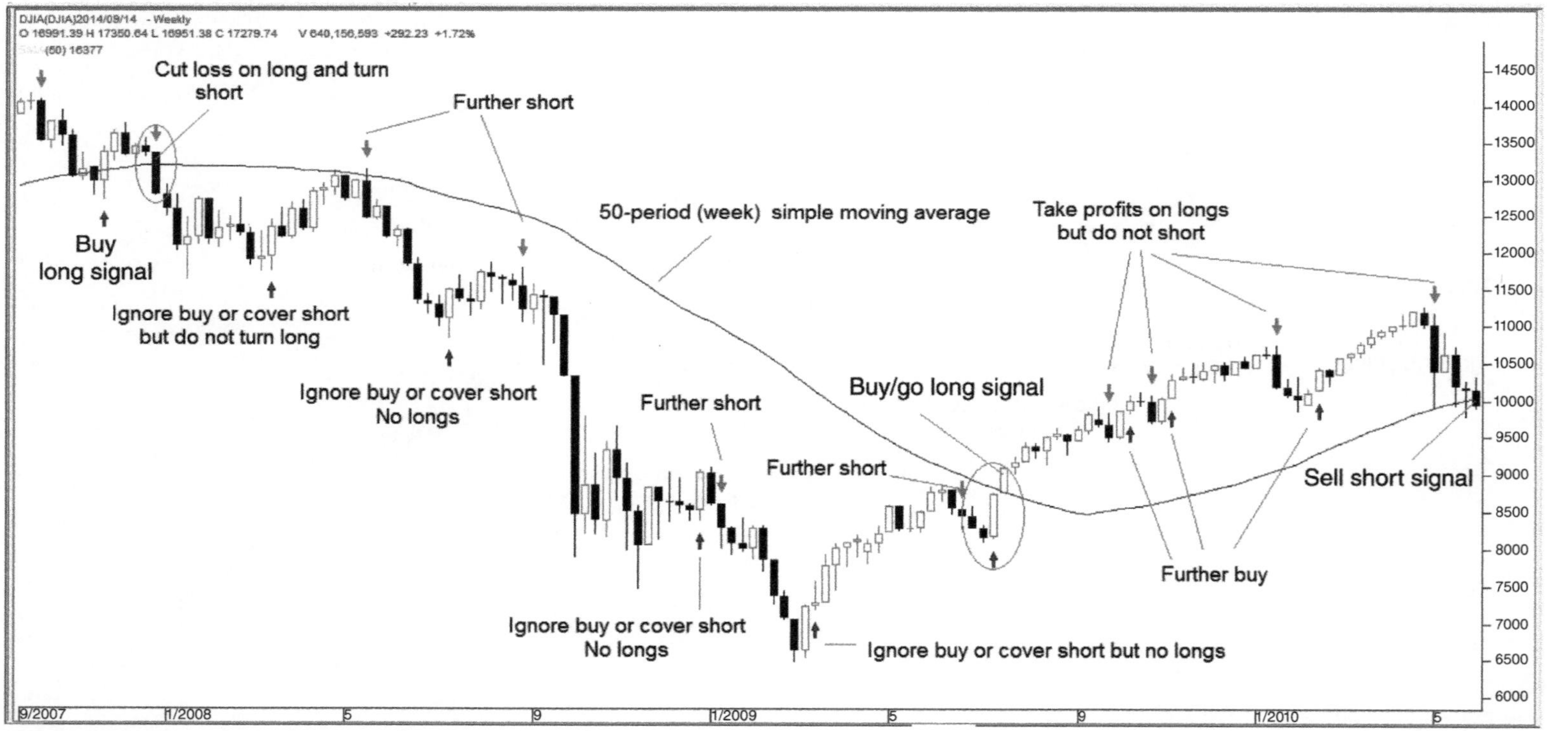
DJIA(DJIA)2014/09/14 - Weekly
O 16991.39 H 17350.64 L 16951.38 C 17279.74 V 640,156,593 +292.23 +1.72%
(50) 16377
Cut loss on long and turn short
Further short
Buy long signal
Ignore buy or cover short but do not turn long
Ignore buy or cover short No longs
50-period (week) simple moving average
Take profits on longs but do not short
Further short
Buy/go long signal
Further short
Sell short signal
Further buy
Ignore buy or cover short No longs
Ignore buy or cover short but no longs
14500
14000
13500
13000
12500
12000
11500
11000
10500
10000
9500
9000
8500
8000
7500
7000
6500
6000
9/2007
1/2008
5
9
1/2009
5
9
1/2010
5

FIGURE 8.3 Crude Palm Oil Futures Daily (2014)—Take all P.I. System Trader sell signals if trend is bearish. Ignore buy signals or at most close shorts but do not go long.

CHAPTER 9

Sakata's Five Methods

Sakata's Five Methods refers to a set of trading rules and methods originated by the great Japanese trader Munehisa Homma in the mid-eighteenth century.

Homma was revered by his contemporaries for his immense success in trading the Japanese rice markets and earned the title "god of the markets."

The word *Sakata* was used to refer to Homma's trading techniques because this is the city where Homma traded rice futures on the local exchange way back in the 1700s. Sakata is a port city in Dewa Province (now known as Yamagata Prefecture) on the west coast of northern Honshu.

■ Sakata's Constitution and Sakata's Five Methods

Sakata's Five Methods originated from the rules and methods that Homma first developed to trade, which were called Sakata's Constitution. During his time, the candlestick chart had not evolved yet and so it was not incorporated into Homma's technique. Later, after Homma began using the candlestick chart, Sakata's Five Methods were developed by fusing Sakata's Constitution with the advanced techniques of the candlestick chart. Homma's secret methods were divided into two groups and have been passed down through many generations of Japanese traders. The two methods are the *Soba Sani No Den* (Sakata's Constitution) and Sakata's Strategies.

Sakata's Constitution (*Soba Sani No Den*)

Rule 1. Without being greedy, think about the time and price ratio by looking at last price movements.

Rule 2. Attempt to sell at the top and buy at the bottom (see Figure 9.1).

Rule 3. One should increase one's position after a rise of 100 bags from the bottom or a fall of 100 bags from the top.

Rule 4. If one forecasts the market incorrectly, one should attempt to identify the error as soon as possible. As soon as the error is discovered, one should liquidate one's position and rest on the side for 40 to 50 days.

Rule 5. One should liquidate 70 to 80 percent of one's profitable positions, liquidating the remainder and changing directions once the price has reached its ceiling or bottom.

Note: Upon execution, all of these methods can be considered Sakata's Strategies. Strategies 4 and 5 are primarily trading principles used to limit one's losses and increase one's profits. Strategies 1, 2, and 3 require the use of a chart and are techniques designed to realistically enhance one's trading ability over time.

The Japanese Method of Three

There is a Japanese saying, "To consult the market about the market." This means that when we are observing the market, we should pay close attention to the market's movement itself rather than observing international affairs and economic policies that may or may not affect the market. The chart is a record of market price movements in a picture form. By studying the chart, one is able to identify the path the market has taken in the past and thus able to predict the future direction of the market.

As divulged by Seiki Shimizu in his book *The Japanese Chart of Charts*, the natural law of market price is the Three Level Fluctuations. This method teaches us that market prices move in three levels: moving up three levels, then moving down three levels, to form a zigzag pattern. The Three Level Fluctuations closely corresponds to the Elliott Wave Theory. There are many unforeseen circumstances that can alter or cause a breakdown in this pattern, such as recent news items, which may cause erratic price movements. We need to be able to adjust to the realities of the future by sorting through the various chart shapes and patterns that have formed and using only those with the highest probabilities. This is where we apply the candlestick technique. The charting technique's task is not to predict exact tops or bottoms, but to instantly assist in confirming market tops or bottoms when they form.

Very early in Japan's cultural history, the number three was considered a mysterious number, and it is thought that a divine power lives within it. This is more than likely where the Sakata Constitution and Sakata's Five Methods attained their mysticism. Sakata's Five Methods consists of *Sanzan* (Three Mountains),

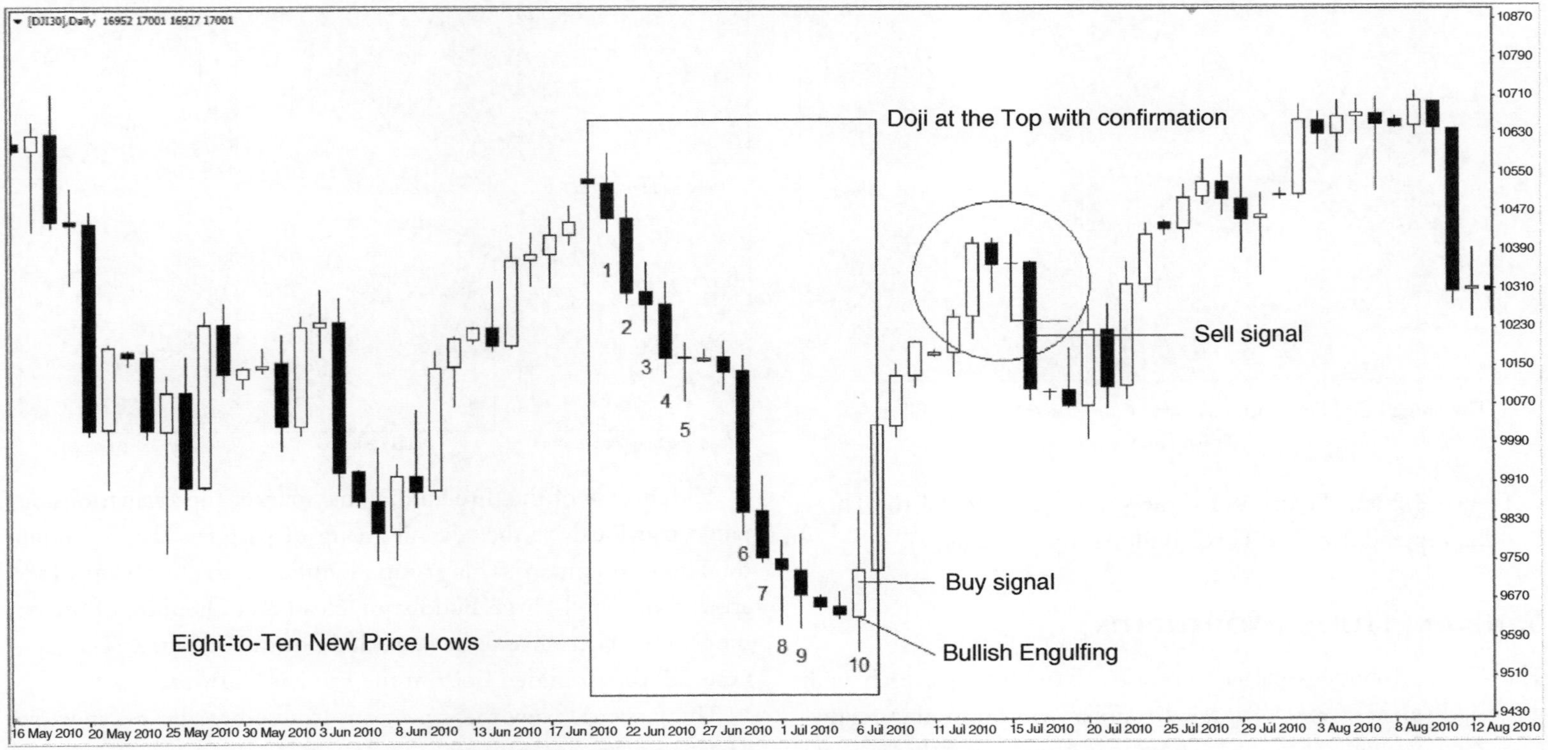
[DJI30],Daily 16952 17001 16927 17001
Doji at the Top with confirmation
Sell signal
Buy signal
Bullish Engulfing
Eight-to-Ten New Price Lows
1
2
3
4
5
6
7
8
9
10
10870
10790
10710
10630
10550
10470
10390
10310
10230
10150
10070
9990
9910
9830
9750
9670
9590
9510
9430
16 May 2010
20 May 2010
25 May 2010
30 May 2010
3 Jun 2010
8 Jun 2010
13 Jun 2010
17 Jun 2010
22 Jun 2010
27 Jun 2010
1 Jul 2010
6 Jul 2010
11 Jul 2010
15 Jul 2010
20 Jul 2010
25 Jul 2010
29 Jul 2010
3 Aug 2010
8 Aug 2010
12 Aug 2010

FIGURE 9.1 Dow Jones Industrial Average Daily (2010)—An example of rule 2: buy at the bottom and sell at the top

Sansen (Three Rivers), *Sanku* (Three Gaps), *Sanpei* (Three Parallel Lines), and *Sanpo* (Three Methods).

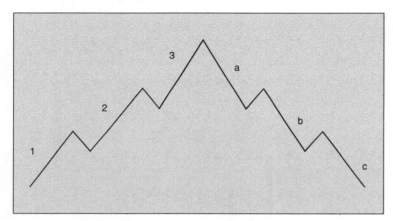

The Three Level Fluctuations Bears Some Resemblance to Elliott's Wave Theory

Figure 9.2 and Figure 9.3 show some examples of the Three Buddha Top and Inverted Three Buddha Top patterns.

Sanzan (Three Mountains)

The Three Mountains pattern consists of two groups, each with three individual shapes of market topping and bottoming formations (see previous diagrams). These two groups directly correlate to the three level fluctuations theory we have already discussed. The Three Mountains pattern is very similar to the Western Triple Top. If the middle mountain is higher than the mountains to its left and to its right, then this pattern is called a Three Buddha Top. Its western equivalent is the Head and Shoulders Top. The Japanese also consider

the Double Top and Rounded Top as variations to the Three Mountains group. The Japanese call the Rounded Top a Dumpling Top.

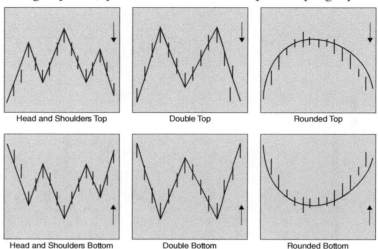

The reverse of the three individual market top formations detailed previously is the second group of patterns that complete the Three Mountains. This group identifies market bottoms. They are the Inverted Three Buddha or Head and Shoulders Bottom, the Double Bottom and the Rounded Bottom or Saucer. The Japanese call the Rounded Bottom the Fry Pan Bottom.

The Japanese view these patterns from a broader perspective. These patterns are attuned to identifying major reversals of trend over a longer time frame. Often, we see these patterns as smaller pieces to a much larger puzzle. When we begin to piece together the puzzle, we can then begin to predict its outcome.

Figure 9.4 and Figure 9.5 show some examples of Fry Pan Bottom and Triple Top patterns.

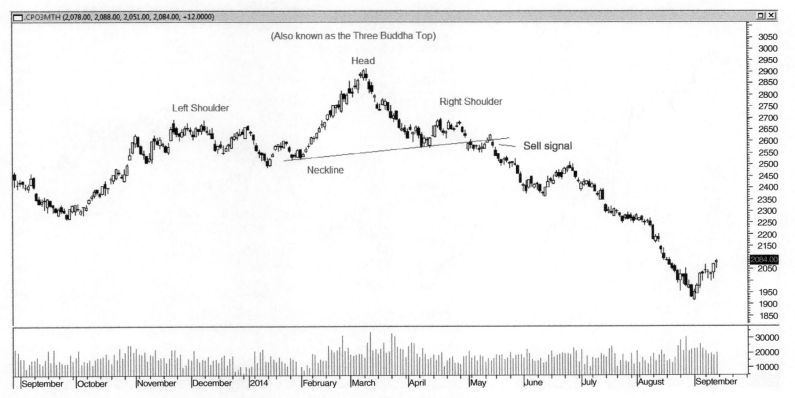

FIGURE 9.2 Crude Palm Oil Futures Daily (2014)—Three Buddha Top (Head and Shoulders Top)

FIGURE 9.3   Kuala Lumpur Composite Index Weekly—Inverted Three Buddha Top (Head and Shoulders Bottom)

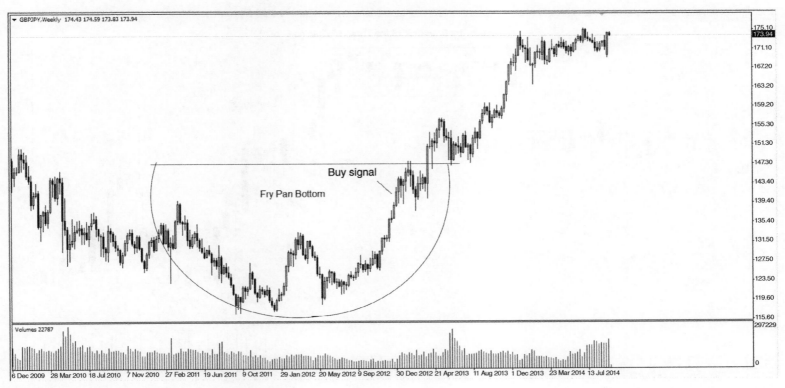

FIGURE 9.4   GbpJpy Weekly (2012)—Fry Pan Bottom

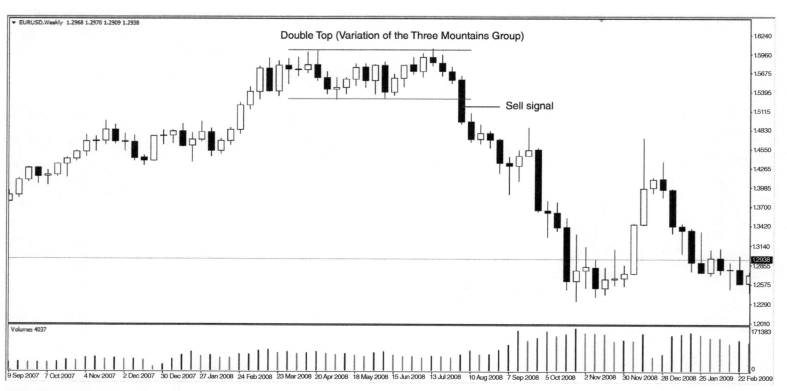

FIGURE 9.5 EurUsd Weekly (2008)—Double Top

Sansen (Three Rivers)

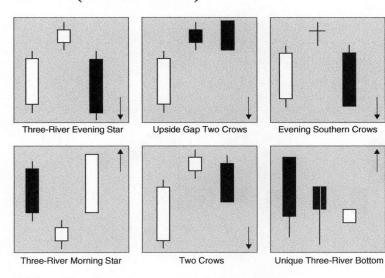

Three-River Evening Star   Upside Gap Two Crows   Evening Southern Crows

Three-River Morning Star   Two Crows   Unique Three-River Bottom

The Three Rivers pattern is based on the theory of using three candles to predict a market's turning point. It forewarns of a complete reversal of price direction. They form in either Morning or Evening positions with many variations. The Three-River Morning Star pattern reflects a bullish reversal of trend or a possible market bottom, whereas the Three-River Evening Star pattern reflects a bearish reversal of trend or a possible market top.

The common formations, as shown in the previous diagrams, often consist of very strong candle types (such as Doji, Bozu, or Marubozu lines). These individual candle types represent some of the strongest single candle types to identify price direction or lack of it. For example, the Doji Line that separates the other two candles within this pattern identifies that the market is unable to continue its current trend. The third candle that completes this pattern confirms the fact that the market trend has reversed.

The variations of the Three Rivers include the Upside Gap Two Crows, the Evening Southern Cross (also called Three-River Evening Doji-Star), the Two Crows, and the Unique Three-River Bottom. Although these variations may appear visually completely different, they reflect the same intention of the market to reverse.

Some literature refers to the Three Rivers to mean the Head and Shoulder bottom, the Double Bottom and the Triple Bottom, but this is not correct.

Figure 9.6 and Figure 9.7 show some examples of Two Crows and Unique Three-River Bottom patterns.

Sanku (Three Gaps)

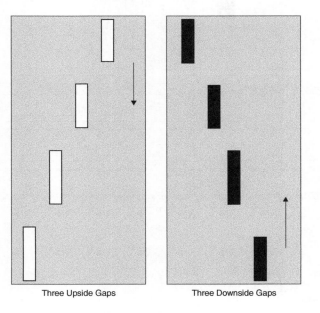

Three Upside Gaps   Three Downside Gaps

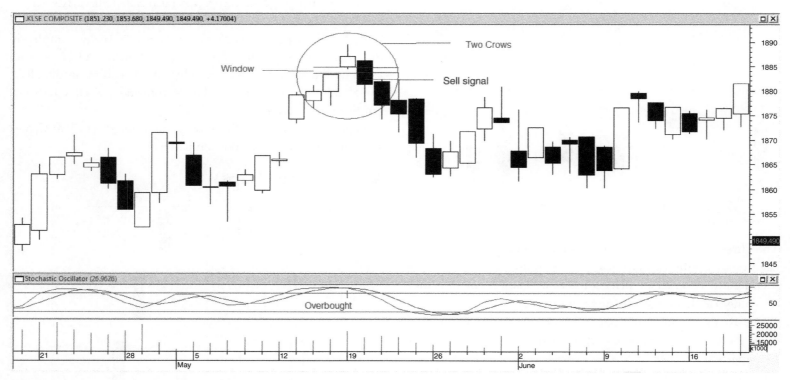

FIGURE 9.6   Kuala Lumpur Composite Index Daily (2014)—Two Crows

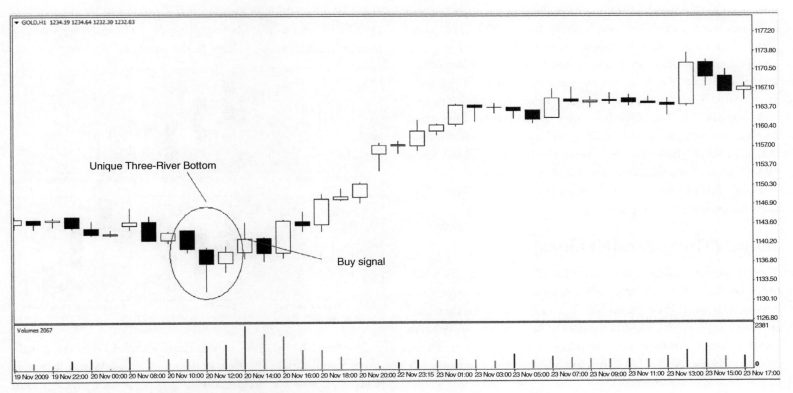

FIGURE 9.7 Gold Hourly (2009)—Unique Three-River Bottom

The Three Gaps pattern consists of three individual gaps in price that occur during a defined trend. The gaps do not need to be consecutive; they may form throughout many days of trading. This pattern signifies that the market has gotten ahead of itself too fast and too soon and the current trend is about to end. The Three Gaps pattern can help to identify trend reversals. Remember that this pattern has a specific correlation to the Three Level Fluctuations theory. The gaps may form during the three individual price advances or declines that support the Three Level Fluctuations theory.

When a Bullish Three Gaps is formed, the Japanese call this *Sanku Fumiage*. It represents a price ceiling, and one should start selling. When a Bearish Three Gaps is formed, the Japanese call this *Sanku Nage Owari* or *Sanku Tatakikomi*, and one should start to buy.

Figure 9.8 and Figure 9.9 show some examples of Three Upside and Downside Gaps pattern.

Sanpei (Three Parallel Lines)

The classic formation of the Three Parallel Lines occurs when three of the same colour candles appear with no price gaps between them. If they are all bullish candles (white), they create the Three White Soldiers pattern. If they are all bearish candles (black), they create the Three Crows pattern. These common types of Parallel Lines are viewed as a continuation of the current market trend.

The variations of the bullish (white) Three Parallel Lines are different in shape and meaning from the classic formations. The White Three-Line Advance Block (*Sakizumari*) differs slightly from the Three White Soldiers, and it represents the possible end of a current bullish price move. It depicts a continuing

bullish price move that is diminishing in strength and likely to reverse. Another variation is the bearish Three Line Star in Deliberation (*Akasansen Shianboshi*). It indicates that the current rally is stalling and is likely to reverse. Often, this pattern may form into a Bearish Engulfing or a Three-River Evening Star indicating strong selling in the market.

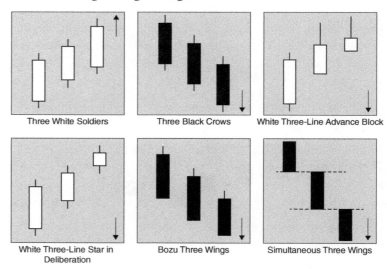

Three White Soldiers

Three Black Crows

White Three-Line Advance Block

White Three-Line Star in Deliberation

Bozu Three Wings

Simultaneous Three Wings

The bearish variations of the Three Parallel Lines are a little more complicated. The first is the Bozu Three Wings. It varies from the Three Crows because of a gap between the first and the second candle and the requirement that all three candles be of the Bozu or Marubozu type. This pattern represents strong bearish price action. The second variation occurs when the second candle's opening price is equal to the first candle's closing price and the third candle's opening price is equal to the second

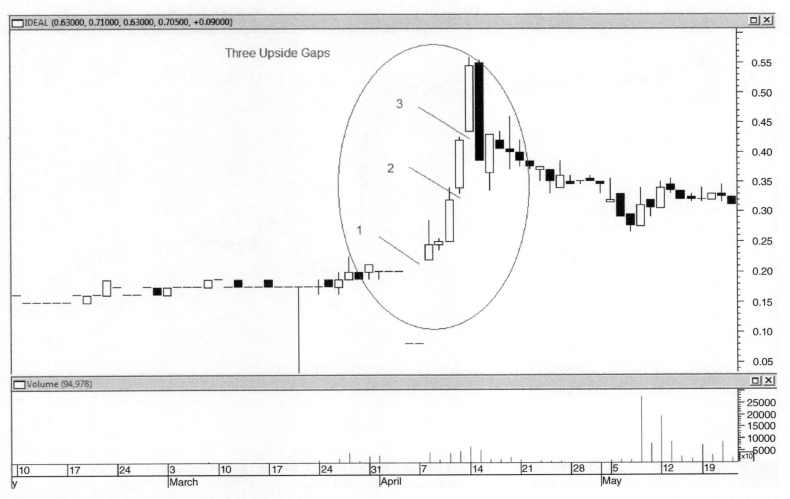

FIGURE 9.8 Ideal Malaysia Daily—Three Upside Gaps

266

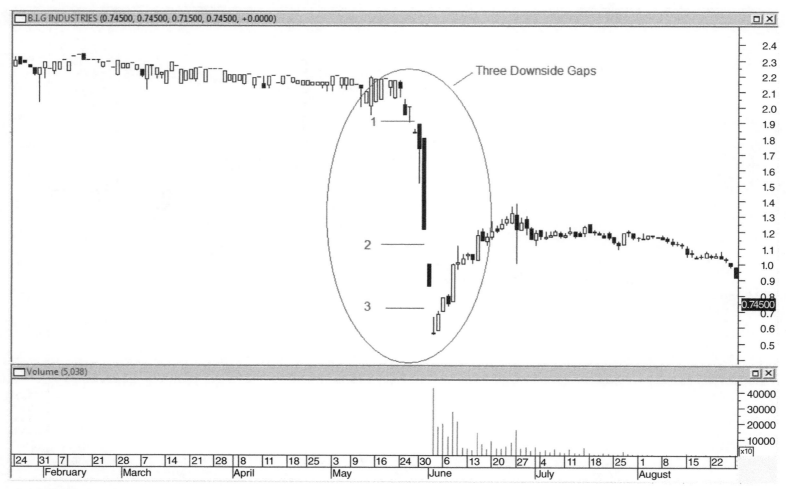

FIGURE 9.9 B.I.G. Industries Daily (2005)—Three Downside Gaps

candle's closing price. In other words, each new candle opens on the previous candle's close. This is called the Simultaneous Three Wings, and is an indication of continued bearish price action.

Figure 9.10 shows an example of the Simultaneous Three Wings pattern.

Sanpo (Three Methods)

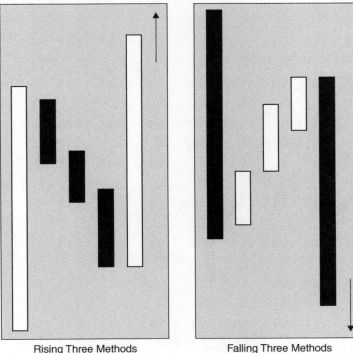

Rising Three Methods

Falling Three Methods

The Three Methods patterns relate to a resting period. These pattern groups indicate a congestion period within the market, and one should wait for confirmation of a new trend, usually in the direction of its prior trend. They are also known as continuation patterns in Western charting theory. *Sanpo* in Japanese means "to take a rest or cease fire in market action."

The two continuation patterns are the Rising Three Methods and the Falling Three Methods. If the Rising Three Methods appears in a rising market, one should expect a short rest before a further climb in price. The opposite is true for the Falling Three Methods. If it appears is a declining market, one should expect a short rebound before a further fall.

The Western chart pattern equivalents of these two Japanese patterns are the Bullish Flag and Bearish Flag.

Figure 9.11 and Figure 9.12 show some examples of the Rising and Falling Three Methods patterns.

■ Conclusion

Sakata's Five Methods are intended to group frequently recurring price patterns to help the trader discern the next market direction. Western classical charting theories have also grouped frequently recurring patterns, but under continuation and reversal patterns.[1]

What is interesting to note is that traders from two entirely different parts of the world and over two different time periods (the

---

[1] Detailed coverage of Western continuation and reversal patterns can be found in Robert Edwards and John Magee, *Technical Analysis of Stock Trends*, 6th ed. (Boston: John Magee, 1991).

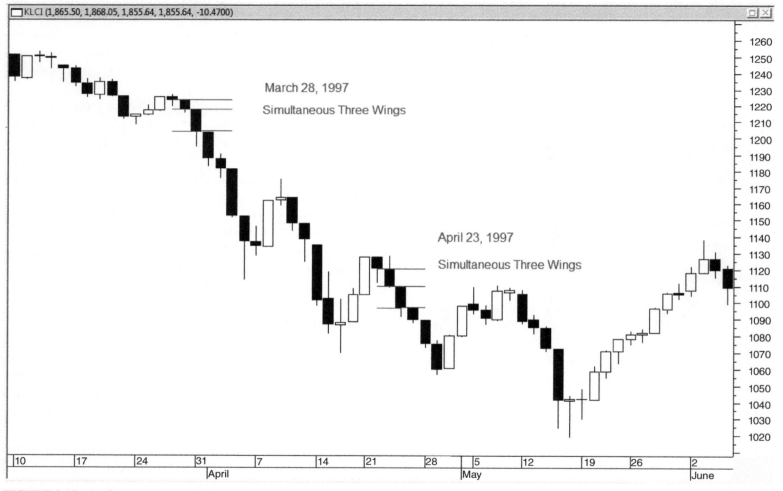

KLCI (1,865.50, 1,868.05, 1,855.64, 1,855.64, -10.4700)

March 28, 1997

Simultaneous Three Wings

April 23, 1997

Simultaneous Three Wings

FIGURE 9.10   Kuala Lumpur Composite Index Daily (1997)—Simultaneous Three Wings

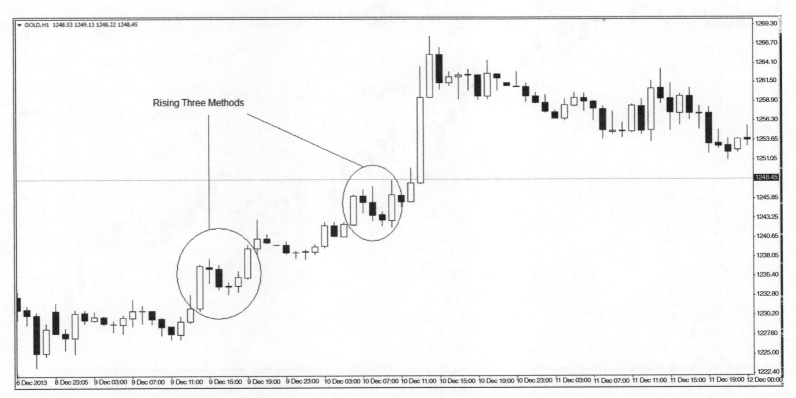

FIGURE 9.11 Gold Hourly (2014)—Rising Three Methods

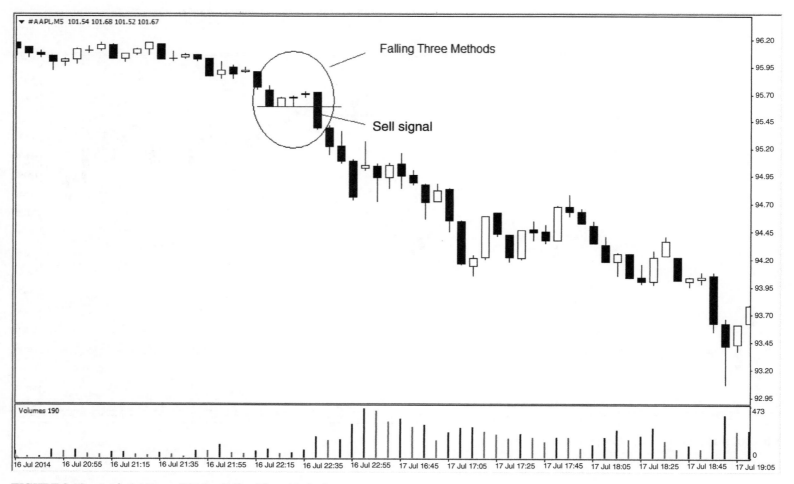

FIGURE 9.12 Apple 5-Minute (2014)—Falling Three Methods

Japanese in the 1700s and the West in the early 1900s) discovered the predictive values of these frequently recurring patterns sufficiently to the extent of documenting them.

These pattern groups, found in both the Eastern and Western techniques, confirm the technician's belief that price patterns on the charts are a mere reflection of the market's psychology.

Correct interpretation of the market's psychology through reading the charts, therefore, holds the key to success in making money in the markets.

As these patterns recur over time and across all markets, the chart can be universally applied, either to predict market turning points or to define market direction.

CHAPTER 10

Computerized Candlestick Forecasting

For over a century, the Japanese candlestick technique was hidden from the Western world until an American analyst, Steve Nison, revealed it in his first book, entitled *Japanese Candlestick Charting Techniques,*[1] in 1991.

Nison's book is credited with revolutionizing technical analysis in the West "by igniting the flames of interest in candles." Before this book, few had ever heard about candlestick charts, except in Japan. Now, the candlestick charting technique is one of the most popular around the world.

Steve Nison is the acknowledged Western authority on the subject of candlestick charting. His two internationally bestselling books, *Japanese Candlestick Charting Techniques* and *Beyond Candlesticks,*[2] have

---

[1]Steve Nison, *Japanese Candlestick Charting Techniques: A Contemporary Guide to the Ancient Investment Techniques of the Far East* (Paramus, NJ: New York Institute of Finance, 1991).

[2]Steve Nison, *Beyond Candlesticks* (New York: John Wiley & Sons, 1994).

been translated into six languages. Nison holds an MBA in finance and investments. He was among the first to receive the Chartered Marked Technician designation from the Market Technicians Association (MTA) and was nominated for the MTA's "Best of the Best" for price forecasting and market analysis.

Nison's work has been highlighted in several finance publications including the *Wall Street Journal*, *Barron's*, *Institutional Investor*, and *Euroweek*. As a sought-after speaker, Nison has presented his trading strategies to thousands of traders and analysts in 16 countries and, by request, the World Bank and the Federal Reserve. He has also been a lecturer at four universities.

Steve Nison is now known worldwide as the father of modern candlestick charting. He not only introduced this exciting and powerful charting method to Western traders, but he also continues training thousands of traders every year. His proven techniques and strategies are ideal for every type of trader.

In the beginning, Nison only offered his expertise through customized technical advisory and on-site seminars to institutional traders and analysts at top trading firms. His clients included J.P. Morgan; Fidelity; Bank of New York; Goldman Sachs; Spear, Leeds & Kellogg; Morgan Stanley; hedge funds; and OTC and NYSE market makers. Currently, Nison is helping individual traders with methods that can help them win in any market conditions. That's because he has proven time and again that candlestick charts are the best tool to see what's going to happen in the market—faster than old-fashioned bar charts. In addition, Nison is an acclaimed Western technical analyst. By combining candle charts with the best Western technical indicators, he teaches his students how to get the most out of every trade and how to trade with more confidence than they ever imagined.

Until recently, practitioners of Japanese candlestick charting were only able to spot candle reversal or continuation patterns manually, even as the candlestick chart is now the de facto standard and the most popular mode of recording price action since 1991, surpassing the popularity of the Western bar chart.

■ The Era of Computerized Candlestick Scanning

One of the main complaints about learning and interpreting candlestick charts is the large number of reversal and continuation patterns. In this book I have described 10 single black-and-white candles, 7 doji, 4 in the umbrella group, 53 reversal patterns, and 14 continuation patterns. Even so, this is not an exhaustive list of patterns available in candlestick literature.

With such a large number of patterns it would be a challenging task, especially for the newbie, to identify them. Even for the professional practitioner of candlesticks, it would be a demanding task to spot candle patterns when you are trading several markets at once and on several time frames.

Even after the Japanese candlestick technique's popularity exploded in 1991, few candlestick analysis programs are currently available in the market to cater to this fast-growing thirst for automatic candle pattern analysis.

Nison recognized it was a challenge for traders to browse through multiple markets on several time frames just to find profitable trade setups. That is when he came up with the idea of computerizing his favorite candle patterns with candle-pattern recognition software to reduce the time needed to find profitable trades from hours to just minutes.

To help meet this challenge, he designed the innovative Nison Candle Scanner in 2013, using the NinjaTrader Platform.[3] NCS is also available on the Trade Navigator and Tradestation platforms. For users of MetaTrader 4, Nison Candle Highlighter is available.

■ Features of the Nison Candle Scanner

The Nison Candle Scanner has several features that are useful in candlestick pattern analysis.

Candlestick Pattern Filtering

With the Nison Candle Scanner, you can filter a universe of markets (stocks, indexes, forex, futures, etc.) for any specific candlestick signal—and then watch as all the markets with that pattern are listed. You will be able to click on a market to view the chart.

Here are the simple steps:

Step 1: Pick one or more of Steve's 28 favorite candle signals. These signals are all preprogrammed and ready to use. In Figure 10.1, the Bullish Engulfing Pattern is selected.

Step 2: Choose a single market or a market group for which you want to find the patterns, such as the S&P 500. You

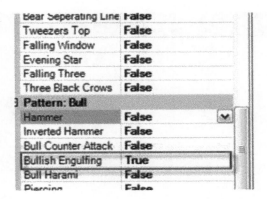

FIGURE 10.1   Picking Bullish Engulfing Pattern in the List of Signals

can even put in your own list of markets to filter (i.e., the 10 markets you track most closely). For this example, the Dow stocks have been selected to filter for a Bullish Engulfing Pattern.

Step 3: All of the markets that are currently in the pattern selected show up in this quick and easy pick list (see Figure 10.2).

Step 4: When you view the chart (in this case MMM), the pattern's signal is highlighted for you to see instantly (see Figure 10.3).

---

[3] See www.ninjatrader.com. NinjaTrader Platform is a free technical analysis platform (down to daily charts), which the Nison Candle Scanner rides on. It is market independent and analyses the world's leading stocks, futures, and forex markets. It can be upgraded into a trading platform for a small fee.

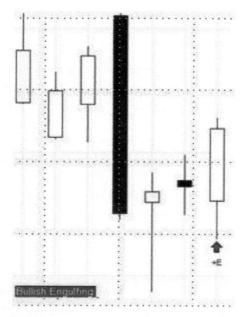

Instrument	Nison Candle Scanner
MMM	Bullish Engulfing
MSFT	Bullish Engulfing
PFE	Bullish Engulfing
T	Bullish Engulfing
VZ	Bullish Engulfing
XOM	Bullish Engulfing

FIGURE 10.2 Quick and Easy Pick List

FIGURE 10.3 The Pattern Is Highlighted on the Chart

Highlighting the Patterns on Your Charts

In addition to finding all of the markets that are currently in a particular candlestick pattern, you can also use the Nison Candle Scanner to quickly identify all of the different candlestick patterns that appear in a specific time frame for any individual stock or market.

There are two ways to have the Nison pattern displayed: the full name of the pattern, or as an abbreviation of the pattern name (see Figures 10.4 and 10.5). If you use the abbreviation of the pattern name, all you need do is click on the abbreviation and the full name is displayed at the lower left.

Custom Chart Alerts

Select a market—or a group of markets—and you will be alerted in real time when any of those markets hit the Nison candle patterns you want to follow. It works in any time frame and is a great time saver.

Step 1: Pick any (or all) of the preprogrammed Nison candle signals to automatically track your market (see Figure 10.6).

Step 2: Customize your alerts with a pop-up window, special audio alerts, and more (see Figure 10.7).

Step 3: Choose the markets you want NCS to automatically track for you and you're ready to go (see Figure 10.8).

Step 4: When any of your Nison candle signals occur on any of your markets, you'll be alerted immediately (see Figure 10.9).

You can also set up your Alert Window to notify you in real time when any of the candle signals and markets you're following hit a candle signal.

In Figure 10.10, the alert is set to show bull candle signals as green and bear signals as red.

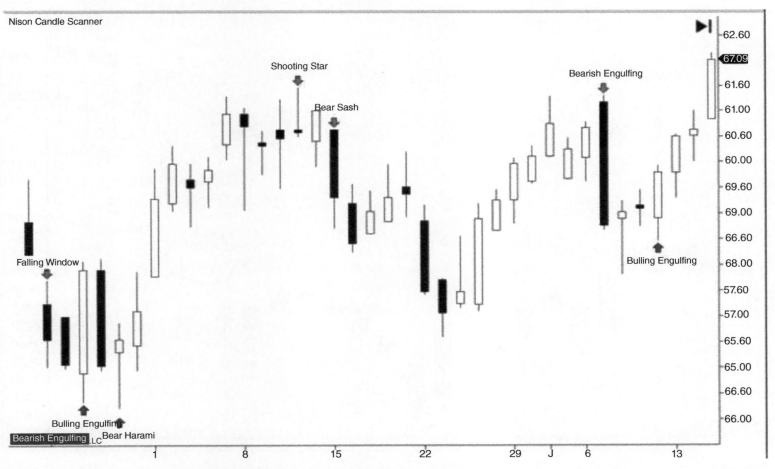

FIGURE 10.4 Nison Candle Scanner Helps Identify All Significant Candlestick Patterns in One Chart

FIGURE 10.5 Combining East and West

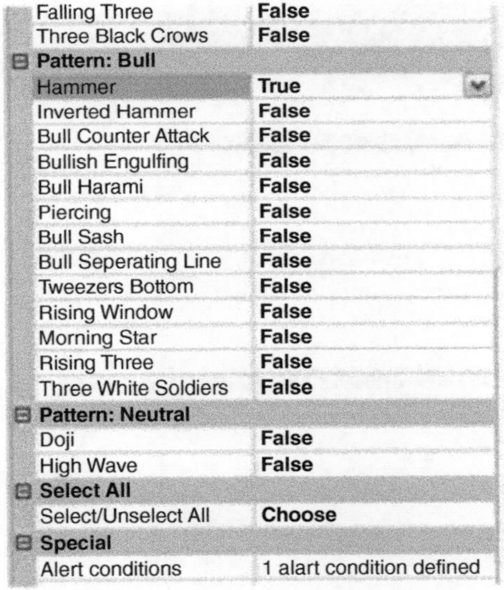

Falling Three	**False**
Three Black Crows	**False**
⊟ **Pattern: Bull**	
Hammer	**True**
Inverted Hammer	**False**
Bull Counter Attack	**False**
Bullish Engulfing	**False**
Bull Harami	**False**
Piercing	**False**
Bull Sash	**False**
Bull Seperating Line	**False**
Tweezers Bottom	**False**
Rising Window	**False**
Morning Star	**False**
Rising Three	**False**
Three White Soldiers	**False**
⊟ **Pattern: Neutral**	
Doji	**False**
High Wave	**False**
⊟ **Select All**	
Select/Unselect All	**Choose**
⊟ **Special**	
Alert conditions	1 alart condition defined

FIGURE 10.6 Track the Market Automatically

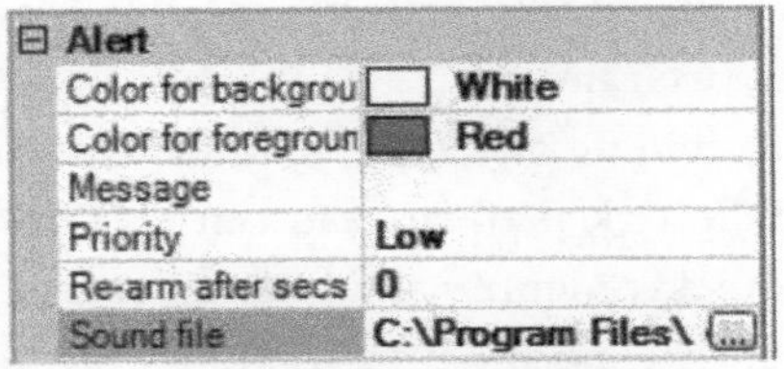

Market Analyzer
Instrument
AA
AXP
BA
BAC
C
CAT
CVX
DD
DIS
GE
GM
HD
HPQ
IBM
INTC
JNJ
JPM
KFT
KO
MCD
MMM
MRK
MSFT

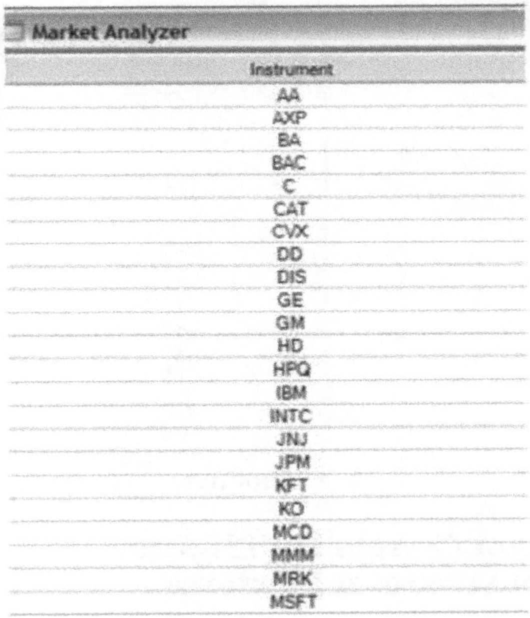

FIGURE 10.8 Choose Markets to Track

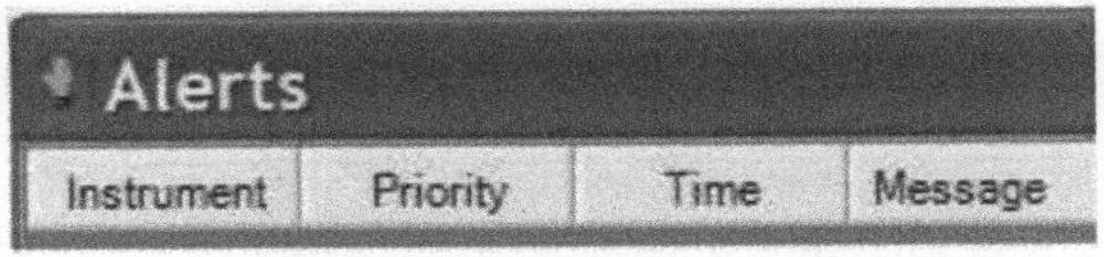

⊟ **Alert**	
Color for backgrou	**White**
Color for foregroun	**Red**
Message	
Priority	**Low**
Re-arm after secs	**0**
Sound file	**C:\Program Files**

FIGURE 10.7 Customize Alerts

Alerts			
Instrument	Priority	Time	Message

FIGURE 10.9 Alerts

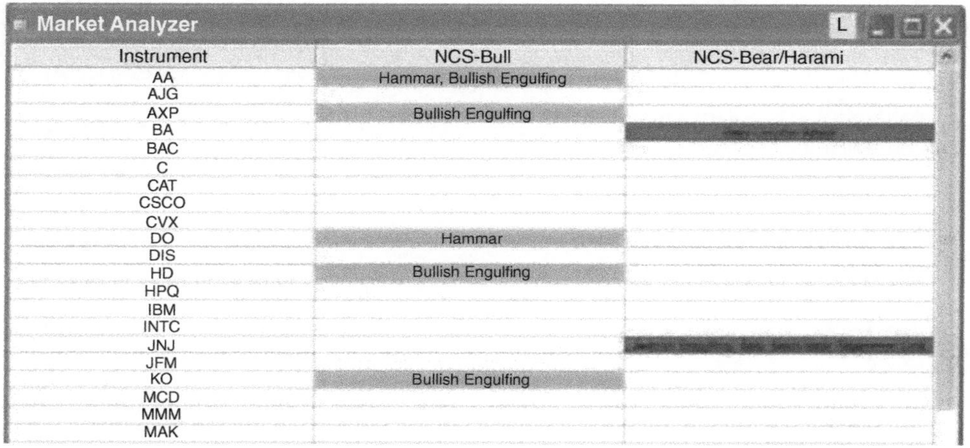

FIGURE 10.10 Bull and Bear Signals

■ Nison Candle Highlighter on MetaTrader 4 Platform

MetaTrader 4 (www.metaquotes.net) is an online trading platform designed to provide brokerage services to customers in forex, CFD, and futures markets.

Nison realized the potential of this platform and, as a result, designed the Nison Candle Highlighter to integrate with this platform.

Features of MetaTrader 4:

- The built-in technical analysis tools are powerful and easy to use.

- It is a free charting platform, which includes live data feeds through the Internet.

- It is very simple to use—even for beginners—yet powerful enough for the most experienced and demanding forex trader.

- MetaTrader 4 plots whatever intra-day or end-of-day charts of instruments the broker you sign up with offers, such as forex, stocks and stock indices, precious metals, crude oil, and so on.

If you trade forex, this innovative software helps you instantly find Nison's favorite candle patterns in your markets and saves you hours of research time.

In addition to finding all of the markets that are currently in a particular candlestick pattern, you can also use Nison Candle Highlighter to quickly identify all of the different candlestick patterns that appear in a specific time frame for any individual stock or market (see Figures 10.11 through 10.13).

FIGURE 10.11a   Different Candlestick Patterns Identified

FIGURE 10.11b (continued) Different Candlestick Patterns Identified

GBPUSD,MS 1.51859 1.51664 1.516648 1.51648

FIGURE 10.11c (continued)

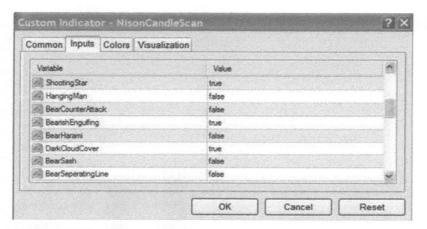

FIGURE 10.12 Custom Indicator

ADVANCED CANDLESTICK TECHNIQUES

Bullish Patterns	Symbol
Hammer	+H
Inverted Hammer	+IH
Bull Counter Attack	+CA
Bullish Engulfing	+E
Bull Harami	+HR
Piercing	+P
Bull Sash	+SH
Bull Separating Line	+SL
Tweezer Bottom	+TB
Rising Window	+W
Morning Star	+MS
Rising Three	+RS
Three White Solders	+3S
Bear Patterns	**Symbol**
Shooting Star	-S
Hanging Man	-HM
Bear Counter Attack	-CA
Bearish Engulfing	-E
Bear Harami	-HR
Dark Cloud Cover	-DC
Bear Sash	-SH
Bear Separating Line	-SL
Tweezer Top	-TT
Falling Window	-W
Evening Star	-ES
Falling Three	-F3
Three Black Crows	-3C
Neutral Patterns	**Symbol**
Doji	D
High Wave	HW

FIGURE 10.13 Patterns and Symbols Key

CHAPTER 11

Conclusion: Facts about Candlesticks

This book should convey to readers the following facts about the candlestick technique:

1. The Japanese candlestick technique had been relatively unknown for the last three centuries, except in Japan, until Steve Nison popularised it in 1991.
2. Candlesticks use the same price data as bar charts, yet the candlestick technique better promotes the ability to recognize complex patterns and interpret what these patterns mean.

3. Candlestick charting is the only technique that generates intuitive text messages (results) about the inner psychology of any market.
4. The candlestick technique is excellent for spotting market turning points and is especially adept at trading Spikes or *V* and inverted *V* formations. It does this job much better than Western charting theory.
5. Candlestick reversal patterns work best if they are found after a rally or decline. They are not useful in forecasting market

direction in a sideways market. In other words, they should not be used all the time.

6. Candlestick continuation patterns are useful in gauging trend continuation.

7. Candlestick patterns are true leading indicators and regularly identify potential market reversals much earlier than Western technical indicators.

8. Candlesticks are attuned to the short-term trend (5 to 15 days). To apply candlesticks to longer-term trending markets, you must use a weekly or monthly chart. For shorter-term trading, intra-day charts, ranging from 1-minute, 5-minute, 15-minute, 1-hour, to 4-hour charts, can be used.

9. The candlestick technique can be used as a standalone technique to trade the markets, but profitability is enhanced when it is combined with Western technical indicators. In other words, candlestick analysis should be used in conjunction with trend analysis. This concept is called candlestick filtering or the Rule of Multiple Techniques.

10. Western trend-line analysis, support and resistance, and Western technical indicators like the Moving Average, RSI, Momentum, MACD, Stochastic, DMI, CCI, Percent R, Bollinger Bands, and Elliott Wave Theory are some of the techniques that should be applied to assist in identifying the primary trend as well as periods when the market is overbought and oversold.

11. The trader should take a candlestick signal in the direction of the primary trend and to ignore a candlestick signal that is counter to the primary trend; otherwise there can be a high degree of failure. Steve Nison shares this principle and I quote this paragraph from page 287 of his book *Japanese Candlestick Charting Techniques*:

Be flexible about chart reading. Where you stand in relation to the overall technical evidence may be more important than an individual candlestick pattern. For example, a bullish candlestick signal in a major bear market should not be used as a buy signal. A bullish candlestick formation, especially when confirmed by other technical signals in a bull market, would be a buying point.

12. Traders who at times find it impossible to identify a market reversal due to the complexity of certain reversal patterns, which cannot be found in this book or in other books on candlesticks, should use my P.I. System Trader to mimic candlestick reversal patterns. This system can be programmed into any charting software.

13. The Nison Candle Scanner can help you reduce the time spent finding profitable candlestick patterns from a universe of markets (stocks, indexes, forex, futures, etc.) from hours to just minutes by using the filtering feature of the scanning software.

Fred Tam studied securities and commodities futures trading techniques in the United States under George Lane, Larry Williams, Steve Nison, Dr. Bill Williams, Jake Bernstein, Joe DiNapoli, Dr. Van K. Tharp, Thomas Dorsey, Professor Hank O. Pruden, and many other prominent U.S. traders.

Mr. Tam uses a combination of Japanese candlestick charting and Western technical indicators to track the markets. He developed his own computerized trading system called the P.I. System Trader or F1 Trader, which mimics candlestick reversal patterns and is excellent for trading fast-moving markets. He also developed the Multiple Time Frame system of trading in 2012 and presented his findings at the International Federation of Technical Analysts (IFTA) 2012 conference in Singapore.

He holds a Master of Philosophy from Multimedia University, Cyberjaya. He is a full member of the Society of Technical Analysts in the United Kingdom and is Malaysia's first recipient of the Master of Financial Technical Analysis from IFTA. Mr. Tam is a Certified Financial Technician from IFTA, and a Certified Accountant from the United Kingdom since 1979.

During his 30 years in the financial industry, Mr. Tam has participated in many conferences and conducted extensive seminars, workshops, and professional courses in association with University Malaya; University Sains Malaysia; University Sabah Malaysia; University Putra Malaysia; Multimedia University, Cyberjaya; Taylor's College; Bursa Station; Bursa Malaysia; stocks and futures brokerage houses; and unit trust companies both within Malaysia and around Asia. He has the distinction of being recognised as the guru of technical analysis in Malaysia.

Mr. Tam has authored six books on technical analysis and was the principal lecturer at Open University Malaysia–IPD's certificate course in technical analysis, the first and only such course conducted at the university level in South East Asia. He has his own website: www.f1traderacademy.com.

Mr. Tam's current research interest is in multiple time frame trading systems programmed into MT4.0. He teaches and promotes technical analysis and makes speaking appearances in Indonesia, Vietnam, and Singapore besides Malaysia. Mr. Tam is now collaborating with Asia e University (AeU) to offer Malaysia's first EMBA (financial technical analysis) course.

Japanese Candlestick Charting

Japanese Candlestick Charting Techniques by Steve Nison (NYIF, 1991)

Beyond Candles by Steve Nison (John Wiley & Sons, 1994)

Japanese Chart of Charts, 2nd ed., by Seiki Shimizu (Tokyo Futures Trading Publishing Co., 1990)

Trading Applications of Candlestick Charting by Gary Wagner and Brad Matheny (John Wiley & Sons, 1994)

CandlePower by Greg Morris (Probus, 1992)

Encyclopedia of Candlestick Charts by Thomas N. Bulkowski (John Wiley & Sons, 2008)

Major Reversal Patterns, Continuation Patterns, and Basic Concepts of Trend

Technical Analysis of Stock Trends, 6th ed., by Robert Edwards and John Magee (John Magee, 1991)

Technical Analysis of the Financial Markets by John J. Murphy (NYIF, 1999)

Technical Analysis Explained, 5th ed., by Martin J. Pring (McGraw-Hill, 2014)

Moving Averages, Volume

Technical Analysis of the Financial Markets by John J. Murphy (NYIF, 1999)

Technical Analysis on Futures by Jack D. Schwager (John Wiley & Sons, 1996)

Technical Traders Guide to Computer Analysis of the Futures Markets by Charles Lebeau and David Lucas (Irwin Professional Publishing, 1992)

Oscillators: Stochastic, RSI, MACD, Momentum, CCI, DMI, Percent R, Bollinger Bands, and More

Martin Pring on Market Momentum by Martin Pring (International Institute for Economic Research, 1993)

Handbook on Technical Analysis by Darrell Jobman (Probus, 1995)

Technical Traders Guide to Computer Analysis of the Futures Markets by Charles Lebeau and David Lucas (Irwin Professional Publishing, 1992)

Technical Analysis of the Financial Markets by John J. Murphy (NYIF, 1999)

Technical Analysis on Futures by Jack D. Schwager (John Wiley & Sons, 1996)

New Concepts in Technical Trading Systems by J. Welles Wilder Jr. (Trend Research, 1978)

Bollinger on Bollinger Bands by John Bollinger (McGraw-Hill, 2002)

Triple Screen

Trading for a Living by Alexander Elders (John Wiley & Sons, 1993)

High Probability Trading by Marcel Link (McGraw-Hill, 2003)

New Trading Systems and Methods, 5th ed., by Perry Kaufmann (John Wiley & Sons, 2013)

Elliott Wave Theory

Elliott Wave Principles by A. J. Frost and Robert Prechter Jr. (New Classic Library, 1998)

R. N. Elliott's Masterworks by Robert Prechter Jr. (New Classic Library, 1994)

Fibonacci Theory

Trading with Fibonacci Levels by Joe DiNapoli (Coast Investment Software, 1998)

Fibonacci Applications and Strategies for Traders by Robert Fisher (John Wiley & Sons, 1993)

R.N. MasterWorks by Robert Prechter Jr. (New Classics Library, 1994)

W. D. Gann Technique

The Trading Methodologies of W. D. Gann: A Guide to Building Your Technical Analysis Toolbox by Hima Reddy (FT Press, 2012)

45 Years in Wall Street by W. D. Gann (Lambert Gann, 1949)

Fractals / MACD Histogram / Elliott Wave

Trading Chaos by Dr. Bill Williams (John Wiley & Sons, 1995)

Point and Figure Charting

Point and Figure Charting by Tom Dorsey (John Wiley & Sons, 2007)

Money Management

The Universal Principles of Successful Trading by Brent Penfold (John Wiley & Sons [Asia], 2010)

Technical Analysis of the Financial Markets by John J. Murphy (NYIF, 1999)

Market Wizards by Jack D. Schwager (Harpers Business Edition, 1993)

New Trading Systems and Methods, 5th ed., by Perry Kaufmann (John Wiley & Sons, 2013)

Rule of Multiple Techniques

Techniques of a Professional Commodity Chart Analyst by Arthur Sklarew (Windsor Books, 1980)